Classical Savannah

Fine & Decorative Arts
1800 – 1840

For Jim, Jody, Alex, Katie, and Adam

Classical Savannah

Fine & Decorative Arts
1800 – 1840

Page Talbott

Telfair Museum of Art / Savannah, Georgia

This book was published by the
Telfair Museum of Art,
Savannah, Georgia in conjunction
with the exhibition
*Classical Savannah: Fine and
Decorative Arts 1800-1840*,
May 16 to November 19, 1995.

The publication was made possible
by generous grants from the
National Endowment for the Arts,
Francis D. McNairy, Chatham Steel
Corporation, and Alvin and Davida
Deutsch.

Author:
Page Talbott
Editor:
Olivia Evans Alison
Editorial Assistance:
Pamela D. King
Susan Emack Alison
Curatorial Assistance:
Thea N. Tjepkema
Designer:
Jeana Aquadro
Design Assistance:
Savitha Bala
Kathleen C. Bolch
Marni Jo Lessa

Printer:
Mercantile Printing Company, Inc.
Bindery:
Acme Bookbinding Company
Distributor:
The University of Georgia Press

ISBN 0-8203-1793-4
Library of Congress Catalog
Card Number: 95-60860

All photographs, unless otherwise
noted, are by Daniel L. Grantham,
Jr. of Graphic Communication,
Savannah, Georgia. Randall
Connaughton produced figure (**26**)
and the image of the facade of the
Richardson-Owens-Thomas House
(page 48) as part of a 1994 photographic survey of the House funded
by the Getty Grant Program and the
Woodruff Foundation.

Cover: detail of built-in sideboard
(**31**), Richardson-Owens-Thomas
House, c. 1819

Contents

ACKNOWLEDGEMENTS

We are deeply grateful to the individuals and institutions who gave their time, talents, and resources to make the Classical Savannah exhibition and catalogue a reality. Foremost is guest curator and author Page Talbott who devoted herself tirelessly to the Classical Savannah project, sharing her vision and her unwavering enthusiasm. We thank her for her long months of hard work and her invaluable contribution to the history of Savannah and American art. Next is graphic designer Jeana Aquadro who created a design of beauty and clarity under formidable time constraints. We also wish to acknowledge the National Endowment for the Arts for the generous grant which made this project possible. Equally important was the expert knowledge, encouragement, and financial support of Francis D. McNairy. Additional support was graciously provided by Alvin and Davida Deutsch and the Chatham Steel Corporation.

Our research interns James A. Buttimer, Helen Eady, Alexandra Wetter, and Lindsley E. Hand deserve particular mention for their careful and thorough efforts. We are also indebted to copy editor Susan Emack Alison, interior designer Caroline Gordon Armstrong, former Telfair curator Feay Shellman Coleman, typist Donna Gilliard, the library staff of the Georgia Historical Society, photographer Daniel L. Grantham, cabinetmaker Gregory Guenther, architectural scholar Lynn Harvey, Telfair curator and editor Pamela King, historian Gordon Smith, and Richardson-Owens-Thomas House curator emerita Agnes M. Tison.

We thank both the families of former donors to the Telfair collection and the lenders of the Classical Savannah exhibition who delved into family and institutional records for genealogical information.

Special recognition is due the following lenders who graciously surrendered their patrimony for the six months of the exhibition:

Emma Walthour Morel Adler
Caroline Gordon Armstrong
Mrs. Lawrence Austin
H. Paul Blatner
Juliette Gordon Low Birthplace
Dorothy Rabey Brantley
Margaret Caldwell and Carlo Florentino
Mr. and Mrs. John Cay III
Michael Everett Collins
Adrian B. Colquitt
The National Society of The Colonial Dames in the State of Georgia
Daniel Denny
Davida Tenenbaum Deutsch
V & J Duncan
Jeanne Morrell Garlington
Georgia Historical Society
Mrs. Walter C. Hartridge
Historic Savannah Foundation
Dorothy Kingery
Elizabeth Layton
Mrs. Lorton Stoy Livingston
Maryland Historical Society
Mrs. M. Heyward Mingledorff
Morris Museum of Art
Mrs. James White Morton, Jr.
James White Morton III
Francis D. McNairy
Ruth Lomel Mullininx
The New-York Historical Society
Sumpter Priddy III, Inc.
Mrs. George Quaile
Will H. Theus
Charlton Theus, Jr.
Mr. and Mrs. O. O. Thompson, Jr.
University of South Carolina
Mr. and Mrs. Lamaund E. Wells
Westville Historic Handicrafts, Inc.
Anna Habersham Wright
Caroline Jones Wright

In addition we would like to thank Bryding Adams, Birmingham Museum of Art; Jim Alley, Savannah College of Art and Design; Craig Barrow, The Wormsloe Foundation; Stephen Bohlin-Davis and Fran Powell Harold, Juliette Gordon Low Birthplace; Sarah Bruce; Judy Cohen, High Museum of Art; Philip G. Correll, National Park Service; Jerry Cotten, University of North Carolina Photography Services; Alice Daily, The National Society of The Colonial Dames in the State of Georgia; Gail Miller DeLoach and Jane Powers Weldon, Georgia Department of Archives and History; Katharine Gross Farnham; Barbara Fertig, Armstrong State College and the Savannah History Museum; George T. Fore; Danielle Funderburk, The Columbus Museum of Arts and Sciences; Thom Gentle; Mary Giles, The Charleston Museum; Sophia Hewryk, Paula Feid, and Maureen Pelta, Moore College of Art and Design; Mary Huber, Bartow-Pell Mansion; Alexandra Klinglehofer, Macon Museum of Arts and Sciences; Bryan Lane, National Gallery of Art; Mills B. Lane IV and Betty Ann Lichner, The Beehive Press; Robert A. Leath, Historic Charleston Foundation; Clermont Lee; Deanne Levison; Johanna Metzgar, Brad Rauschenberg, Martha Rowe and Wes Stewart, Museum of Early Southern Decorative Arts; Dean Owens; Stephen Patrick, Hammond-Harwood House; Jessica M. Pigza and Jennifer A. Bryan, Maryland Historical Society; Henry N. Platt; William Rutledge; the staff of the Savannah College of Art and Design Graphic Design Production Lab; the reference department of the Savannah Public Library, Sam Simpson; Jane Webb Smith; Margaret Tamulonis, The New-York Historical Society; Neville Thompson, The Henry Francis duPont Winterthur Museum; Rita Trotz; Catherine Wade Wahl, Morris Museum of Art; and Deborah Dependahl Waters, the Museum of the City of New York.

Finally we express our gratitude to the entire staff of the Telfair Museum of Art particularly Edward Blanchard, Nathan Conrad, and Matt Jenkins, art handlers; Harry Delorme, curator of education; Jane Espy, bookkeeper and computer consultant; Sandra Hadaway, administrator; Pamela King, curator of fine arts and exhibitions; Diane Lesko, director; Jennifer Marsik, administrative assistant; Beth Moore and Candice Moore, curatorial assistants; Jeanette Overstreet and Eleanor Haynes, housekeepers; Milutin Pavlovik, exhibition designer; Colleen Rice, education assistant; Tania Sammons, registrar and copy editor; Letty Shearer, development officer; and, Gregory Allgire Smith, former director. Interns Jennifer DeLelle, Jeff Foos, Jason Hawkins, Scott Knight, Tami Lamberg, John Preece, and David Zona were a great help. All the docents of Richardson-Owens-Thomas House deserve specific mention, but especially Sara Cabaness and Nancy Cabaness Warth. Thea Tjepkema, my talented assistant, merits special thanks for her extraordinary contribution to this project. The dedication and cooperation of the Telfair staff is evident in the outstanding exhibition and book Classical Savannah: Fine and Decorative Arts 1800-1840.

Olivia Evans Alison

3

The significance of *Classical Savannah: Fine and Decorative Arts 1800-1840* stretches far beyond the boundaries of the beautiful city which it chronicles. The exhibition and catalogue record the impact of the Classical Revival in the South and thus contribute to national, regional, and local history. Recent scholarship on neoclassicism in America has focused on the Northeastern United States where many classically inspired goods were manufactured. *Classical Savannah* documents the influence of these products on a thriving Southern port which imported most of its fine consumables. The origins of these goods reveal fascinating links between Savannah and the rest of the world and hint at parallel situations in other Southern ports.

In a city long celebrated for its architecture, the *Classical Savannah* exhibition and book offer a view of the art and furnishings behind Savannah's imposing nineteenth-century facades. Furniture in Savannah was first discussed by Will H. Theus (Mrs. Charlton) in her 1967 and 1968 publications. Katherine Gross Farnam's 1967 Winterthur thesis and Marilyn Johnson's 1968 *Winterthur Portfolio* article were equally significant contributions. The three major exhibition catalogues include the Atlanta Historical Society's 1983 *Neat Pieces: The Plain-Style of Furniture of Nineteenth Century Georgia*; The Georgia Museum of Art's 1984 *Georgia's Legacy: History Charted Through the Arts*; and the High Museum of Art's 1990 *Hidden Heritage: Recent Discoveries in Georgia Decorative Art*.

The Telfair's own 1992 catalogue *Nostrums for Fashionable Entertainments: Dining in Georgia 1800-1850* by Feay Shellman Coleman provides a tantalizing glimpse into the Savannah interiors of this era, yet *Classical Savannah* gives us a broader perspective, taking us from the dining room and kitchen through the rest of the house and out into the community. Emphasis is placed on the domestic oeuvre of architect William Jay (1792-1837) since the two museum buildings,

the Richardson-Owens-Thomas House and the Telfair House, were designed by Jay; and the Telfair and Thomas bequests form the nucleus of the institution's decorative arts collection.

The *Classical Savannah* exhibition grew out of the Telfair Museum of Art's preservation plans for the Richardson-Owens-Thomas House. Extensive conservation repairs of the historic house afforded an opportunity to display its furnishings in gallery settings at the art museum. The neoclassical design of these objects and the houses which they originally adorned provided a scholarly theme for the exhibition. Further research yielded an extraordinary body of surviving fine arts and decorative objects in the classical taste, many still linked to the Savannah residences and families for which they were acquired in the nineteenth century. The resulting exhibition is the largest ever organized by the Telfair Museum of Art and the first to combine fine and decorative arts.

The accompanying *Classical Savannah* catalogue is an incredible achievement. Produced in less than a year, *Classical Savannah* is a testament to the richness of Savannah's historical record and the perseverance and scholarship of author Page Talbott. For the convenience of the reader, the essays in the first two chapters are each followed by their particular notes and catalogue entries. The essay on furniture in the third chapter incorporates the catalogue information into the illustration captions. A checklist of additional objects in the exhibition, with an emphasis on provenance, follows.

We hope that *Classical Savannah: Fine and Decorative Arts 1800-1840* will encourage further study of this rich period in Savannah, the South, and the nation.

Olivia Evans Alison
Curator of Decorative Arts and the Richardson-Owens-Thomas House

The Classical Taste
in the
Early Nineteenth Century

ITS ANCIENT ORIGINS

The idealization of the democracy of ancient Greece and the glory of ancient Rome has sparked the admiration, imagination, and emulation of mankind in the Western world for centuries. During the Renaissance, sculptors evoked the elegant and serene statues of the Romans; poets recalled the epic masterpieces of Homer, Virgil, and Plato; and architects looked to the antique buildings of Athens and Rome as sources for both decorative vocabulary and spatial organization.

Italy

With the discovery of the cities of Herculaneum (1709) and Pompeii (1748), their pasts frozen in time under a shroud of volcanic ash, and the subsequent archaeology that ensued, a renewed fascination with the ancient world precipitated a century of classical enthusiasm and inspiration that affected all aspects of European and American culture (1).

The tradition of travel to the birthplaces of Western civilization, which began in England in the 1730s, fostered a growing awareness of antique masterpieces. Tourists who could afford lavishly illustrated architecture and travel books and copies of ancient statues and artwork brought them home to their houses. Italy was the principal destination of these early Grand Tourists (Greece was under the rule of the Turks and was rarely visited by Westerners). There, observers compiled encyclopedic volumes of drawings with accompanying descriptions, which led to the development of a style known today as Neoclassicism.

The Neoclassical style in architecture and household articles can be described in two phases: Early Classical Revival, characterized by antique decoration applied to traditional forms, and Late Classical Revival, in which the form as well as the ornament imitated Greco-Roman examples.

The Early Classical Revival owes its origins to the Roman Empire and was inspired by archaeological excavations. Particularly influential in the spread of Roman classicism to England and France was the Italian designer and artist Giovanni Battista Piranesi (1720-1778), whose precise engravings were catalogues of classical ornament that influenced Western designers.[1] In both France and England architects and craftsmen applied decorative motifs derived from antique sources to traditional forms of architecture and decorative arts. Later, during the third quarter of the eighteenth century, classicism began to influence the form as well, straightening out the curves of the Rococo style and lightening the overall concept of the design.

Greece

During the second half of the eighteenth century increased interest and scholarship focusing on Greek architecture and art slowly influenced the burgeoning Neoclassical style. Publications by travelers to Greece provided dramatic evidence of the beauty and idealism of that ancient country.[2] Excavations that unearthed Greek vases of the fourth through six centuries B.C.E. provided models for a linear style of painting that widely influenced artists both in England and on the Continent. Through the influence of persuasive and authoritative writers and taste-makers such as Johann Joachim Winckelmann (1717-1768) and Anton Raffael Mengs (1728-1779), Greek art became widely considered superior to Roman(2).[3]

At the end of the eighteenth century, however,

The choice of ancient modes to be imitated came to be determined primarily by the associative values which they possessed. An admiration for the whole of Greek culture resulted in the widespread adoption of her architectural style in England, Germany and Scandinavia, but in Italy and France, ancient Rome continued to be the chief source of stylistic inspiration.[4]

By that time other ancient civilizations were being studied and emulated. Among the best known sourcebooks documenting ancient art and architecture were the seven volumes by Comte de Caylus, *Recueil d'antiquités égyptiennes, étrusques, grecques et romaines*, published in Paris between 1752 and 1767. This series included illustrations of bas-reliefs, coins, placques, utensils, paving stones, jewelry, and ceilings from throughout the ancient world and "made available to designers and architects an immense repertory of entirely new motifs."⁵ The Egyptian ornament illustrated in this work became widely popular in both Europe and America.

1

Attributed to Charlotte McCord
Cheves (1818-1879)
American (Charleston)
Sale of Loves
c. 1835-1840
Watercolor on paper

2

Samuel C. Barnard (n.d.)
American (Savannah)
Apollo and the Muses on Parnassus
1829
Graphite on paper

TRANSMISSION OF STYLE

Early Classical Revival

In the evolution of Early Classical Revival style, the developments in England and France are closely interrelated. During the 1750s the English designer Robert Adam (1728-1792) traveled to Italy, meeting Piranesi and visiting classical ruins. Returning to England in 1759, Adam launched a "stylistic revolution there by applying his newly acquired knowledge of ancient architecture to the planning and decoration of domestic interiors."[6] The classically inspired ornament used in his innovative designs included urns, vases, scrolls, arabesques, griffins, swags, and husks, which were applied to furniture, ceiling decoration, lighting, and other elements of interior decoration.

Adam's other principal contributions to neoclassicism were his juxtaposition of oval and rectanglar forms in decorative schemes of interiors and their furnishings, and the introduction of the straight classical leg for furniture (3). With the facility to combine elements of Pompeian (Roman) and Hellenistic (Greek) motifs within a single interior, Adam became what some believe to have been the greatest of English neoclassical architects. The far-reaching influence of Adam's "antique motifs" can be found in European and American decorative arts of the period.

Simultaneous with Adam's innovations were the furniture designs of 1766 by the Parisian sculptor Jean Louis Prieur for the King of Poland.[7] Prieur's drawings of classical beds, chairs, and case furniture indicate that it is impossible to determine if this new style originated in England or France. As was the case in England, classical ornaments such as the Greek key and egg and dart moldings were lavishly applied to French furniture of the period (4).

Late Classical Revival

Classicism proceeded to introduce furnishings that were directly imitative of ancient art. The new archaeologically inspired style reached its height in France in the 1780s. French designers of the *style étrusque* first incorporated specific elements of Greco-Roman furniture, such as legs or backs, and later created pieces intended to precisely replicate Roman furniture. This new type of furniture can be seen in the paintings of Jacques-Louis David (1748-1825), court painter to Emperor Napoleon (1769-1821), whose studio props were made to the artist's specifications by the cabinetmaker Georges Jacob (1739-1814).[8]

4
Detail, Wall light with Greek key motif
1816-1819
Savannah, Georgia
North wall, dining room
Richardson-Owens-
Thomas House

8

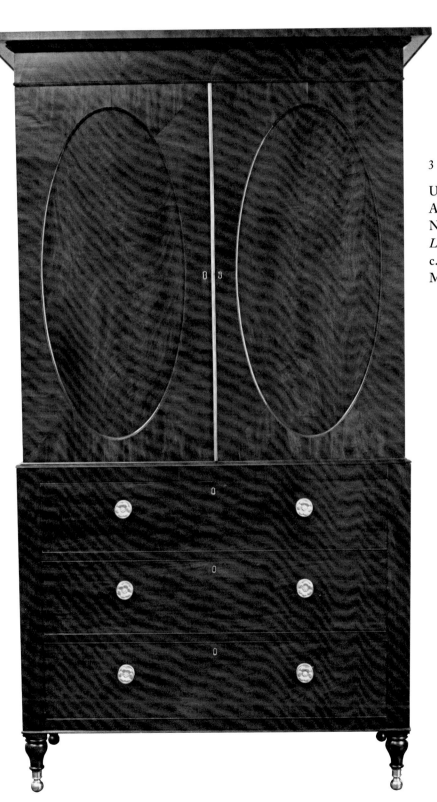

3

Unknown maker
American (Philadelphia or
New York)
Linen press
c. 1810-1820
Mahogany; mahogany, pine

Napoleon's military campaigns allowed him to see firsthand many of the ruins of Rome, Greece, and Egypt. The Emperor's official court architects and decorators, Charles Percier (1764-1838) and Pierre François Léonard Fontaine (1762-1853), largely created what is now often referred to as the Empire style.[9] At the time, however, this second phase of Neoclassicism was most often called Grecian. Other terms occasionally used include "antique," "classical," or "modern."

Sources for the designs of Percier and Fontaine included Egyptian grave steles, Greco-Roman sarcophagi, and antique figural vases. The fifth-century Athenian klismos chair was copied extensively, as were sofas and settees of late Roman design. Their decorative vocabulary included elements from actual archaeological sites: caryatid figures, dolphins, wreaths, swans, and monumental animal legs and feet (**5**).

In England the fashion for archaeologically correct furniture was led by Thomas Hope (1769-1831) — banker, collector, patron, gentleman, scholar, designer, and friend of Percier and Fontaine. Having traveled extensively throughout the eastern Mediterranean, Hope collected antiquities, contemporary neoclassical sculpture, and Dutch and Italian paintings, which he displayed in his house in Surrey. On view there, as he said, was "the entire assemblage of productions of ancient art and of modern handicraft, thus intermixed, collectively, into a more harmonious, more consistent, and more instructive whole."[10]

Hope's published line drawings were important in the development of the Classical style in England, not as the basis for exact models of furniture for popular consumption but as inspiration for contemporary designers and cabinetmakers. His designs and theories for the adaptation of antique forms were the foundation of the so-called English Regency style, enthusiastically embraced by English designers.[11]

George Smith (active 1800-c. 1830) was one Englishman who popularized Hope's designs in a number of books featuring drawings of furniture and interior decoration that expanded and elaborated on Hope's ideas for applied motifs and furniture construction. Smith's books present furniture that typifies what is thought of today as the Regency style.[12] The main features of this new mode were extreme simplicity of outline with large uninterrupted surfaces, subordination of ornament to a minor role, and an emphasis on solidity. The favorite methods of decoration were metal inlay and reeding (**6**).

At first, Greek, Roman, and Egyptian antiquities were all sources for neoclassical design, but as time went on, the Greek model characterized by its severity, simple straight lines, and bold curves won out. International interest in Greece was intensified by the 1816 discovery of the Parthenon sculptures, and by the 1821 Greek revolt against the Turks, which particularly drew the attention of democratic-minded Americans.

6

Unknown maker
American (Philadelphia)
Astragal-end worktable
c. 1815-1825
Mahogany; poplar, white pine, mahogany, beech

5

Unknown maker
English (probably Staffordshire)
Cream pitcher
c. 1810
Pink lusterware

THE IMPACT OF NEOCLASSICISM ON THE UNITED STATES

Consumers and craftsmen in the United States were in no way immune to the stylistic changes experienced throughout Europe. While the delay for style changes to reach the American colonies was considerable in the eighteenth century, by 1800 it took little time for American cabinet-makers, silversmiths, and painters to incorporate the innovations of their peers in England and on the Continent. American Federal style architecture and furniture was thus dramatically influenced by the work of Robert Adam, by the English pattern books of Thomas Sheraton (1751-1806) and George Hepplewhite (d. 1786), and by the products of French cabinetmakers during the reign of Louis XVI (1754-1793).

By the early nineteenth century, American intercoastal as well as intercontinental shipping brought word of new trends from one area to another in a matter of weeks, plus the import of actual goods. The transmission of stylistic influences was accomplished in several ways: immigration of foreign-trained craftsmen to this country; importation of European pattern books; and access to American furniture price books, which emulated those of Europe.[13] Rarely can one identify the precise European source for a specific American-made object, but it is certain that foreign influences abounded.

New York, Philadelphia, Boston, and even the more distant ports of Richmond, Charleston, and Savannah were the destinations of ships bearing cargoes of both necessities and luxuries that reflected current European fashions in fabrics, wallpapers, decorative items, and building materials. These goods were incorporated into the homes of the wealthy throughout the Eastern seaboard.

To what extent were American consumers aware of the classical precedents for many of the household furnishings they imported? The same could be asked of their European counterparts. It is certain that they were well aware of the prestige of subscribing to the newest fashions and of following the guidelines in the latest design books. It is also clear that the educated gentleman in any major American port was well versed in the classics and fully aware of the European fascination with the lives of the ancient Greeks and Romans.

Classical Education

While a national debate about the advantages and disadvantages of a classical education caught the attention of such well-known luminaries as President John Adams (1735-1826) and Dr. Benjamin Rush (1746-1813) of Philadelphia, most young men born in the United States between 1790 and 1840 received the standard training in Greek, Latin, and classical literature and philosophy endured by their fathers and their grandfathers.[14] The lists of books owned by Americans of means of the early nineteenth century indicate their familiarity with classical writers, such as Cicero, Euclid, Homer, Ovid, Plutarch, Pliny, Seneca, and Virgil.[15]

Libraries in Savannah, for example, featured such volumes by Greek and Roman writers as Pliny's *Natural History*, Homer's *Works*, and Seneca's *Morals*, in addition to eighteenth- and early nineteenth-century histories of the Roman Empire (Gibbons's and Rollins's), of ancient Greece (Gilles's and Goldsmith's), and descriptions of antiquities (Adam's *Roman Antiquities*, Kennett's *Romae Antiquae Notitia*, and Volney's *Ruins*).[16] While English translations of the Greek and Latin texts were increasingly popular, the mythological and moralistic stories told therein were the basis of much of the literary and pictorial imagery of the period.[17]

It stands to reason, therefore, that specific references to Greek and Roman gods and goddesses as well as more subtle uses of classical ornament on furniture, silver, textiles, and ceramics were understood and appreciated by American consumers eager to appear knowledgeable and up-to-date in their attire and in the art and furnishings they selected for their homes (7).

7

Unknown maker
English (probably Staffordshire)
Teapot
c. 1810-1820
Transfer printed earthenware

8

Unknown artist
American
Nathaniel Alexander Adams
c. 1820-1825
Watercolor on ivory; brass case;
gold-colored foil

Considering that during the first quarter of the nineteenth century five to ten ships arrived weekly at the Savannah docks, orders for purchases of all kinds could be quickly filled and desires for all that was *à la mode* were easily gratified.

Classical Portraiture

As for painting, portraiture was by far the most prolific expression of American artists of the neoclassical period. This was certainly the case in Savannah, where the vast majority of works that survive from the first four decades of the nineteenth century are portraits, either in oil on canvas or in watercolor on ivory. Some done by known artists, others by anonymous painters, as a group the works are relatively homogenous, representing the prevailing taste in English portraiture of the eighteenth century in the Grand Manner.

    With composure and grace, the sitters are impeccably dressed and arranged in static poses against a formulaic background of columns, drapery, or a view of the sea. All of these conceits were known and accepted both

9

John Carlin (1813-1891)
American
Ann Wylly Adams Habersham
c. 1835
Watercolor on ivory; original
painted glass and wooden frame

in the United States and abroad. The Savannah sitters are captured in ideal likenesses tempered by some degree of realism (**8,9**).[18] And, while in America the concept of an aristocracy was anathema, the first families of Savannah were inclined to perpetuate the long tradition of imperious portraiture that was a part of their colonial heritage.

Classical Furniture

Of all the articles of household furnishings remaining in Savannah from the first four decades of the nineteenth century and reflecting the classical taste, furniture is the most abundant. Almost entirely of American manufacture (but little locally made), these tables, chairs, sofas, and sideboards are similar to those owned by wealthy people in every East Coast city of that period (**10**).

The American Late Classical style in furniture incorporates elements of both the English Regency and the French Empire. In addition to cabinetmakers' design books, both styles were spread via periodicals available in America—the Regency style by Rudolph Ackermann's *Repository of the Arts*, published between 1809 and 1828, and the French Empire by Pierre La Mésangère's *Collection des Meubles et Objets de Goût*, published between 1802 and 1835, for example. A preference for chairs in the klismos form; for tables with simple pedestals or turned or veneered columns; for case pieces with extensive, highly figured veneered surfaces; and ornament in the classical vein (urns, lyres, putti, and swags) all point to the ubiquitous influence of these and other sources for neoclassicism in the major U.S. cities at this time.

In Savannah it was no different. Newspaper accounts from the period indicate that the majority of the furniture in the latest style, arriving in Savannah almost daily,

came primarily from New York, followed by Providence, Philadelphia, Boston, and Portsmouth. Cabinetmakers, brokers, and ship captains alike all found a ready market for the newest designs in this small yet cosmopolitan city. In January 1820, for example, D. Williford informed the public of his stock of "fashionable New York furniture" consisting of card tables with roped legs and those with claw feet as well as a wide selection of dining, tea, night, and ladies' worktables.[19] Likewise in the chair department, F. W. Heinemann carried the latest in a variety of forms, including harp back with cane seats, flat top, imitation mahogany, double back, mortise top, and Baltimore patterns (all made in Boston).[20]

Furniture in Savannah was sold in a variety of ways and venues. Ship captains with cargo room to spare sold chairs, primarily from ship board, advertising their goods in local newspapers. Auctioneers offered quantities of furniture that were consigned to them by out-of-town as well as local merchants. A well-known and successful auctioneer, J. B. Herbert, offered in April 1835, "20 doz. Fancy Chairs landing on [the ship] *Magnolia* from Boston," and a few months later advertised "400 chairs, 3 bureaus," also from Boston.[21]

Local cabinetmakers made their own wares, served as agents for Northern craftsmen, and traveled to New York and Philadelphia to purchase furniture on speculation to market locally. Among these entrepreneurs, the best known was Isaac W. Morrell, a furniture-maker in his own right who was the Savannah agent for New York cabinetmakers P. J. Arcularius, J. L. Brower, John Hewitt, and Duncan Phyfe; chairmakers J. K. Cowperthwaite, Charles Frederick(s) and Benjamin Farrington, and Stephen Wheaton and Robert Davies, all of New York; and for pianoforte makers Alpheus Babcock of Boston and Samuel L. Speisseger of New York.[22]

10

Unknown maker
English
Recamier sofa
c. 1815-25
Mahogany; beech, spruce

General merchants imported furniture along with a host of other goods, sometimes selecting the objects themselves but more frequently assigning that task to an agent in the North. The citizens of Savannah had a number of different opportunities to buy new household furniture in their own city. Furthermore, many individuals with Northern contacts of their own preferred to commission a friend or relative to act on their behalf by making appropriate purchases directly from a cabinetmaker, based on specific or more general requests and requirements.

A few tantalizing letters describing these transactions remain, suggesting the successes and frustrations linked to this way of selecting household items. In 1830, writing to her friend George Jones Kollock (1810-1894) in Philadelphia, Maria Hull Campbell requested "a few commissions," including some Rose Soap and 1/2 lb. of Brown's Tooth-powder, in addition to two copies of *Lady of the Manor* by Mrs. Sherwood.[23] At the same time she expressed her dismay at the turn of events concerning a wardrobe, recently received from "Cooke and Parsons" of Philadelphia.[24] She writes:

I requested [them] to put a "ketch" on my wardrobe, similar to your Aunts [sic], & showed him that, which he promised to do. He put a hook instead — and in attempting to hook the Wardrobe, the hook flies off —This has always been the case. But now the wood has shrunk so much, that neither lock nor hook is of any use —for the doors do not meet. I must trouble you to ask them to send me a ketch like your Aunts [sic], & I will get it fixed I hope by a Cabinet maker in this place.[25]

Homemade Classicism

With the abundance of imported items available in Savannah shops, there was nonetheless a respectable market for some locally made goods. Identifying these items today, however, is a difficult task for a number of reasons. In the case of furniture, few pieces are marked with the maker's name, so attribution to place of origin is based solely on style, construction, and woods used. No single element is definitive. A small group of furniture by Savannah cabinetmaker John Wilkins (1808-1886) has descended in his family and represents one of a scant number of examples of documented locally made pieces reflecting the influence of classicism. Less fashionable than the imported furniture, the local product contains certain decorative elements, notably twisted reeding and acanthus leaf carving, that suggest an awareness of the Classical style, albeit in a provincial vein (**11**).

Several silver artisans retailed imported silver as well as made their own, marking both these products with their own imprint. The relative sophistication of the marked Savannah hollowware and its similarity to documented pieces made in New York and Philadelphia, in particular, suggest that these examples were made in the

North, shipped to Savannah, and marked by the silversmith who sold them. Current scholarship suggests that with the exception of some flatware, almost all early nineteenth-century Georgia silver was imported.[26]

Ceramics, silver, furniture, brass, lighting — almost all these products were bought elsewhere and arrived in Savannah by ship. Only a few objects included in this exhibition can be firmly attributed to local makers: notably a small number of items of furniture, drawings, miniatures, and oil portraits. Of the latter two categories, many of the artists were actually Northern natives who traveled to Southern cities, plied their trade for a few weeks, and eventually returned home.

The widespread influence of the classical taste assured that no form or material of household goods was exempt from an overlay of this style. The objects documented in this exhibition and catalogue were almost entirely imported by the wealthier citizens of Savannah during the first four decades of the nineteenth century, and they reflect an awareness and desire for the most up-to-date fashions in the classical mode.

11

John Wilkins (1808-1886)
American (Savannah)
Washstand
c. 1835
Mahogany and mahogany veneers;
yellow pine

17

NOTES

1

Piranesi (1720-1778) published a series of engravings, *Antiquities of Rome [Le Antichità Romane]* (1756), depicting the ruins of ancient Rome. According to art historian Rudolf Wittkower, these etchings are said to have had "no equal" when they were published, even "when other artists of considerable merit were attracted by similar subjects, stimulated, more than ever before, by a public desirous to behold the picturesque remains, true and imaginary, of Roman greatness." [Rudolf Wittkower, *Art and Architecture in Italy: 1600-1750* (Baltimore: Penguin Books, 1958), p. 236]. Piranesi also published *Views of Rome [Vedute di Roma]*, beginning in 1748.

2

Two of the best known publications were those by LeRoy (*Les Ruines des plus Beaux Monuments de la Grèce*, 1758) and by James Stuart and Nicholas Revett (*Antiquities of Athens*, 1762, 1789, 1795).

3

Considered by many to have been "the father of classical archaeology," German antiquarian and scholar Winckelmann (1717-1768) was the author of *The History of Ancient Art*, published in 1764, and director general of Roman antiquities for Pope Clement XIII (1758-69). [Wittkower, 1958, p. 236] Together with his friend, writer and painter Anton Raffael Mengs (1728-1779), Winckelmann was highly influential in the development of the Neoclassical taste in Europe.

4

Henry Hawley, *Neo-classicism: Style and Motif* (Cleveland: Cleveland Museum of Art, 1964), p. 16.

5

Peter Thornton, *Authentic Decor: The Domestic Interior 1620-1920* (New York: Viking, 1984), p. 92.

6

Hawley, 1964, p. 17.

7

Robert C. Smith. "The Classical Style in France and England 1800-1840," *The Magazine Antiques*, v. 74, # 5 (November, 1958), p. 430.

8

Among the best known of David's paintings showing "Antique" furniture is his famous portrait of Madame Récamier painted in 1800. The sitter is seen lounging on a settee of late Roman design, a form which later took the name of the lady sitting upon it.

9

The designs of Percier (1764-1838) and Fontaine (1762-1853) were later published in *Recueil de décorations intérieures comprenant tout ce qui a rapport à l'ameublement* (in 1801 in serial form, and later as a book in 1812).

10

Thomas Hope, *Household Furniture and Interior Decoration* (London: Longman, Hurst, Rees and Orme, 1807), pp. 4-5.

11

Most accurately used to describe the nine years when the Prince of Wales ruled as Prince Regent from 1811 to 1820, the term "Regency," when applied to decorative arts, is more typically used to describe the popular style in England from 1795 to 1820. In his thorough treatment of the subject, Frances Collard expands the period of the Regency to 1840 [*Regency Furniture* (Suffolk, GB: Antique Collectors' Club, 1985)], as does John Morley in his discussion of the style. [*Regency Design* (London: A. Zwemmer Ltd., 1993)]

12

George Smith's books include *A Collection of Designs for Household Furniture and Interior Decoration* (London: J. Taylor, 1808), considered to be one of the most important pattern books for cabinetmakers in England during the Regency period. He also published *A Collection of Ornamental Designs after the Manner of the Antique* (London: J. Taylor, 1812) and *The Cabinet-Maker and Upholsterer's Guide* (London: Jones & Co., 1826 [28?]).

13

For a discussion of European antecedents of American neoclassical furniture, see Donald L. Fennimore, "American Neoclassical Furniture and its European Antecedents," *The American Art Journal*, v. 13, # 4 (Autumn, 1981), pp. 49-65.

14

For a discussion of this issue and an overview of scholarship on classical traditions in early America, see Meyer Reinhold, *Classica Americana. The Greek and Roman Heritage in the United States* (Detroit: Wayne State University Press, 1984), pp. 1-48.

15

Howard Mumford Jones has written that the notion that "the classical past has exerted an important influence on the culture of the United States seems to many absurd;" he cautions that only a small elite minority was endowed with a veneer of "gentlemen's culture." However he acknowledges that the classics served an important political and historical function in the development of American culture. [*O Strange New World. American Culture: The Formative Years* (New York, 1952), pp. 227-272; discussed in Reinhold, 1976, p. 19] While this proviso is noteworthy, the material evidence in Savannah suggests that a substantial part of the population was exposed to, and interested in, the various contemporary interpretations of classical civilization as represented in books, prints, and decorative arts.

16

This list of books was selected from two of the many Chatham County wills containing references to books on classical subjects: John J. Evans, Inventory, Chatham County Inventory and Administration Book F, May 24, 1813 and Stephen C. Greene, Inventory, Chatham County Inventory and Administration Book H, April 30, 1833.

17

Translations of classical texts owned by attorney Joseph H. Stephens of Savannah, for example, included Lealand's version of Demosthenes, Davidson's Virgil, and Duncan's Cicero. [Chatham County I & A Book F (May 24, 1806)]

18

In her discussion of neoclassical portraiture, Ann M. Hope observed that it was the role of the portraitist to "go beyond actual nature in quest of an ideal, was free, was indeed required to omit defects and to make good what deficiencies he might."

She quotes Jonathan Richardson as writing, "To make a wise man to be more wise, and a brave man to be more so, a modest discreet woman to have an air something angelical, and so of the rest; and then to add that joy, or peace of mind at least, and in such manner as is suitable to the several characters is absolutely necessary to a good face painter." [Quoted in Ann M. Hope, *The Theory and Practice of Neoclassicism in English Painting: The Origins, Development and Decline of an Ideal* (New York and London: Garland Publishing, Inc., 1988), p. 117]

19

Columbian Museum and Savannah Daily Gazette (January 31, 1820).

20

Daily Georgian (November 3, 1840).

21

Daily Georgian (April 10, 1835); *Ibid.* (December 23, 1835).

22

Georgian and Evening Advertiser (May 2, 1821); *Columbian Museum and Savannah Daily Gazette* (January 4, 1822; June 12, 1822); *Savannah Georgian* (October 29, 1825); *Daily Georgian* (November 25, 1834). Also Inward Coastal Manifests, National Archives, Record Group 36 [NA ICM 36/ Boxes 2-21] Isaac W. Morrell was thought to have come to Savannah from New England. The earliest record of his importing furniture into Savannah is the arrival on Feb. 2, 1811 of one case of furniture sent by John Hewitt of New York. [NA ICM 36/2] He continued in business for many years and died in Savannah in 1865.

23

Maria Hull Campbell was later wed to Judge W. W. Montgomery of Augusta, Georgia. After marriage she lived next to the southwest corner of South Broad (now Oglethorpe Avenue) and Whitaker Streets.

24

Thomas Cook and Richard Parkin were Philadelphia cabinetmakers who may have come from England. During their partnership (1819-1833), they made furniture in the Regency style that relates closely to designs in English pattern books known to have been owned in this country. An example of their work is illustrated in

Wendy Cooper, *Classical Taste in America* (Baltimore: Baltimore Museum of Art, 1993), p. 56. A table made for Margaret Telfair by Thomas Cook is illustrated here (**90**).

25

Maria Campbell to George J. Kollock, 297 Spruce St., Philadelphia, Pa., March 5, 1830, in "The Kollock Papers, Part III," *Georgia Historical Quarterly*, v. 31, # 1 (January, 1947), pp. 41-2.

26

Among those Savannah silversmiths who were known to import silver from Northern cities were David B. Nichols, Josiah Penfield, Moses Eastman, and Frederick Marquand. While all these men were craftsmen in their own right, there is every reason to believe that the majority of their business was in imported silver from the North and abroad. [see Katharine Gross Farnham and Callie Huger Efird, "Early Silversmiths and the Trade in Georgia," *The Magazine Antiques*, v. 99, # 3 (March, 1971), pp. 380-385]. In addition to silver, most men who called themselves silversmiths also sold jewelry, watches, keys, and small decorative items such as snuff boxes, spectacles, and seals.

CATALOGUE ENTRIES

1

**Attributed to Charlotte McCord
Cheves (1818-1879)
American (Charleston)**
Sale of Loves
**c. 1835-1840
Watercolor on paper
Framed: 5 ¾ x 5 ¾ in.
(14.6 x 14.6 cm.);
image: 2 ½ in. dia. (6.4 cm.)**

*Provenance: Charlotte McCord
Cheves; to her niece Louisa Rebecca
McCord Smythe (1845-1928);
to her daughter Hannah M. Smythe
Wright (1874-1955); to her son
David M. Wright (1909-1968);
to his wife Caroline Jones Wright
(b. 1911).
Loan from Caroline Jones Wright*

20

When Charlotte Cheves chose
this subject to paint for this delicate watercolor, she joined a succession of artists whose work was
indebted to the archaeological
excavations of Pompeii, Herculaneum, and Stabiae. With the
uncovering of these long-buried
cities came a wealth of information about classical art in a variety
of media, including painting. Of
these, one of the most popular
motifs was "Sale of Loves," a subject taken from a wall painting in
Stabiae, a site in the Italian
Campania region, not far from
Herculaneum.

Depicting a woman selling cupids
as love charms, this theme became
a popular one for decorative arts
of all kinds: patch boxes, fans,
jewelry, porcelain, textiles. A variety of interpretations were given
to this scene. Maréchale, for
example, "insisted that the figures

represented Venus, her three sons,
and their nursemaid; the three
cupids corresponded to the three
aspects of human love: desire,
need, and possession."[1]

Among the most common objects
using this theme were small
ceramic plaques, such as the jasper
wares manufactured in abundance
by Josiah Wedgwood (1730-1795).
These plaques were made for
insertion into boxes, or tops of
canes and umbrellas.[2] His source
may have been the engraving by
Carlo Nolli for *Antichità di
Ercolano* (published by the
Accademia Ercolanese under the
command of the King of Naples,
1757-1762).[3] So widespread was the
circulation of this work that by
1767 everything was said to be

*made à la greque, which is the same
as saying 'à Erculanum.'... All the
bronzes, engravings and paintings
are copied from Ercolano. I have seen
that painting of a woman selling
cherubs as chickens at least ten
times.[4]*

Mrs. Charlotte Cheves was an
amateur artist, known as an artful
copyist, who was born in
Columbia, South Carolina. Later
she moved south where she spent
the warmer months in Charleston,
and the rest of the year on the rice
plantation across the river from
Savannah owned by her husband's
family. Langdon Cheves Jr. (1814-
1863) was the son of Langdon
Cheves I (1776-1857), a lawyer,
politican, and planter who was at
one time president of the Second
Bank of the United States in

Philadelphia. The senior Cheves
returned to South Carolina in
1829 where he purchased property
along the lower Savannah River
that became the largest and most
consistently successful rice plantation in the area, the 2,762 acre
Delta plantation. His friends and
neighbors included two of the
wealthiest and most influential
men in South Carolina and
Georgia, Dr. James Proctor
Screven (1799-1859) **(97)** and Judge
Daniel Huger (1779-1854).[5]

Charlotte Cheves's miniatures
were described at the time as
"excellent likenesses, and finished
with great delicacy."[6] She was also
known to paint in oil and to excel
in pastels as well as pencil sketch-
ing. Like other women artists of
her day she "might have gained
celebrity had her life been given
to the study of painting."[7]

1
*Pompeii as Source and Inspiration: Reflections
in Eighteenth-and Nineteenth-Century Art;
An Exhibition Organized by the 1976-1977
Graduate Students in the Museum Practice
Program* (Ann Arbor, MI: The University
of Michigan Museum of Art, 1977), p. 18.
The authors illustrate a bracelet and a
printed French textile using this theme.
2
Examples of these plaques are illustrated in
Elizabeth Bryding Adams, *The Dwight and
Lucille Beeson Wedgwood Collection at the
Birmingham Museum of Art* (Birmingham,
AL: Birmingham Museum of Art, 1992),
pp. 399 and 511, and date from c. 1770-
1800. The artist responsible for Wedg-
wood's "Sale of Cupids" is not known, but
it has been suggested that it may have been
Lady Templeton. A number of drawings
for small domestic scenes and "amorini"

are attributed to her, but others were also known to have supplied such images to Wedgwood. [Henry Barnard, *Chats on Wedgwood Ware* (New York: Frederick A. Stokes Company, Publisher, 1924), p. 222]

3
Objects found at other Campanian sites, including Stabiae and Pompeii, were included in this publication, falling under the general heading of "antiquities of Herculaneum and its environs." [Richard Brilliant, *Pompeii: The Treasury of Rediscovery* (New York: Clarkson N. Potter, 1979), p. 40]. Nolli, a Neopolitan painter and engraver, died in 1770.

4
From a letter from the Abbey Ferdinando Galiani to Bernardo Tanucci, quoted in *Rediscovering Pompeii: an Exhibition by IBM-ITALIA* (Rome: L'erma di Bretschneider, 1990), p. 1.

5
Lawrence S. Rowland, "'Alone on the River:' The Rise and Fall of the Savannah River Rice Plantations of St. Peter's Parish, South Carolina," *South Carolina Historical Magazine*, v. 88, # 3 (July, 1987), pp. 136-137. Included in the property Cheves purchased was Smithfield plantation, purchased from the estate of Edward Telfair of Savannah.

6
Mrs. Ellet, *Women Artists in All Ages and Countries* (New York: Harper and Brothers Publishers, 1859), p. 344. For more on women artists in South Carolina, see Anna Wells Rutledge, "Artists in the Life of Charleston, through Colony and State from Restoration to Reconstruction," *American Philosophical Society Transactions*, new ser. 39 (November, 1949), pp. 101-126.

7
Ellet, 1959, p. 344.

2
Samuel C. Barnard (n.d.)
American (Savannah)
Apollo and the Muses on Parnassus
1829
Graphite on paper
19 ⅞ x 27 ¼ in. (20 x 69.2 cm.)

Inscriptions: signed l.r. "Samuel C. Barnard/Savannah 22 Jan. a.d. 1829."; l.c. "Polyhymnia Clio Erato Melpomene/Apollo and the Muses on Mount Parnassus/Terpsichore Urania Calliope Thalia Eurterpe"

Provenance: found in Savannah; Terry Lowenthal, 1970s; Robert Powell Coggins Collection; Robert Powell Coggins Art Trust, Morris Museum of Art.
Loan from Morris Museum of Art

Three centuries removed from its ultimate artistic source, this drawing reflects thorough knowledge of classical subjects as well as eighteenth century culture and scholarship. Apollo, son of Zeus and Leta, was the god of light, purity, and the sun. The patron god of musicians and poets, he is pictured here playing the lyre, the attribute most often associated with him. He stands on Mount Parnassus, the site sacred to him, presiding over the pastimes of the muses who surround him.

Derived from Anton Raffael Mengs's famous ceiling fresco *Apollo at Parnassus* in the apartment of Cardinal Albani (1760-1761), Barnard's direct source is not known. It is doubtful that he had traveled to Rome to actually

examine the original, but considering the widespread influence of this painting, it is not surprising that a citizen of nineteenth-century Savannah would have known of it through a print or an illustration in a book. While Kenneth Clark referred to Mengs's fresco as "insipid... fundamentally frivolous," at the time it was completed, this painting personified the glorification of all that was Greek and an aesthetic that placed Hellenic art at the pinnacle of discriminating taste.[1]

In fact Mengs's *Parnassus* is considered to be "nothing less than the first manifesto of the neoclassical movement in painting."[2] His painting was in turn directly derived from a work by Raphael, Mengs's namesake along with Antonio Corregio, another artistic giant of the Italian Rennaissance. Raphael's painting, an allegory of poetry, was painted for Pope Julius II in the Stanza della Signatura in the Vatican.

1
Kenneth Clark, *The Romantic Rebellion*, quoted in Estill Curtis Pennington, *A Southern Collection* (Augusta, GA: Morris Communications Corporation, 1992), p. 127.

2
Julius S. Held and Donald Posner, *Seventeenth and Eighteenth Century Baroque Painting, Sculpture, Architecture* (Englewood Cliffs, NJ: Prentiss-Hall, Inc.; New York: Harry N. Abrams, Inc., n.d.), p. 355.

3
Unknown maker
American (Philadelphia or
New York)
Linen press
c. 1810-1820
Mahogany; mahogany, pine
90 x 48 x 24 ¼ in.
(228.6 x 133.7 x 61.6 cm.)

Provenance: part of the original furnishings of Hermitage plantation, owned by the McAlpin family of Savannah; Miss Margaret Vernon Stiles; Susan and Walter Hartridge; Francis D. McNairy.
Loan from Francis D. McNairy

The McAlpin linen press incorporates a number of elements of the Adamesque vocabulary that began to have an impact on Federal design following the Revolution. Two important innovations of this style are the use of the oval and rectangle within one form and the contrast of light and dark. Large expanses of highly figured contrasting mahogany veneer accentuate the juxtaposition of rectangle and oval in this elegant yet restrained linen press. And while the doors are veneered with only one type of wood, the selection of horizontal and vertical grains gives the appearance of a variation of light and dark.

Other New York and Philadelphia examples, most with outward-raking French feet, can be found in many museum collections. Similar examples were also made in the South, notably in Charleston and Savannah.[1] One of the few documented Savannah-made pieces of furniture is a secretary desk in The Columbus (Georgia) Museum of Arts and Sciences made by Owen Strange (1776-1814) between 1801 and 1809.[2] This secretary incorporates many of the Adamesque details seen in the linen press. The linen press may have belonged to Henry McAlpin (1780-1851), whose inventory of 1851 includes "one mahogany wardrobe."[3] This and other fashionable furniture were part of the furnishings of the Hermitage, the McAlpin's estate near Savannah.

1
New York examples can be found in the Metropolitan Museum of Art and the Diplomatic Reception Rooms, Department of State, Washington, and the Winterthur Museum. Philadelphia examples are in the Metropolitan Museum and the Philadelphia Museum of Art. The horizontal overhanging cornice relates to documented New York examples, such as the Phyfe secretary owned by the Telfairs (**65**) and the Olmstead secretary desk (**66**).
2
This signed desk and bookcase is illustrated in Jane Webb Smith, *Georgia's Legacy: History Charted Through the Arts* (Athens, GA: University of Georgia Press, 1985), p. 135.
3
Henry McAlpin, Will and Inventory, Book M-3, #321, pp. 1406-69 (July 7, 1851).

4
Detail, Wall light with Greek key motif
1816-1819
Savannah, Georgia
North wall, dining room
Richardson-Owens-
Thomas House

The Greek key (or meander) convex cutout on the north wall of the "Dining Room or Large Parlour" of the Richardson-Owens-Thomas House, currently interpreted as a dining room, is backed with amber glass, providing a source of additional light to supplement the light from the pair of windows at the front of the room.[1] This decorative motif is one of many classical elements used by William Jay (1792-1837) in his Savannah houses. Other commonly used ornaments include anthemia, Corinthian columns, egg and dart moldings, and urns.

1
This room was described as "Dining Room or Large Parlour" in the inventory of the sale of the contents of the house in December 1822. [Chatham County Deeds Book 2L, p. 43]

5
Unknown maker
English (probably Staffordshire)
Cream pitcher
c. 1810
Pink lusterware
5 x 6 x 3 ⅜ in.
(12.7 x 15.2 x 8.1 cm.)
**Print source: perhaps based on
drawings of Adam Buck.**

*Provenance: found in the Savannah
area; Regency Shop at the
Richardson-Owens-Thomas House;
Telfair Museum of Art.
Telfair Museum of Art Study
Collection*

Perhaps adapted from the series of
"Sportive Prints" published by
English artist Adam Buck (1759-
1833), the transfer print on this
small lusterware cream pitcher
shows a woman in Regency dress
reclining on a Grecian couch.
Buck was a student and collector
of the antique and is best known
for his drawings of ladies and
children. As props, he frequently
uses klismos chairs and other classical furniture and motifs, such as
lyres and chariots.[1] English ceramics had a ready market in
America, and Savannah was no
exception. Earthenwares of all
varieties were imported in abundance into this port in the early
decades of the nineteenth century.

In the case of this pitcher, the
decoration was achieved through
two methods: the transfer print
and the luster decoration. Most
popular from 1805 through 1825,
the metallic luster process was an
English invention of the late
eighteenth century that involved

painting a solution of acid and
gold or platinum over a pre-glazed
surface. Firing the pitcher created
a reaction that caused the gold or
platinum to fuse into a thin film.[2]

1
A tea service featuring Buck's engravings
(c. 1790-1810) is illustrated in Wendy A.
Cooper, *Classical Taste in America*
(Baltimore: Baltimore Museum of Art,
1993), p.199. For a discussion of the influence of Greek vase painting on Adam
Buck see Ian Jenkins, "Adam Buck and the
vogue for Greek vases," *The Burlington
Magazine*, v. 130, # 1023 (June, 1988), pp.
448-457.
2
John W. Keefe, "English Lusterware from
the Duckworth Collection," *The Magazine
Antiques*, v. 96, # 3 (September, 1969),
p. 382. For a discussion of the process of
transfer printing, see (**36 a-d**).

6
Unknown maker
American (Philadelphia)
Astragal-end worktable
c. 1815-1825
**Mahogany; poplar, white pine,
mahogany, beech**
30 ½ x 23 ⅝ x 13 in.
(77.4 x 60 x 33 cm.)

*Inscription: verso of top drawer, in
pencil, in script "Timothy G.
Barnard/April 17, 1829"*

*Provenance: descended in the White-
Jackson families of Savannah;
Telfair Museum of Art.
Bequest of Mary White Jackson,
1951, OT 12.1959*

This table combines many elements of the English Regency
style: the use of reeding (here on
the legs and the face of the cabinet); the vase-shaped support;

large uninterrupted veneered surfaces; and an overall emphasis on
vertical and horizontal lines juxta-
posed against ovals. The astragal
shape of the case and the top were
features produced in relatively
sophisticated urban shops in the
mid-Atlantic region, for local consumption or as venture cargo.[1]
The reeded pilasters on the case
and the bulbous turning of the
vase suggest a Philadelphia maker.

Tables such as this were used for a
variety of purposes, as writing
desks or for storage of sewing and
other handwork.[2] Worktables did
not become common in America
until the end of the eighteenth
century, when they usually had
fabric bags for storage of sewing
materials, which, being attached
to a frame that was fit to a sliding
mechanism, could be pulled out
for easy access. The bag hung
between four tapered legs.[3] Later
examples such as this one often
featured side compartments with
hinged tops and single pedestals
for support. Inside the smaller
drawer are a group of movable
wooden partitions that make compartments for storage of sewing
implements, thread, etc., while the
larger drawer is deep and open
and would have held fabric or
items being mended.

The name "Timothy G. Barnard"
appears on the underside of a
drawer on this worktable. The
1849 will of a man of this name
appears in the Chatham County
records where the deceased is
referred to as Doctor, married
to Mary Ann Mongin.

23

A Dr. Timothy Barnard, son of Timothy Barnard (d. 1842) and Amelia Guerard, is mentioned in the Steele White Papers in the Georgia Historical Society.[4] Nothing more is currently known about this man who was likely the owner of the worktable.[5]

1
Another New York table of almost identical form and detail was also shipped to Savannah, this to the Charlton family, and is illustrated in John Bivins, "A Catalog of Northern Furniture with Southern Provenance," *Journal of Early Southern Decorative Arts*, v.15, #2 (November, 1989), pp. 43-91.

2
The interior writing surface is a modern replacement.

3
David Barquist, *American Tables and Looking Glasses in the Mabel Brady Garvan and Other Collections at Yale University* (New Haven: Yale University Press, 1992), p. 274. Barquist knows of no American worktable which can be dated before 1800, either based on its maker's working dates or by history of ownership.

4
Ms. Collection # 965 (Colonial Dames Collection: Steele White Papers). The donor, Mary White Jackson (d. 1951), was the great-granddaughter of Steele White (1784-1823) and Anna Matthews Guerard (d. 1861). Amelia Guerard Barnard may have been her sister and the daughter of Godin Guerard.

5
Will, Timothy G. Barnard, 1849, Chatham Country Probate Court, Microfiche B-3, 522-524.

7
Unknown maker
English (probably Staffordshire)
Teapot
c. 1810-1820
Transfer printed earthenware
5 ½ x 9 ½ in. (13.9 x 24.1 cm.)
Print sources: the figure is perhaps derived from one in George Richardson's *A Collection of Ornaments in the Antique Style*, published posthumously by his son in 1816. It is also related to Richard Westall's illustration for Sir Walter Scott's *Lady of the Lake*, published in London in 1810.

Provenance: found in the Savannah vicinity.
Loan from Will Theus

While the precise print source for this teapot is not known, the identity of the reclining woman is quite certain. She is Demeter (or Ceres to the Romans), goddess of agriculture and summer, holding two attributes associated with her: a scythe and a sheaf of wheat; she is crowned with a wreath of poppies. The educated American would have been familiar with her story from the Homeric hymn "To Demeter," through Virgil and Pausanius.[1] The purchaser would no doubt have known the captivating story of Demeter's search for her daughter Persephone, who had been carried off to the underworld by Hades. Although Demeter appears benign in this transfer print, she would also have been remembered as the wrathful mother responsible for making the earth infertile until Persephone returned to her.

Combined with the picture of Demeter on this teapot is a decorative motif with an equally ancient history: the cluster of feathers forming a band at the top of the body and around the lid. Known to some as "Prince of Wales feathers," this ornament relates to a design copied by Robert Adam from the Temple of the Sun at Palmyra, Greece.[2] The same motif was used on chair backs and as an inlay on the top of table legs in Hepplewhite's furniture designs.

1
Jane D. Reid, *The Oxford Guide to Classical Mythology in the Arts 1300-1900's* (New York: Oxford University Press, 1993), p. 338.

2
Philippa Lewis and Gillian Darley, *Dictionary of Ornament* (New York: Pantheon Books, 1986), p. 126.

8
Unknown artist
American
Nathaniel Alexander Adams
c. 1820-1825
Watercolor on ivory; brass case; gold-colored foil
2 ⅝ x 2 ⅝ in. (6.6 x 5.7 cm.)

Provenance: Nathaniel A. Adams (1800-1846); to his daughter Julia Mildred Adams Walker; to her granddaughter Mrs. Reginald Scott Fleet, early 1930s; to her daughter Julia B. Fleet, 1987; Telfair Museum of Art
Gift of Julia Bolton Fleet, 1990, in memory of her mother, Mrs. Reginald Scott Fleet, 1990.1

9
John Carlin (1813-1891)
American
Ann Wylly Adams Habersham
c. 1835
Watercolor on ivory; original
painted glass and wooden frame
Framed: 6 ⅜ x 7 ⅜ in.
(16.2 x 18.8 cm.)

Inscriptions: signed l.l. "J. Carlin"

*Provenance: Ann Wylly Adams
Habersham (1795-1876); to her
daughter Josephine Habersham
Habersham (1821-1893); to her
daughter Anna W. Habersham Jones
(1849-1888); to her son George Noble
Jones (1874-1955); to his daughter
Frances Jones Luquer (b.1905); to her
niece Anna Habersham Wright
(b. 1950).*
Loan from Anna Habersham Wright

Seated in a painted fancy chair so
commonly imported into
Savannah in the early nineteenth
century, young Nathaniel
Alexander Adams (1800-1846) (**8**)
was the brother of Ann Wylly
Adams Habersham (1795-1876)
(**9**), wife of Dr. Joseph Clay
Habersham (1790-1885). With this
marriage two well-known
Savannah families were united.
The Adams children were grand-
children of Colonel Richard
Wylly, who served in the Georgia
Continental Line during the
Revolution. The Habersham fami-
ly was a distinguished one, and
many likenesses of its members
have been preserved as well,
including that of Joseph
Habersham II (**41**) and Joseph
Habersham (**59**).

Painted by different artists, both
these miniatures reflect the
wealth, stylishness, and dignity of
the sitters.[1] Ann Adams
Habersham's portrait was painted
by John Carlin, a deaf mute
painter who worked primarily in
Philadelphia and New York.[2]
In its original painted glass mat,
Carlin's portrait is painted in his
typical delicate stipple technique,
in a palette known for its brilliant
color.[3] Both miniatures are
sophisticated renderings of prominent Savannahians.

[1]
The portrait of Nathaniel Adams has been
attributed to miniaturist Cornelius
Schroeder (active c. 1802-1826), who visited
Savannah in 1807, 1809, and 1817. For 15
dollars he warranted "Likenesses as accu-
rate as can be obtained in any part of the
union." [*Republican and Savannah Evening
Ledger* (March 21, 1809)] Like many other
American miniature painters of the period,
such as Raphael and Rembrandt Peale,
Picot de Clorivière and Edward Greene
Malbone, Schroeder traveled throughout
the South, visiting in addition to
Savannah, Richmond, and Alexandria,
Virginia; Augusta, Georgia; and Halifax,
North Carolina. Nathaniel Adams looks to
be in his early twenties in this portrait,
making the attribution to Schroeder ques-
tionable. As very few documented works
by Schroeder are known, it is difficult to
make an attribution to this artist based on
style.
[2]
George Groce and David H. Wallace, *The
New-York Historical Society's Dictionary of
Artists in America 1564-1860* (New Haven:
Yale University Press; London: Oxford
University Press, 1957), p. 109. Carlin was
also an author of some success, best known
for the *Scratchside Family* (New York:
W. L. Stone & J.T. Barron, 1868) and the
poem, "The Mute's Lament," published in
Deaf Mute's Journal [April 30, 1891].

[3]
Dale T. Johnson, *American Portrait
Miniatures in the Manney Collection*
(New York: Metropolitan Museum, 1990),
pp. 90-91.

10
Unknown maker
English
Recamier sofa
c. 1815-25
Mahogany; beech, spruce
37 ¾ x 75 x 26 in.
(95.9 x 190.5 x 66 cm.)
Mark: stamped, recto, right of
median rail "WB"

*Inscription: c. median rail, in chalk,
in script "G.GS (Y?)"; on red-edged
paper label "Mrs. Julian/119"
(missing last name and rest of
address); on adhesive tape "131"*

*Provenance: descended in the
Wilder-Anderson family; to Ann
Page Wilder Anderson (1874?-1958);
to her daughter Page Randolf
Anderson Platt (1899-1984);
Telfair Museum of Art.
Gift of Mrs. Henry W. Platt,
1958.3.1-3*

Perhaps one of a mirror-image
pair, this sofa descended in the
Wilder and Anderson families of
Savannah. The raised arm and
high curvilinear back are typical of
the form called a "Grecian squab"
or "Grecian couch" in Thomas
Sheraton's *Cabinet Dictionary*
(London, 1803).[1] Sheraton and
other English designers, in turn,
adapted the form from Roman
banqueting couches, as seen on
antique vase paintings and other
archaeological sources.

Somewhat unusual on this sofa is the rounded lower end, a different solution from the more typical inward scroll seen on most couches of this period, and a feature rarely seen on American furniture. The broad reeding on the front surfaces is a common feature on both New York- and Baltimore-made furniture of the period, as are the shape of the legs and the use of brass lion's paw casters, but the form of the sofa and the presence of beech and spruce as secondary woods suggest an English origin. Perhaps original, the patterned horsehair cover fixed to the frame with brass nail heads was a typical upholstery treatment. Made primarily for reclining, such couches were ubiquitous in the finer houses in America in the early decades of the nineteenth century. A form popular in America in the late seventeenth century and early eighteenth century, sofas serving the function of day beds were much in fashion in this period. They were primarily placed against a wall, with only one side finished with reeding.

I

Plates 49 and 50. Other English publications refer to this form as a "chaise longue" [George Smith, 1805] or a "couch" [Thomas Hope, 1807]. See Michael Flanigan, *American Furniture from the Kaufman Collection* (Washington: National Gallery of Art, 1986), # 58 (p. 154).

II
John Wilkins (1808-1886)
American (Savannah)
Washstand
c. 1835
Mahogany and mahogany veneers; yellow pine
30 ½ x 15 ¾ x 15 ¾ in. (77.5 x 40 x 40 cm.)

Provenance: John Wilkins; to his daughter E. Catherine Wilkins Rabey (1855-1936); to her son D. Wilkie Rabey (1895-1977); to his daughter Dorothy Rabey Brantley (b. 1927).
Loan from Dorothy Rabey Brantley

John D. Wilkins arrived in Savannah prior to 1830 when he was married to Rebecca Ann Lavendar. A widower by 1839, he remarried Mary Catherine Gnann. A number of pieces made by Wilkins have descended in his family, including two washstands, a bureau and dressing glass, a sideboard, a drop-leaf worktable, a gentleman's dressing table, and a group of cabinetmaker's tools (marked "W."). These tools include glass and mold cutters, a bit brace, and two jack planes.[1]

While the date of this washstand is not known, the rather thick legs and heavy diagonal reeding suggest that it was probably made in the 1830s, a somewhat old-fashioned interpretation of the Federal style, imitating the form of New York examples of washstands popular in the first two decades of the nineteenth century.

I
Pamela Wagner, *Hidden Heritage: Recent Discoveries in Georgia Decorative Art, 1733-1915* (Atlanta: High Museum of Art, 1990), p. 23.

26

Savannah, Georgia

1800 – 1840 / 1800

Its Colonial Legacy

Located on a 40 foot bluff overlooking a river, the city of Savannah was the site of the first English settlement in the colony of Georgia. The land was purchased from the native inhabitants and granted to nineteen "Trustees for establishing the colony of Georgia in America." Among them was General James Oglethorpe (1696-1785), who landed there with 116 settlers on February 12, 1733.[1] Oglethorpe named the town Savannah after the Yamacraw Indian word for the "great river on the S.W. bank of which it is sited."[2]

King George II's motives for establishing this newest colony were numerous. The settlement would serve as a buffer between the Carolinas to the north and Spanish Florida to the south.[3] The first settlers were to be the "worthy poor" of England, for whom the new country would offer respite and hope. These colonists were also potential consumers of goods produced by the mother country and eventual providers of such desirable products as silk and wine.[4] The additional colony of Georgia also gave England a stronger foothold in North America.

Savannah was laid out in a carefully organized grid plan intersected with a series of squares. The original town, or "tything," lots were 60 by 90 feet, fronted by parallel streets and backed by service lanes. The larger "trust" lots faced the squares and were initially reserved for public buildings. In addition to town lots, settlers were granted five-acre garden plots just outside the city and 45 acre farm lots beyond. The plan provided a framework for future development, which was followed fairly closely until the mid-nineteenth century.[5]

Its Location

Savannah became the principle port for the new colony as well as its capital. The strategic location fifteen miles from the mouth of the Savannah River possessed a deep harbor that could accommodate boats "drawing 14 feet water...larger vessels take in their cargoes 3 miles below."[6] To the south were the fertile Sea Islands, where black seed or "sea-island" cotton grew along with oranges, lemons, sugarcane, and arrowroot. In the tidal swamplands of the Altamaha, Ogeechee, and Savannah Rivers, large crops of rice were also cultivated; inland were vast stands of timber. These crops provided the colonial settlers with the economic resources to buy large quantities of imported goods, principally from England, but also from Northern American cities, mainly New York and Philadelphia.

In 1788 the town of Augusta, 120 miles upstream from Savannah, became the capital of the new state of Georgia, but Savannah retained its prominence as a port and trade center. The increasing importance of Sea Island cotton as an exportable commodity secured for the city a significant geographic advantage over Charleston, its neighboring rival which had long enjoyed economic superiority. Not only had Charleston been a center for direct trade with London since early in the eighteenth century, but also the city had fostered a local community of craftsmen straight from London whose products were far superior to anything then made in Savannah.[7] By the beginning of the new century, however, Savannah, though much smaller than Charleston, was beginning to enjoy an improved economic position on the Southern coast, a position which was to improve steadily during the ensuing six decades.

Its People

In mid-May 1791, Savannah was favored by a visit from President George Washington (1732-1799).[8] Although unimpressed with the physical status of the town, which he found uncomfortably warm, windy, and sandy, Washington was contented with his lodging and pleased by the enthusiastic, nearly ecstatic, greeting from Savannahians. According to one early account:

Ten miles above the city the President and his escort were met by a large number of gentlemen in boats, and as the President passed by them a band played the celebrated song "He comes, the Hero comes," accompanied by several voices. On his approach to the city the "concourse on the bluff and the crowds which had pressed into the vessels evinced the general joy which had been inspired by the visit of this most beloved of men and the ardent desire of all ranks and conditions of people to be gratified at his presence." [9]

Among those who welcomed the President were the most prominent citizens of Savannah, many of whom had served in the Revolutionary War and had helped establish the new United States government (**12**). The members of the Society of the Cincinnati, former officers of the American army, entertained the President at a ball and dinner peopled by ninety-six ladies who were "elegantly dressed, some of whom displayed infinite taste in the emblems and devices on their sashes and head-dresses, out of respect to the happy occasion." [10] Preceding each of the numerous toasts were salutes from the Chatham Artillery, one of the earliest volunteer artillery companies in the United States, established in 1786 (**13**).[11]

12

Unknown artist
American
William Gibbons
c. 1800
Watercolor on ivory; copper case;
woven hair; glass

13

Unknown maker
American
*Cross belt plate
worn by a member of the
Chatham Artillery*
c. 1790-1810
Cast brass

Officers at an earlier soirée at Brown's
Coffee House included Colonels Steele White
(1784-1823) (**14**), Noble Wimberly Jones (1787-
1818), Joseph Habersham (1751-1815), and Major
Pierce Butler (1744-1822) (**15**). Absent from the
festivities was the recently deceased General
Nathanael Greene (1742-1786) (**16**), whose wife
Catherine Littlefield Greene (1755-1814) (**17**)
received Washington at her nearby plantation,
Mulberry Grove, upon both his arrival and
departure from the city.[12]

Two years later, the home of "Caty"
Littlefield Greene became even more famous as
the birthplace of the cotton gin invented by Eli
Whitney, the young law student who tutored
Mrs. Greene's children at the plantation (**18**).
This machine revolutionized the cotton industry
and initiated the prosperity that Savannah
enjoyed for most of the next half-century, despite
periods of adversity, including yellow fever epi-
demics, occasional economic depressions,
and most notably, the disastrous fires of 1796
and 1820.

30

14

Joseph-Pierre Picot de Limoëlin
de Clorivière (1768-1826)
French
General [Colonel] Steele White
c. 1803-1806
Watercolor on ivory; copper case

15

Samuel Williamson
(d. 1843; active 1794-1813)
American (Philadelphia)
Tankard
c. 1794
Coin Silver

16

Thomas Addison Richards
painter (1820-1900)
American (New York)
James Smillie
engraver (1807-1885)
American (New York)
Greene Obelisk, Johnson Square
c. 1844
Steel engraving

32

17

Attributed to James
Frothingham (*1786-1863*)
American
Catherine Littlefield Greene Miller
c. 1800-1814
Oil on panel

18

Attributed to Edward Greene
Malbone (1777-1807)
American
Martha Washington Greene
Nightingale
c. 1796
Watercolor on ivory; copper case
and initials; woven hair, verso;
encased in glass

19

Attributed to Edward Greene
Malbone (1777-1807)
American
Robert Bolton
c. 1800
Watercolor on ivory; copper case
and initials; blue glass, verso;
woven hair, verso

The first of the two major fires that devastated Savannah occured on Saturday night,
November 26, 1796. In the ensuing conflagration,
229 buildings were destroyed and "hundreds of
families were rendered houseless and hundreds
thrown out of employment. The suffering and
distress was great, notwithstanding the generous
donations of money and provisions from all parts
of the State."[13] From this terrible disaster resulted a few positive outcomes. Fire-proofing for
new structures was introduced, and officials
began to mandate the presence of fire-buckets in
all dwellings. Among those advertising fire-proof
buildings were Savannah merchants John (1774-
1838) and Robert Bolton (1757-1802), the latter of
whom had himself suffered devastating losses in
the fire (**19**).[14]

The project of rebuilding Savannah began immediately; however reconstruction took many years. One improvement was initiated in 1800: the planting of pride-of-India trees, thereby beautifying a devastated landscape and providing much-needed shade. Aiding the recovery was the sustained high price of cotton. Although other ports received this commodity, cotton was routinely brought to Savannah "where the best prices could be secured, and cotton remained above 20 cents per pound until 1810."[15]

The optimism generated by the thriving cotton market was accompanied by the decision to erect a City Exchange. Its cornerstone was laid on June 4, 1799, by the members of the Grand Lodge of the Free and Accepted Masons, No. 1 A.F.M., known locally as "Solomon's Lodge," the third oldest lodge in the United States. That same year the Masons erected their own meeting place, a modest two-story wooden building that was torn down in the mid-nineteenth century. In this unpretentious structure many prominent Savannahians regularly met under the leadership of a series of Grand Masters. The written records of the Lodge, beginning in 1785, include such well-known Georgia surnames as Berrien (**20**), Bulloch, Butler, Habersham, Jackson (**21**), Jones (**22**), McAllister, and Sheftall.[16]

By the turn of the century, Savannah could best be described as a recovering town of about 6,000 inhabitants. The census of 1798 lists 618 houses, 415 kitchens, 218 outhouses, and numerous shops and stores. With the exception of a few memorable events, notably the 1802 visit of Vice-President Aaron Burr (1756-1836) and the 1804 hurricane, which devastated many of the local island plantations—the first decade of the nineteenth century was a quiet one of slow and steady growth.

A visitor to Savannah in 1809 gave the following unflattering description of the town:

Soil of the City – Loose sand. Streets not paved, patrolled by hundreds of Turkey Buzzards, tame as common dunghill fowls, which scour the city of every kind of putrefaction.

Surface – Dead level, extending from the Bluff, back, quite over the common far into the woods.

Buildings – Greatest part wood: not compact, many squares in S end of town not half occupied.

No. Inhabitants – Not over 5000. ⅓ or more blacks. ½ the men of business Northern men.

Richest citizens – Bolton, Gibbons, Stiles, Anderson, Young, & c.

First Merchants – Bolton, Anderson, Burrows & Sturges, Richardson and some names I don't rec'l't. Eloquence dwells only with Berrien, Science with very few, Speculation with every body.

Ruling Characteristic is to get money and display it in a fashionable hospitality.

Amusements for Gentlemen – are to get money – dance – gamble – run horses.

Amusements for Ladies – spend money – play piano – contemplate their own beauty.[17]

To some observers, the Savannah of 1809 may have appeared to be culturally unsophisticated and shallow, but few could fail to acknowledge the advances in architecture, art, and education accomplished in the first decade of the new century.

34

20

Unknown maker
American
Badge of the Anacreontic Society
1804–1810
Silver; gilt wash

21

Unknown
American
Mourning pendant
c. 1802
Watercolor and dissolved hair on
ivory; brass case

22

Unknown maker
French or English
Chocolate pot and cup and saucer
c. 1780–1810
Paste porcelain with overglaze
enamels and gilt

NOTES

1
Kenneth Coleman, "Savannah-Georgia's Port City," *The Magazine Antiques*, v. 91, # 3 (March, 1967), pp. 322-323.

2
J.C. Kayser and Co., Commercial Directory of the United States (Philadelphia, 1823), p.36.

3
The Battle of Bloody Marsh commanded by Oglethorpe and fought on nearby St. Simons Island, July 7, 1742, established English dominance over Spain on the southern frontier of the colonies.

4
Georgia was envisioned as a "silk colony" and early became famous for its acres of mulberry trees which grew all around the town of Savannah. [Federal Writers' Project, *Savannah* (Savannah: Review Printing Co., 1937), p. 5]

5
For a comprehensive discussion of Savannah's town plan see John W. Reps, "C2 + L2 = S2?: Another Look at the Origins of Savannah's Town Plan," in Harvey H. Jackson and Phinizy Spalding, eds., *Forty Years of Diversity: Essays on Colonial Georgia* (Athens, GA: University of Georgia Press, 1984), pp. 101-109.

6
Kayser, 1823, p. 37. According to one source, the bar "outside of the mouth of the river... has on it a greater depth of water than on any on the Southern coast." This statement is based on a survey of the bars from Charleston, SC, to St. Marys, GA (c. 1840) conducted by the Department of the Navy. [F.D. Lee and J.L. Agnew, *Historical Record of the City of Savannah* (Savannah: J.H. Estill, 1869), pp.73, 75]

7
For more on English imports into Charleston, see M. Allison Carll, "An Assessment of English Furniture Imports into Charleston, S.C., 1760-1800," *Journal of Early Southern Decorative Arts*, v. 11, # 2 (November, 1985), pp. 1-18. See also Milby Burton, *Charleston Furniture 1700-1825* (Charleston, SC: Charleston Museum, 1955), pp. 7-10, 22-24.

8
Shortly after his inauguration, Washington decided to visit all the states currently in the Union. The purpose of his trip was "to gather information on the natural resources, economic and agricultural developments, to meet the people and find out their main thoughts, and with all to build up a loyalty to the national government and strengthen the Union." His first trips were to Northern states; he did not set out on his Southern tour until March 21, 1791. [Merton E. Coulter, "Presidential Visits to Georgia During Ante-Bellum Times," *Georgia Historical Quarterly*, v. 55, # 3 (Fall, 1971), p. 331]

9
Internal quotations from *The Georgia Gazette* (May 19, 1791), quoted in Lee and Agnew, 1869, pp. 69-70.

10
Ibid., p. 70.

11
The Brigadier General of Georgia's First District, James Jackson (1757-1806), issued a public accolade to members of the Chatham Artillery on the day following Washington's departure. He announced "to the Artillery the very general applause they received on Saturday, and, what ought to immortalize the Corps, the approbation of their conduct expressed in the warmest terms by the Commander in Chief of the United States." [Adelaide Wilson, *Historic and Picturesque Savannah* (Boston: Boston Photogravure Co., 1889), p. 94] No higher praise could have been expressed than this. The words of approval were echoed by a tangible award when two six-pound bronze cannons were delivered to the Chatham Artillery as a gift from Washington, henceforth referred to as the "Washington Guns." These cannons had been captured at the Battle of York Town, October 18, 1781. Today the guns are on view in the Strand on East Bay Street.

12
Mulberry Grove had been a gift to Nathanael Greene from the State of Georgia, in recognition of his service in the Revolutionary War. [Coulter, 1971, p. 333]

13
Lee and Agnew, 1869, p. 73.

14
"Fire proof stores to let" were advertised by Robert and John Bolton in the *Columbian Museum and Savannah Advertiser* (February 7, 1800) and watchmaker John Rice gave his business address as "Bolton's Brick Buildings, nearly opposite the Exchange on the Bay." [*Ibid.* (January 21, 1804). Both quoted in Jane Webb Smith, *Georgia's Legacy:History Charted Through the Arts* (Athens, GA: University of Georgia Press, 1985), p. 62] John Bolton (1774-1838), a native of Chestertown, MD, went into partnership with his cousin Robert Bolton in 1796. [*Columbian Museum and Savannah Advertiser* (April 29, 1796)] The name of the firm, known as R. and J. Bolton, continued unchanged after Robert Bolton's death in 1802.

15
Federal Writers' Project, 1937, p. 31.

16
Solomon's Lodge was chartered in 1735, only 18 years after the establishment of the constitutional Grand Lodge of London. The history of Solomon's Lodge has been published by the members and is available at their headquarters.

17
Letter from Daniel Mulford to Levi Mulford, January 28, 1809. [Daniel Mulford Papers, 1803-1812, MS Collection 579, Georgia Historical Society]

12

Unknown artist
American
William Gibbons
c. 1800
Watercolor on ivory; copper
case; woven hair; glass
3 x 2 ½ in. (7.6 x 6.5 cm.)

Inscription: verso, c., in bright-cut
copper script initials, on woven hair
inset "WG"

Provenance: William Gibbons; to his
brother-in-law Dr. George Jones
(1766-1838); to his son Noble
Wimberly Jones (1787-1818); to his
son George Noble Jones (1811-1876);
to his son George F. Jones (1841-
1876); to his son George Noble Jones
(1874-1955); to his daughter Caroline
Jones Wright (b. 1911).
Loan from Caroline Jones Wright

William Gibbons (1754-1804),
a lawyer and member of the
Continental Congress from 1784-
1786, served in the House of
Representatives and as the
president of the Georgia
Constitutional Convention.
He came from an illustrious
Savannah family and was related
by marriage to two of Savannah's
most distinguished citizens,
Edward Telfair (c. 1735-1807) [hus-
band of Sarah Gibbons (1758-
1827)] and Dr. George Jones
(1766-1838) [husband of Mary
Gibbons (1762-1792)]. It was in
the Jones family that this miniature locket descended.

Gibbons was a man of great
wealth and vast land holdings.
On one of his rice plantations

along the Savannah River, he was
visited by Revolutionary War hero
General Nathanael Greene[1] (16).
At his house in town, Gibbons
was known for his great hospitality and his elegant furnishings.[2]

Painted near the end of Gibbons's
life, the miniature locket shows an
elderly man in a rust-colored coat
and ruffled jabot. He is painted
against a light-blue background in
the style typical of English-
trained artists of the day: finely
drawn, delicate strokes, attention
to detail, transparent washes, and
vibrant highlights. As one art historian has written: "The English
preferred to treat the ivory as a
light shining behind transparent
hatches and washes, and cultivated
the linear rhythms which are
equally apparent in the contemporary watercolour drawings of this
elegant age."[3] On the back of the
oval copper frame is plaited brown
hair, overlaid with glass and
engraved brass initials "W.G."

1
William J. Northen, ed., *Men of Mark in*
Georgia (Atlanta: A. B. Caldwell,
Publisher, 1907-1911; reprint: Spartanburg,
SC: Reprint Co., 1974), v. 1, p. 103.
2
Gibbons's household memo, listing many
of his purchases, is included in the Telfair
family papers, 1751-1875, MS Collection
793, Georgia Historical Society.
3
Graham Reynolds, *English Portrait*
Miniatures (Cambridge: Cambridge
University Press, 1988), p. 142.

13

Unknown maker
American
Cross belt plate worn by a member
of the Chatham Artillery
c. 1790-1810
Cast brass
2 ½ x 3 ¼ in. (6.4 x 8.3 cm.)

Inscription: engraved on face in
bright-cut script "C.A./1786"

Provenance: excavated in downtown
Savannah, 1920s.
Loan from H. Paul Blatner

Engraved with the founding date
and initials of the Chatham
Artillery company, this brass
buckle plate is considered to be
the earliest militia plate from the
state of Georgia. Featuring the
bright-cut style of engraving popular during the late eighteenth
and early nineteenth century, the
belt plate may have been made
and engraved by a Savannah
jeweler.

Chatham Artillery was the oldest
of Savannah's volunteer militias;
their first major military service
was during the War of 1812 when
members were "constantly on
duty."[1] Although the city was
never invaded, its proximity to the
ocean made it a strategic location,
likely to be under assault at any
time. Indeed, in May 1814, the
headquarters for the British fleet
in Southern waters was
Cumberland Island, only a short
distance to the south. From this
location the commander of the
fleet, Sir George Cockburn (1772-
1853), authorized marauding and
slave-trading along the coast.[2]

Fortifications were built around the city of Savannah in September 1814, and the citizens continued to anxiously await the worst until peace was declared in February 1815. The Chatham Artillery played a major role in two Presidential visits to Savannah, firing welcoming salutes and escorting both Washington and Monroe on their visits, the only two United States Presidents to make appearances in the city before the Civil War.

1
Lee and Agnew, 1867, p. 75.
2
The British headquarters were at Dungeness, a plantation owned by General Nathanael Greene (**16**) and his wife, Catherine Littlefield Greene (**17**).

14

Joseph-Pierre Picot de Limoëlin de Clorivière (1768-1826)
French
General [Colonel] Steele White,
c. 1803-1806
Watercolor on ivory, copper case
2 ⁷/16 x 2 in. (6.19 x 5 cm.)
Signed: recto, l.r., in watercolor
"Picot" [1]

Inscriptions: verso, in script on (partially torn) paper "General/Steele White son/of Ro[bert and]/Jean [McAllister] White b. Dec. 5, 1784. d. March 29/1823"

Provenance: Steele White (1784-1823); to his daughter Mary Amelia White; to her daughter Mary Amelia Fairchild; to her daughter Mary White Jackson (d. 1952); Telfair Museum of Art.
Bequest of Mary White Jackson, 1952

Colonel Steele White (1784-1823) was an officer of the Savannah Volunteer Guards (organized in 1802) with whom he served an active role in the defense of coastal Georgia during the War of 1812. White, the son of Jane McAllister and Robert White, wrote many letters to his wife, Ann Matthews Guerard, reporting the progress of the war. He died prematurely in a riding accident. In tribute to him, his fellow guardsmen were said to have worn black arm bands for 30 days.[2]

This elegant miniature of White as a young man was painted during the years that Picot, a French immigrant, worked in Savannah (1803-1806). A former officer of the French army and a principal

figure in the unsuccessful plot to assassinate Napoleon in 1800, Picot fled to the United States in 1803. He earned his living as a miniaturist, first in Savannah and Charleston, and then in Baltimore. In the latter city he studied for the priesthood and was ordained in 1812.[3]

Picot's training is unknown, but it is assumed he painted miniatures before he arrived in the United States.[4] *Steele White* is characteristic of the artist's portraits with its opaque gray background. Picot's technique of linear and precise delineation was shared by other Continental expatriates who made their home in the young republic. White's collar and vest are carefully articulated as are his fine features and thick, curly hair.

1
Clorivière variously signed his work "de Clorivière," "Picot," and "Guitry."
2
Marion Converse Bright, *Early Georgia Portraits 1715-1879* (Athens, GA: University of Georgia Press, 1954), p. 299.
3
Anna Wells Rutledge, "A French Priest, Painter, and Architect in the United States: Joseph-Pierre Picot de Limoëlin de Clorivière," *Catalogue* (Charleston, SC: Carolina Art Association, 1939), pp. 126-7.
4
Martha R. Severens, *The Miniature Portrait Collection of the Carolina Art Association* (Charleston, SC: Gibbes Art Gallery, 1984), pp. 2-21.

15

Samuel Williamson (d. 1843;
active 1794-1813)
American (Philadelphia)
Tankard
c. 1794
Coin Silver
5 ¼ x 3 ¾ in. (13.3 x 9.5 cm.)
Mark: verso, stamped in rectangle in
Roman capitals "WILLIAMSON"

Inscription: engraved in script on
front of tankard "To/Maurice/
from/P. Butler/for/His faithful,
judicious and Spirited Conduct/in
the Hurricane on the 8th of
September 1804;/whereby the Lives
of more than one hundred
persons/were, by Divine permiSsion
Saved."

Provenance: gift to Pierce Butler's
slave known as "Driver" Morris
(d. 1822); to his son; to his grandson,
John Bull Sampson; to his great-
grandson, Morris Seagrove; to Alice,
Lady Butler, great-great-grand-
daughter of Major Pierce Butler.
Loan from the heirs of Alice, Lady
Butler, OT 7.1962

Major Pierce Butler (1744-1822),
the son of the Fifth Baronet of
Cloughrenan in Ireland, with his
wife Mary Middleton, owned
countless acres of land in South
Carolina, Georgia, and
Pennsylvania. Formerly a commis-
sioned officer in the British army,
Butler also served as Adjutant
General of South Carolina during
the Revolution, a delegate to the
Constitutional Convention in
Philadelphia, and as South
Carolina's first United States

Senator. The family's prosperity
depended, in large measure, on
the great number of slaves who
lived and worked on Butler plantations.[1] One of these slaves was
Morris (or Maurice) of Hampton
plantation on St. Simons Island,
Georgia. During the fatal coastal
hurricane of September 1804,
Morris prevented 100 slaves from
fleeing Little St. Simons Island by
using his driver's whip to force
them into a small hurricane shel-
ter where they weathered the
storm unharmed.[2] His bravery and
quick thinking were rewarded by
the gift of this tankard, made in
Philadelphia by silversmith
Samuel Williamson.[3]

Williamson is known to have
engaged extensively in coastal
trade, including to Southern
towns such as Alexandria,
Georgetown and Richmond,
Virginia, so it is possible that this
cup was shipped directly to
Savannah. Butler also lived part of
the year in Philadelphia, where he
would have had easy access to the
silversmith's shop as well.[4]
Tankards made in this form,
which imitated hooped and staved
wooden barrels, were common
presentation pieces. Somewhat
old-fashioned in style, they typically have a plain cylindrical body
hooped in two places with a
domed cover and a flat or pierced
thumb piece. Most commonly
made in Philadelphia, they look
backward to the colonial period
rather than reflecting the new
Classical style. Tankards of the

late eighteenth and early nineteenth century were made in a
new way. They were made of sheet
metal seamed along one side to
form the body and fitted with a
separate bottom soldered on.
Earlier tankards had been made
completely of one piece of silver.[5]

1
For a complete history of the Butler family
in the South, see Malcolm Bell, Jr., *Major*
Butler's Legacy: Five Generations of a
Slaveholding Family (Athens, GA and
London: University of Georgia Press,
1987).
2
The "hurricane house," built to withstand
tropical storms, was the only structure on
the island. Usually each evening the slaves
would cross the river to their homes on St.
Simons Island. [Margaret Davis Cate, *Our*
Todays and Yesterdays (Brunswick, GA:
Glover Brothers, 1930; Spartanburg, SC:
The Reprint Co., 1972), pp. 148-150]
3
Morris was also offered his freedom, a
proposition he refused because it did not
include freedom for his wife and children.
[Bell, 1987, p. 143]
4
Ellen Beasley, "Samuel Williamson:
Philadelphia Silversmith, 1794-1813"
(Unpublished thesis, University of
Delaware, Winterthur Program in Early
American Culture, 1964), pp. v-vi.
5
Donald L. Fennimore, *Silver and Pewter*
(New York: Alfred A. Knopf, 1984), p.158.

16
Thomas Addison Richards,
painter (1820-1900)
American (New York)
James Smillie, engraver (1807-
1885)[1]
American (New York)
Greene Obelisk, Johnson Square
  c. 1844
Steel engraving
6 x 9 ⅞ in. (15.2 x 25.1 cm.)

Inscriptions: l.l. "Drawn by J.
Smillie from a sketch by T. Addison
Richards."; l.r. "Engraved by
Rawdon, Wright, Hatch &
Smillie."; l.c. "PULASKI MONU-
MENT-EPISCOPAL CHURCH./
SAVANNAH./Grahams' Magazine
1844./Published in 1850"
Loan from V & J Duncan

40

Nathanael Greene (1742-1786) was
a distinguished officer in the
Revolutionary War, having risen
from Private to Brigadier General
"in a few day's time, thanks to raw
ability and a shortage of dedicated
men."[2] Greene, originally from
Rhode Island, served as
Commander of the Southern
Army for the colonial forces in
the Carolinas and Georgia and
was "justly considered the saviour
of the South in our revolutionary
struggle."[3] Both General Greene
and his wife Catherine Littlefield
Greene (**16**), spent the winter of
1778 with George Washington at
Valley Forge.

Following the war, Greene was
granted a silk plantation, valued
at £50,000, which had been con-
fiscated from the Royalist
Lieutenant Governor John
Graham (c. 1718-1795). The

Greenes moved to Mulberry
Grove plantation in 1783, but the
general had only a short time to
enjoy this gift; Greene died of
sunstroke in 1786. His wife was
left an estate riddled with large
debts incurred repaying merchants
from whom Greene had borrowed
during the war to purchase clothing for his troops.[4] Greene's
remains were accompanied by the
Chatham Artillery to the place of
burial, John Graham's family vault
in Colonial Cemetery in
Savannah.[5]

Greene was honored with a monument in Johnson Square, the cornerstone of which was laid by
General Marquis de Lafayette
(1759-1834) when he visited
Savannah in 1825 to honor his
"dear companion and friend, the
great and good Greene."[6]
According to colorful descriptions
at the time, the celebrations
included five hundred little boys
and girls, the boys dressed in "blue
coatees and white pantaloons" and
the girls in "plain white frocks
with blue sashes."[7] Subsequently,
donations were solicited for the
construction of this and a second
monument, to Revolutionary War
hero Brigadier General Count
Casimir Pulaski (1748-1779).

In 1826, the Georgia State
Legislature approved a lottery for
the purpose of raising the $35,000
needed to build these monuments.
When the necessary monies had
not been secured by 1829, a single
monument was erected in honor
of both heroes and was called the
"Pulaski and Greene Monument."[8]

The simple, 50-foot-high obelisk
was designed by William
Strickland (1788-1854), the
Philadelphia architect. Many years
later a separate monument to
Pulaski was erected in Monterey
Square.[9]

Johnson Square, pictured in the
Smillie engraving, was "the center
of Oglethorpe's original campsite,
the place where colonists gathered
to name the streets and wards of
the town, where a draft of the
Constitution with Alexander
Hamilton's cover letter was read to
the public," and "was the center of
business and social life in the early
nineteenth century."[10]

1
James Smillie was born in Scotland, later
lived in Quebec, and worked in New York
City from 1829 until his death in 1885,
where he became particularly well-known
as an engraver of banknotes. He was also
widely known for his steel engravings of
landscapes and figure pieces by notable
artists such as Thomas Cole and Alden
Weir. [Groce, p. 1957, p. 585]
2
Glen McCaskey, "Caty Greene: Kiawah
During the American Revolution," *Kiawah
Island Legends*, v. 1, # 1 (Spring/Summer,
1990), p. 87.
3
*An Account of the Reception of General
Lafayette*, March 19, 1825 (Savannah: n.p.,
1825), p. 33.
4
John F. and Janet Stegeman, *Caty: A
Biography of Catherine Littlefield Greene*
(Providence: Rhode Island Bicentennial
Foundation, 1978), pp. 8, 11.
5
The site of Greene's interment was lost for
over 100 years until rediscovered in 1901.
Later his remains were moved to Johnson
Square, where they were placed under the
monument to him. [*Savannah Morning
News* (February 29, 1948)]

6
Lafayette, 1825, p. 19.
7
Joseph Frederick Waring, *Cerveau's Savannah* (Savannah: The Georgia Historical Society, 1973), p. 9.
8
Lee and Agnew, 1869, p. 169.
9
By the end of the nineteenth century the unadorned neoclassical obelisk was no longer thought a fitting memorial for Greene. A movement began to tear the monument down or have it "suitably ornamented and inscribed" as was the 1854 obelisk to Casimir Pulaski by Robert Eberhard Launitz (1806-1870). Local poet G.M. Williams admonished in 1871, "Oh! Let the chisel do its work, bid the dumb marble speak,/That it may tell the travelers what else where they now seek./Give to the senseless stone a tongue that it may ever be/A monument of him who died for liberty." In 1886 on the centennial anniversary of the Chatham Artillery, four bronze bas reliefs depicting the life of Greene by Giovanni Turini (1841-1899) were installed on the faces of Strickland's obelisk.
10
Mills Lane, *Savannah Revisited: A Pictorial History* (Athens, GA: University of Georgia Press, 1969), p. 17. This image of the obelisk in Johnson Square was first printed in J.H. Hinton, *History and Topography of the United States* (London: I.T. Hinton & Simpkin & Marshall, 1830-1832). [See *Ibid.*]

17
Attributed to James Frothingham (1786-1863)
American
Catherine Littlefield Greene Miller
c. 1800-1814
Oil on panel
32 ¾ x 25 ¾ in. (83.2 x 65.4 cm.)

Inscriptions: verso, frame, u.r., label "43./PORTRAIT OF MRS. NATHANAEL GREENE/ *after Gilbert Stuart/by* FROTHINGHAM"

Provenance: Catherine Littlefield Greene Miller; to her great-granddaughter Frances Cunningham Nightingale; sold at Parke-Bernet, November 20, 1947, No. 902, as Mrs. Nathanael Greene; Telfair Museum of Art.
Museum purchase, 1947.2

"Caty" Littlefield Greene (1755-1814) was from all accounts a remarkable woman. While the somberness of this portrait of the middle-aged widow of General Nathanael Greene does not reflect the flamboyant, flirtatious, energetic woman described in contemporary accounts, the set of her mouth and expression in her eyes suggest her warmth and bravado.[1] Married in 1774 and widowed in 1786, Caty Greene inherited the huge debts incurred by her husband during the Revolutionary War (**16**).

Left with four small children, Mrs. Greene petitioned Congress on March 5, 1790 to "indemnify the Greene estate for the indebtedness that her husband had incurred when he stood surety for the bankrupt contractor whom he had engaged to supply his army."[2] She was referred to Secretary of the Treasury Alexander Hamilton, who, along with Congressman Jeremiah Wadsworth of Connecticut, favored a concession to satisfy the claim. Other supporters and admirers included George Washington, Henry Knox, Anthony Wayne, Edward Rutledge, the Marquis de Lafayette and Aaron Burr. Nonetheless, Mrs. Greene's petition was denied in 1790, and four other times. She never did receive any compensation for her husband's extraordinary personal sacrifice.[3]

In 1796 she married Philadelphian Phineas Miller (1764-1803), ten years her junior and Eli Whitney's classmate at Yale. Miller, who had previously served as the Greene children's tutor, invited Whitney to Mulberry Grove in 1792. It was during his stay in Georgia that Whitney invented the cotton gin. Due to disastrous land purchases, Miller was forced to sell Mulberry Grove plantation and move to Dungeness House, Cumberland Island, one of the "Golden Isles" off the coast of southern Georgia. Like Caty Greene's first husband, Miller died a relatively young man in 1803.[4]

This painting has long been attributed to James Frothingham, a coach painter who later studied under Gilbert Stuart. He is known to have worked in Boston, Salem, New York, and Brooklyn and was admitted to the National Academy of Design in 1831. If Frothingham is indeed the author of this portrait, it would have been one of his early works, executed near the end of Catherine Littlefield Greene Miller's life.

1
According to one early account, Caty had "glossy black hair, brilliant violet eyes, clear-cut features, transparent complexion, with exquisitely moulded hands and feet, all uniting to make her lovely." [*Savannah Morning News* (February 29, 1948)]. Two miniatures of Mrs. Greene, very similar to this portrait, were painted and signed by Picot de Clorivière, one at the Metropolitan Museum, New York, and the second at the New Orleans Museum of Art.

2
Margaret C.S. Christman, *The First Federal Congress*, 1789-1791 (Washington: Smithsonian Institution Press, 1989), p. 167.

3
Ibid., pp. 165-167.

4
This information was taken from notes compiled by Gordon B. Smith, 1994.

18
Attributed to Edward Greene Malbone (1777-1807)
American
Martha Washington Greene Nightingale
c. 1796
Watercolor on ivory; copper case and initials; woven hair, verso; encased in glass
2 ⅝ x 2 in. (6.7 x 5.1 cm.)

Inscription: verso, c., on woven hair inset, bright-cut copper script initials "MN"

Provenance: descended in the Nightingale family; Mrs. Thomas B. Gannett; Mark Bortman, purchased at Parke-Bernet Galleries, 1946 (Catalogue # 814); Telfair Museum of Art.
Museum purchase, 1947, 1940.1

This miniature of the lovely eldest daughter of Nathanael and Caty Greene is included in the catalogue of Malbone's work by Ruel P. Tolman as an example of Malbone's early work, minutely finished and detailed against an opalescent background.[1] Miniaturist Edward Greene Malbone was only 29 at the time of his death in Savannah in 1807. He left behind a remarkable number of portraits, including this of Martha Washington Greene Nightingale (b. 1775?) and other members of prominent Savannah families (including Robert Bolton, **19**).[2] Born in Newport, Rhode Island, Malbone worked in Providence, Boston, Philadelphia, Charleston, New York, and England in addition to Savannah.

He is considered by many to be the foremost American miniature painter, despite his short life, producing delicate, luminous portraits that were as highly valued as full-size portraits in oil.[3]

Martha Washington Greene, named after the wife of her father's great friend and fellow patriot, married John Clark Nightingale (1771-1806) on April 12, 1795. They had three daughters and one son. Following Nightingale's death on Cumberland Island, she married Dr. Henry Edward Turner (1787-1862), with whom she had four more children, the last of whom was born in 1822.

1
Ruel Pardee Toleman, *The Life and Works of Edward Greene Malbone 1777-1809* (New York: The New York Historical Society, 1958), p. 217. This portrait was also illustrated in Jean Lambert Brockway, "Malbone, American Miniature Painter," *The American Magazine of Art*, v. 20, # 4 (April, 1929), p. 186; and in Toleman, "Newly Discovered Miniatures by Edward Greene Malbone," *The Magazine Antiques*, v. 16, # 5 (November, 1929), p. 379. According to Toleman, "a second very similar miniature of the same lady, owned by the Metropolitan Museum of Art, represents a more mature person. Its readier technique likewise points to a slightly later date" (p. 378).

2
157 miniatures by him are listed in Theodore Bolton, *Early American Portrait Painters in Miniature* (New York: F.F. Sherman, 1921), pp. 101-110. These miniatures were those listed in an account book begun in Charleston in December, 1801. In one ten-week stay in Charleston in 1801, Malbone painted 31 miniatures.

42

[Severens, 1984, p. 89]. According to Dale T. Johnson, Malbone produced "hundreds of elegant, graceful portraits." [American Portrait Miniatures in the Manney Collection (New York: Metropolitan Museum of Art, 1990), p. 22]

3
Mantle Fielding, *Dictionary of American Painters, Sculptors, and Engravers* (New York: J.F. Carr, 1965), p. 574. For an introduction to the history of American portrait miniatures, see Johnson, 1990, pp. 13-26.

19
Attributed to Edward Greene
Malbone (1777-1807)
American
Robert Bolton
c. 1800
Watercolor on ivory; copper case and initials; blue glass, verso; woven hair, verso
2 ⅝ x 2 ⅛ in. (includes ring for chain at top) (9.22 x 6.7 cm.)

Inscription: verso, center, on woven hair inset, bright-cut copper script initial "B"

Provenance: descended in the Bolton and Jackson families of Savannah[1]; Mary White Jackson (d. 1951); Telfair Museum of Art.
Bequest of Mary White Jackson, 1952.3

Savannah cotton merchant Robert Bolton (1757-1802) was a member of a distinguished Georgia family which figured prominently in the development of the city.[2] He was the third Robert in direct descent in America, the second to live in Savannah. Life was not easy for Bolton; he lost his house, church, and nearly lost his warehouses in the fire of 1796. The house on Oglethorpe Avenue was rebuilt on the same lot, but from that time forward the family spent their summers in the town of Washington, Wilkes County, Georgia. It was not long thereafter that Bolton died at the age of 45.

This portrait on ivory by Malbone is contained in a brass case, on the reverse of which is engraved the initial "B." On the top of the case is a brass loop so that the miniature could be suspended on a chain or a ribbon and tucked into a bodice or pocket and retrieved for private viewing. As is the case for the vast majority of Malbone's work, this portrait is unsigned.

1
According to a letter from George W. Bolton to Mrs. Mary A. Jackson, June 28, 1896, "there was a great deal of marrying and intermarrying between the Jacksons and Boltons." [Steele White Papers, Colonial Dames Collection (MS Collection 965, Georgia Historical Society)] Robert Bolton married Sarah McLean in 1761, whose first husband was Dr. Jackson.

2
Among those members of the Bolton family who are represented in this catalogue are Nathaniel Adams (**8**) who married Ann Bolton, Robert's sister; Frances Lewis Bolton, daughter of Robert Bolton, who, with her husband Richard Richardson, were the original owners of the Richardson-Owens-Thomas House; Reverend Robert Bolton, son of Robert, and his wife Anne Jay Bolton, whose portraits were painted by William Etty (**23, 24**) and were responsible for the architect William Jay practicing in Savannah.

20
Unknown maker
American
Badge of the Anacreontic Society
1804-1810
Silver; gilt wash
3 ⁶/₁₆ x 1 ⅞ in. (8.5 v 4.8 cm.)

Inscription: recto, c., engraved in script "John M/Berien [sic]"; l., engraved in Roman capitals "SAVAN-NAH"; r., engraved in Roman capitals "ANACREONTIC SOCIETY"; verso, rough etched "17"

Provenance: John McPherson Berrien, descended in the Berrien family to his great-granddaughters Misses Cecil and Gene Burroughs; Georgia Historical Society Loan from the Georgia Historical Society.

In one of her fact-filled and interesting articles on Savannah's history, Anna C. Hunter wrote,

The story of music in Savannah is the story of personalities who flash across the screen of time in dramatic, solemn or humorous light. The years have seen many changes but the pattern has always repeated itself, fluctuating from inspired effort to goal of achievement and then lapses and a change of personalities. That there was a flourishing culture in the city before 1800 we feel sure, and by 1804 we have charming and characteristic evidence that concerts were being given by the Anacreontic Society.[1]

The Anacreontic Society, Savannah's first poetry and music society, does, indeed, appear as a "flash" in history, having existed for a mere six years. But during its heyday, its members were among the finest of Savannah's citizens, including John McPherson Berrien (1781-1856), Richard M. Stites, Oliver Sturges (**42**), P.D. Petit de Villiers, and William Dudley Woodbridge.[2]

The first notices of the Society's activities appeared in 1804, advertising meetings and concerts that occurred regularly. One such advertisement read:

The members of the Savannah Anacreontic Society, are requested to meet at the Long Room of the Exchange, on Monday Evening next, precisely at 6 o'clock, it being a regular meeting. By Order of the President. J.M. Willson, Sec'ry. The Members of the Society are requested to send to the President for their Tickets on or before 12 o'clock on Monday.[3]

The final mention of the organization appeared on March 15, 1810, when the committee "appointed to settle the affairs of the defunct" Anacreontic Society announced their intentions to settle their debts:

They have done so, as far as possible. With proceeds of the effects, they will be enabled to pay all the smaller debts in full, and have declared a dividend to creditors with large accounts at 69 per cent. A number of due bills are on hand; some of them are bad enough, although the makers were fond of good music; others are very doubtful, and from the best, about one hundred dollars may possibly be recovered.[4]

The Society was named after Anacreon (582-485 B.C.E.), the last great lyric poet of ancient Greece. While only a few fragments of his poems survive, he is best known for his songs in praise of love and wine, and the organizations he inspired were known as much as drinking societies as they were for their musical endeavors. The original Anacreontic Society was founded in London in 1766. Meetings were held at the Crown and Anchor Tavern in the Strand, and concerts were given "fortnightly during the season and were followed by a supper, after which the president or his deputy sang the constitutional song 'To Anacreon in Heaven', a tune now familiar to Americans as that of the 'The Star Spangled Banner.'"[5] The society dissolved in 1796 owing to the annoyance of members, "a restraint having been placed upon the performance of some comic songs which were considered unfit for the ears of the Duchess of Devonshire, the leader of the *haut-ton* of the day . . ."[6]

As the symbol of music and poetry, the lyre was the obvious choice for the silver badge of Savannah's Anacreontic Society. Although the Society itself was short-lived, its legacy has survived in the form of these treasured medals, passed down for nearly two centuries in Savannah's most illustrious families.

One such family was that of John McPherson Berrien, a prominent attorney whose father Major John Berrien "saw service in Georgia during the Revolution, and moved to Savannah in 1783."[7] Following graduation from Princeton, the younger Berrien was admitted to the bar in 1799 at the age of seventeen, and joined the Anacreontic Society when he was barely in his twenties. He went on to a legal career of note, serving as Solicitor General and Judge of the Eastern Circuit, Georgia State Senator, United States Senator, and Attorney General under Andrew Jackson (1767-1845).[8]

1
Anna C. Hunter, "Savannah's Musical Heritage," *Savannah Morning News Magazine* (October 26, 1958), pp. 6.

2
Oliver Sturges's Anacreontic Society medal is owned by his ancestor, Mrs. Lorton Stoy Livingston. Like Berrien's, William Woodbridge's medal is in the Georgia Historical Society, gift of Miss Caroline Lamar Woodbridge (**77**). Petit de Villiers was President of the Society in 1807, as indicated by a bond of $2000 held by him from Alexander S. Roe, secretary and treasurer of the Anacreontic Society who was paid a salary of $100 as administrator. [Georgia Historical Society]

3
Columbian Museum and Savannah Advertiser (November 17, 1804).

4
Ibid. (March 15, 1810).

5
Eric Bloom, ed., *Grove's Dictionary of Music and Musicians* (New York: St. Martin's Press Inc., 1954), p. 143.

6
Ibid.

7
Horace Montgomery, ed., *Georgians in Profile: Historical Essays in Honor of Ellis Merton Coulter* (Athens, GA: University of Georgia Press, 1958).

8
Northen, 1974, pp. 140-144.

21
Unknown
American
Mourning pendant
c. 1802
Watercolor and dissolved hair on ivory; brass case
2 ½ x 1 ⅞ in. (6.4 x 4.8 cm.), includes ring

Inscriptions: painted on plinth, in script "RSRB"; verso, on hair, in copper letters, in script (cutout) "JJ" [possibly John Jackson]

Provenance: descended in the White and Jackson families of Savannah. Bequest of Mary White Jackson, 1952.6

Few urns or other decorative details remain on the early tombs in Colonial Cemetery, so if this monument remains, it is not as it appeared in the early nineteenth century. Said by the donor to have been the "McAllister Tomb," the large plinth with urn and weeping mourner are a typical device on pendants of this type.[1] The overall design for the picture may have come from such popular works as Angelica Kauffman's *Andromache Weeping over the Ashes of Hector*, based on a classical story, or *Fame Decorating the Tomb of Shakespeare*, also by Kauffman. Less specifically, the typical mourning picture of the late eighteenth century borrowed from classical Greece and Rome the motifs of the urn, the plinth, the tree, and the mourner, all together expressing heroic death.

While the artist who crafted this delicate watercolor may not consciously have borrowed the iconography of Pompeii and Herculaneum, the artifacts depicted in this pendant were, in fact, related to the designs of the ancients. These emblems became part of American iconography as well, representing "the state of mourning [which] gradually became as beautiful as it was virtuous, embodying Christian, patriotic, and personal meanings as a new art form . . . born from ancient motifs and ideas."[2]

The back of the pendant is decorated with a lock of hair, over which is glass and an engraved metal monogram "JJ," most probably the initials of the deceased memorialized by this miniature.

1
This miniature was the bequest of Mary White Jackson. Research has not as yet revealed the exact descent of this pendant, but it is known that Jane McAllister White and Robert White were the parents of Colonel Steele White (**14**) who appears to have been a direct ancestor of the donor. Mrs. Jackson suggested that the initials "JJ" may have stood for John Jackson.

2
Anita Schorsch, "Mourning Art: A Neoclassical Reflection in America," *American Art Journal*, v. 8, # 1 (May, 1976), p. 3.

46

22

Unknown maker
French or English
Chocolate pot and cup and saucer
c. 1780-1810
Paste porcelain with overglaze
enamels and gilt
Pot: 10 ¹/₁₆ x 6 x dia. of base 3 ¼
in. (25.6 x 15.2 x 8.3 cm.); dia. of
cup: 2 ½ in. (6.4 cm.); dia. of
saucer: 5 ½ in. (14 cm.)

Provenance: Mary Elizabeth Dulles
Cheves (d. 1837); to her daughter
Louisa S. Cheves McCord (1810-
1879); to her daughter Louisa
Rebecca McCord Smthye (1845-
1928); to her daughter Hannah
McCord Smythe Wright (1874-1955);
to her son David M. Wright (1909-
1968); to his wife Caroline Jones
Wright (b. 1911).
Loan from Caroline Jones Wright.

The cylindrical shape of the cup
and ovoid, footed form of the
chocolate pot suggest a late eighteenth-century date for these
pieces, as does the decoration in
the style of French painter
Francois Boucher whose "dancing
cupids" inspired porcelain decorators in his own country as well as
abroad.[1]

The scenes on the pot and the cup
are all based on classical mythology. The chubby boy on the cup
may be Ganymede, cup-bearer
of the gods, who was the beautiful
Trojan youth abducted by Zeus in
the guise of an eagle.[2] The young
nymphs covorting around a vat of
grapes and decorating the statue
of Pan are clearly classical in
derivation.

These particular images may have
been adapted from paintings of
Angelica Kauffman, the celebrated
Swiss artist whose pictures
inspired an extensive print market.
A series of stipple engravings after
Kauffman with Latin titles, such
as "Olim truncus eram ficulnus
inutile lignum" (I used to be the
trunk of a fig tree, a useless piece
of wood), were allegorical scenes
of love that made their way onto a
variety of decorative arts including
furniture and ceramics.[3] Most of
these, like the scenes on the
chocolate pot and the cup, were in
a circular format.

The Bacchanalian overtones of
the puttis' poses points to the
dilution of classical inspiration, as
Cupid, the Roman god of love,
gradually became the model for
generically chubby, sentimental
children engaged in a variety of
playful activities.[4]

[1]
Michel Bloit, *Trois Siecles de Porcelaine de
Paris* (Paris: Editions Hervas, 1988), pp.
61-2.
[2]
Catherine B. Avery, ed., *The New Century
Classical Handbook* (New York: Appleton-
Century-Crofts, Inc., 1962), p. 491.
[3]
Wendy Wassyng Roworth, ed., *Angelica
Kauffman: A Continental Artist in Georgian
England* (London: Reaktion Books, in
association with Royal Pavillion, Art
Gallery & Museums, Brighton, 1992), p.
136.
[4]
Lewis and Darley, 1986, pp. 96-97.

Savannah, Georgia

1800 – 1840 / 1820

Richard Richardson House

48

Bulloch–Habersham House

Scarbrough House

Telfair Academy

In 1820 there was another disastrous fire, in which 463 houses were destroyed. In this same year Savannah was visited by a severe equinoctial storm and an epidemic of yellow fever. Pretty hard luck for a struggling little city of seven thousand to have three such calamities in one year! Don't you think so?[1]

WILLIAM JAY'S SAVANNAH

Despite these tragedies, a "Golden Age" began in the city after the War of 1812. Peace with England in 1815 ended the economic hardships caused by embargoes and naval conflicts. Savannah's merchants thrived anew, residential and commercial building projects were vigorously initiated, and local citizens faced the future with optimism and confidence. It was in this favorable climate that the 25-year-old British architect, William Jay III (1792-1837), arrived from London on the ship *Dawn* on December 29, 1817. Although Jay stayed only a short four years in the city, his bold architecture influenced forever the landscape of Savannah. Nowhere is Jay's work "more stunning, free and rich; better preserved, remembered, chronicled, imitated, and appreciated" than in Savannah.[2] One visitor remarked in 1839:

The greater number of the dwelling houses are built of wood, and painted white; but there are many handsome and commodious brick buildings occupied as private residences, and a few mansions, built by an English architect, Mr. Jay — son of the celebrated divine of that name at Bath — which are of beautiful architecture, of sumptuous interior, and combine as much of elegance, and luxury as are to be found in any private dwellings in the country.[3]

As the chronicler noted, Jay was a native of Bath and the eldest son of Reverend William Jay II (d. 1855), a nonconformist British minister. The well-known cleric had a large following, including Robert Bolton (1788-1857) of Savannah (**23**), who married Reverend Jay's daughter Anne (1793-1859) in 1810 (**24**).[4] It is likely that this

family relationship and business connections between Savannah and Liverpool brought the younger William to Georgia. Jay's first architectural design associated with Georgia was a "sketch of a church now erecting in Savannah, in America" which was exhibited at the Royal Academy in London, two months before his departure for the United States. It has long been speculated that this lost design was for the Independent Presbyterian Church (**25**). In fact, the commission was awarded to William Holden Green (1777-1850), an architect from Providence, Rhode Island, and the church was well under construction when Jay arrived in Savannah.[5]

23
William Etty, R.A. (1787-1849)
English
Reverend Robert Bolton
1818
Oil on canvas

50

INTERIOR OF THE PRESBYTERIAN CHURCH, SAVANNAH.

25
Drawn by William Goodacre
(active 1820-1835)
American (New York)
Engraved by Fenner, Sears and
Co.
English (London)
Interior of William Holden Green's
Savannah Independent
Presbyterian Church
c. 1831
Published in: John Howard
Hinton, ed., *History and*
Topography of the United States
v. 2 (London: I. T. Hinton,
Simpkin, & Marshall, 1830-1832),
pl. 73.
Steel engraving

24
William Etty, R.A. (1787-1849)
English
Anne Jay Bolton and children,
William and Anne
c. 1818
Oil on canvas

Richard Richardson's House

Richard Richardson (1785-1833) and his wife,
Frances Lewis Bolton Richardson (Robert
Bolton's sister) (1794-1822), were William Jay's
first patrons in America. Richardson was a
wealthy merchant, attorney, and bank president.
His house, today known as the Richardson-
Owens-Thomas House, was perhaps begun in
1816 and finished by 1819.[6] The Richardson
House was innovative in a number of ways:
it is the finest American house in the English
Regency style; it is an early example of the
emerging Classical Revival; and it is one of the
first American structures that incorporated both
sophisticated plumbing systems and cast-iron
construction (**26**).[7]

The Richardson House, a two-story
stucco residence on a raised basement, occupies
the northeast trust lot on Oglethorpe Square.
Flanked by curving stone steps with wrought
iron railings, the bowed entrance porch is supported by four Ionic columns and two pilasters
with rare coade stone capitals.[8] The glazed front
doors are set into a shallow semicircular niche
and open onto an entrance hall decorated with
egg and dart cornice molding and marbleized
and wood-grained finishes. Two marbletop console tables (**27**) display plaster busts of George
Gordon, Lord Byron (1788-1824) (**28**) and Sir
Walter Scott (1771-1832) (**29**), as they have since
the 1830s. A pair of Corinthian columns with
gilded capitals screen the central staircase, which
splits into a double flight. The mahogany
handrails and oak stair treads are inlaid with
brass, and the delicate, cast-iron balusters were
originally treated with verdigris paint and powdered bronze gilding. An unusual matching
bridge springs over the upper stairwell to con-
nect the front and rear portions of the second
floor.[9]

26
Photograph, cast-iron balcony
Richardson-Owens-Thomas House
c. 1819

27
Unknown maker
English
Consoles (pair), c. 1819
White pine; marble (mahogany
replacement element on
1951.152.2)

28
After Bertel Thorvaldsen
(1770 -1841)
Danish
Lord Byron
after 1817
Plaster, painted to simulate
bronze

29
After Sir Francis Legatt Chantrey
(1781-1841)
English
Sir Walter Scott
after 1821
Plaster, painted to simulate
bronze

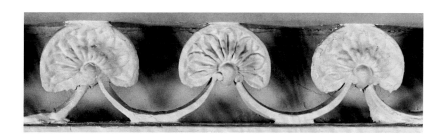

The "Dining Room or Large Parlour" north of the entry is one of the most remarkable neoclassical interiors in America.[10] The D-shaped room is crowned with a freestanding plaster cornice of anthemia (**30**), a motif also seen on the cornice of the exterior balcony (**26**) and in other Jay buildings. The curved east wall is articulated with a black marble fireplace flanked by doors surmounted with demilunette openings. On the north wall is a unique convex window (**4**) with amber glazing in a Greek key pattern which bathes the concave niche below in soft golden light. Installed in this concavity is an unusual marbletop serving table with a brass gallery and a single elaborately carved support (**31**). Unusual, too, are the chased brass push plates in the Egyptian style mounted on the three dining room doors (**32**). All of these elegant features reflect the most fashionable taste of the period.

The "Front Parlour or Drawing Room South," to the right of the entry, is equally stylish. Here, fluted corner pendentives and concentric Greek frets ringing a floriated center medallion create the illusion of a domed plaster ceiling.[11] Framed by shallow arched niches in the east wall is a white marble mantelpiece (**33**) featuring two classically draped female figures. The mantelpiece has been attributed to British sculptor Richard Westmacott, Jr. (1775-1856), based on its similarity to a drawing signed by him (**34**). This work includes two women in classical garb: Judith holding the head of Holofernes and Sappho with her lyre. The drawing was found in Savannah rolled with a signed sketch by William Jay, suggesting an association of these two artisans beyond their Royal Academy days.[12]

30
Anthemia, cornice frieze
dining room, Richardson-Owens-Thomas House
c. 1819

57

32
Unknown maker
English
*Door push plates in the Egyptian
style (one of three)*
c. 1818
Brass

31
Unknown maker
English
Built-in marbletop sideboard
c. 1819
Mahogany; white pine; brass;
marble

58

34
Sir Richard Westmacott (1775-1856) or his son Richard Westmacott
(1799-1872)
English
Drawing of chimney surround
c. 1820

33
Photograph, white marble figural fireplace
front parlour/drawing room
Richardson-Owens-Thomas House
c. 1819

The distinctive architectural features of the house and a small number of objects associated with it are all that remain of Richardson's material splendor in the few years between the completion of his mansion in 1819 and the loss of his wife and fortune in 1822. Documenting the sumptuous furnishings in the house is a room-by-room inventory recorded upon the sale of its contents in 1822 to Durham Hall, a business associate of Richardson.[13] Listed in the tally are the most fashionable and modern household goods, including Grecian lamps, Brussels carpets, lounging chairs, ottomans, marble bath, and Chinese floor stands. Not mentioned specifically, but assumed to have been among the "Whole amt of Sterling" recorded in the kitchen story, is a handsome tea service bearing the initial "R" and the inscription "F.L.B. Richardson" (Frances Lewis Bolton Richardson) (35).

The furniture remained in the house until 1823, when it was purchased from Hall by John H. Morel, Esq.[14] For the next seven years the villa served as a boarding house, run by Mrs. Mary Maxwell and owned by the Savannah branch of the Bank of the United States. It was during this period that Savannah welcomed one of its most illustrious visitors, the returning hero, the Marquis de Lafayette. The choice of Mrs. Maxwell's for Lafayette's accommodations was directly related to its superb design, the notable architect, the spaciousness of the rooms, and the modern comforts. Georgia governor Troup also lived there when he was in Savannah.[15] It is fitting that Lafayette spent his nights in Savannah, which he deemed an "interesting and classic city," in the most celebrated of Savannah's buildings, Jay's Richardson House.[16]

To all who participated in Lafayette's visit to Savannah, the occasion was memorable. Like other Americans, the people of Savannah thought of the Revolutionary War general as a hero of epic and classical proportions, an "illustrious model of virtuous behavior" of the likes of George Washington and Benjamin Franklin.[17] The Frenchman Lafayette was memorialized in all media, including textiles, ceramics, and silver.

His yearlong triumphal tour to all 24 of the United States in 1824-25 sparked the production of souvenirs, many of which were purchased and owned by Savannahians. They include ceramics (**36 a,b,c,d**) and engravings (**37 a,b,c**). Lafayette memorabilia of a more personal nature was also collected and preserved, as testimony to the historic nature of this visit (**38 a,b,c**). The loyalty and admiration of the people of Savannah toward Lafayette continued unabated long after the Marquis returned to his native France, and, upon his death in 1834, Savannah's citizens turned out once again to honor the noble hero (**39**).

36 a
Unknown maker
English (Staffordshire)
Pitcher
c. 1825-1835
One side: *Portrait of LaFayette*
Other side: *Cornwallis resigning his sword at Yorktown*
On front under spout: *Cluster of fruit*
Copper lusterware
36 b
Unknown maker
English (Staffordshire)
Pitcher, smaller version of above

60

36c
Richard Hall & Son
English (Staffordshire)
Pitcher
c. 1825-1832
One side: *Portrait of Lafayette*
Other side: *Portrait of Washington*
Under the spout: *American eagle*
Transfer printed creamware

35
John Crawford (active in New
York 1815-1836 and Philadelphia
1837-1843)
American (New York)
Tea service (four pieces)
c. 1815-1820
Sterling silver

36d
Enoch Wood and Sons
(active 1818-1846)
English (Burslem, Staffordshire)
Retailed by Harris & Chauncey
New York
Small Tureen with saucer
c. 1826-1829
On both sides of tureen, on lid
and on saucer: *Lafayette at
Washington's Tomb*
Transfer printed creamware

M. DE LA FAYETTE.

37c
Anker Smith (1759-1819)
painter and engraver
English
General Marquis de Lafayette
c. 1790-1810
Engraving

37b
Fairman, Draper, Underwood
& Co. (active 1823-1827)
engravers
American (Philadelphia)
*Copper plate, ten and twenty
dollars currency*
1823-1827
Copper

37a
Ary Scheffer, (1795-1858) painter
German/French
Jean Marie Leroux, (1788-1871)
engraver, French
General Marquis de Lafayette
1824
Steel engraving

38a
Unknown maker
English or American
Miniature bird
c. 1825
White opaque glass

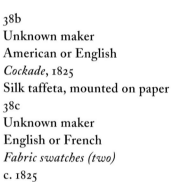

38b
Unknown maker
American or English
Cockade, 1825
Silk taffeta, mounted on paper
38c
Unknown maker
English or French
Fabric swatches (two)
c. 1825

64

39
Unknown maker
American or English
Engraved invitation with classical border
c. 1834
Paper

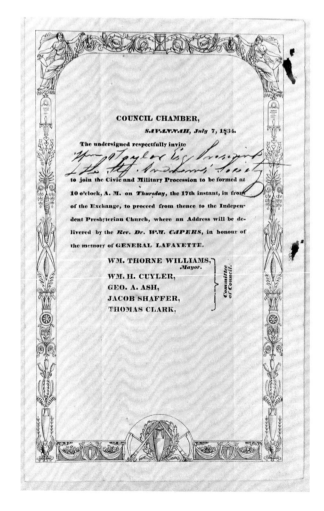

COUNCIL CHAMBER,
SAVANNAH, July 7, 1834.

The undersigned respectfully invite

Wm. Taylor Esq. President
of the St. Andrew's Society

to join the Civic and Military Procession to be formed at
10 o'clock, A. M. on *Thursday*, the 17th instant, in front
of the Exchange, to proceed from thence to the Independent Presbyterian Church, where an Address will be delivered by the *Rev. Dr. WM. CAPERS*, in honour of
the memory of GENERAL LAFAYETTE.

WM. THORNE WILLIAMS,
Mayor.
WM. H. CUYLER,
GEO. A. ASH,
JACOB SHAFFER,
THOMAS CLARK,

Committee of Council.

William Scarbrough's House

Another early commission for William Jay was
a residence for William Scarbrough (1776-1838),
a young wealthy merchant whose firm of
Scarbrough and McKinne imported goods from
all over the world (**40**). Begun in 1818 and completed in 1819 the Scarbrough House faces east at
41 West Broad Street (now Martin Luther King,
Jr. Boulevard). The austere facade has an
entrance porch of Greek Doric distyle in antis
with arched side openings. The form of the
recessed segmental arch at the portico base is
echoed by the Diocletian window directly above.
To the north is a reconstructed arched carriage
gateway with smaller pairs of Doric columns and
a simplified entablature. A south gallery with
cast-iron Corinthian columns identical to those
of the Richardson House balcony features cast-
iron railings in an exuberant foliated scroll pattern, and an interior cast-iron stairway.

    Jay used an interesting T-shaped plan for
the Scarbrough House in which the long axis
was divided into three parts: a grand two-story
atrium entrance hall, its gallery supported by
four massive fluted Doric columns on bases with
corresponding pilasters; and a D-shaped drawing
room on either side. Perpendicular to the atrium
is a rectangular ballroom or banqueting hall. The
original trompe l'oeil ceiling with clerestory
lighting over the atrium was destroyed in the
nineteenth century. In spite of all its alterations,
the brilliant classicism of Jay's Scarbrough House
is still apparent.[18]

40
Attributed to Samuel John
Stump (d. 1863)
English
William Scarbrough
c. 1800-1810
Watercolor (gouache?) on
ivory; silver gilt brass case;
clear and blue glass; hair

65

66

41
Attributed to Nathaniel Jocelyn
(1796-1881)
American
(in Savannah 1820-1822)
Joseph Habersham II
c.1820-1822

Perhaps most significant for Savannah's history was Scarbrough's involvement with the SS *Savannah*. This enterprise reflected the overwhelming optimism of the period and the risky nature of maritime ventures as well as the transient nature of wealth. With a group of investors, including prominent Savannahians Archibald Stobo Bulloch (c. 1775-1859), Andrew Low, Sr. (d. 1849), Isaac Minis (1780-1856), Robert (b. 1783) and Joseph Habersham II (1785-1831) (**41**), and Oliver Sturges (1777-1824) (**42**), Scarbrough formed the Savannah Steam Ship Company in May 1818, with the intention of outfitting a 320-ton sailing ship with steam engine, bent smokestack, and side paddle wheel.[19] This vessel became the first steamship to cross the Atlantic Ocean, departing Savannah for Liverpool, England, and St. Petersburg, Russia, on May 22, 1819.

Scarbrough's ship and new house were both completed in time for the May 1819 visit of President James Monroe (1758-1831). The President stayed at Scarbrough's new residence and sailed downriver aboard the SS *Savannah* to Tybee Island to inspect the city's fortifications and river defenses.[20] Like Washington's visit in 1791 and Lafayette's stay in 1825, Monroe's sojourn in Savannah was a cause for extravagant celebration and the temporary transformation of the city to welcome so notable a visitor. In fact, William Jay himself was commissioned to build a temporary pavilion in Johnson Square where a ball and dinner were held on May 12. The large and sumptuous pavilion was marveled over:

The interior was truly magnificent and beautiful. The ceiling consisted of a single Flag of immense size. The walls were lined with crimson, set off with fluted pilasters made of muslin, which, by candlelight, might be mistaken for fine marble and alabaster. The hall was brilliantly lighted with large chandeliers and lustres.[21]

Like Richardson, Scarbrough experienced financial disaster only shortly after the completion of his house. The SS *Savannah*, despite its successful maiden European voyage, proved a failure because too few passengers were willing to risk overseas passage on so innovative a vessel. Scarbrough's house and its contents were sold at a sheriff's sale, but fortunately all was purchased by his business associate and relative, Robert Isaac, and thus remained in family hands.[22] After the steamship debacle, Scarbrough never regained his financial footing.

42
Joseph-Pierre Picot de Limoëlin
de Clorivière (1786-1826)
French
Oliver Sturges
c. 1805
Watercolor on ivory; brass

Archibald Bulloch's House

Perhaps the most classical of William Jay's domestic architecture was the now demolished mansion of Archibald Stobo Bulloch. Bulloch was another of Savannah's noted citizens whose fortune deteriorated after 1820. By 1822 he was forced to sell his new home on the southwest trust lot of Orleans Square and its luxurious furnishings.[23] Those furnishings included a large quantity of furniture purchased in 1819 from New York cabinetmaker Charles-Honoré Lannuier.[24]

The Bulloch House was also a two-story stucco villa over a raised basement in the English Regency style. The building had a semicircular entry portico with conical roof. Its array of six Corinthian columns recalled the Temple of Vesta in Rome. Jay completed the circular entrance space by setting the front doors in a shallow apsidal niche. The house had a broad central hall with two twenty-foot-wide rooms on each side, a circular domed drawing room, a spiral staircase cantilevered within a circle of six Corinthian columns, unusual tripartite windows on the main floor, and a double drawing room with Corinthian and Ionic columnar screens. A figural mantel in the style of Richard Westmacott, Jr.,

graced the northeast drawing room, and carved Egyptian masks were part of the decorative vocabulary.[25] Today the only remains of the Bulloch House are a few architectural fragments (**43**), a set of gilt window cornices (**44**), and a number of photographs.[26]

43
Unknown maker, possibly by
George James Bubb (1782-1853)
English
Ionic capitals (pair)
c. 1818
Coade stone

44
Unknown maker
English or American
Curtain rod
c. 1819
White pine, gesso; gilt

Alexander Telfair's House

Another residential commission designed by
William Jay and completed in 1819 was the home
of Alexander Telfair (1789-1832).[27] Located on
the northwest trust lot facing St. James Square
(now Telfair Square), the house was lived in con-
tinuously by members of the Telfair family until
1875 when, at Mary Telfair's bequest, the building
became The Telfair Academy of Arts and
Sciences. Alexander Telfair, Mary's beloved
brother (**45**), was one of five surviving children of
the governor of Georgia, Edward Telfair (c. 1735-
1807), and his wife, Sarah Gibbons (1758-1827).
The governor was a man of considerable wealth
whose fortune allowed his son Alexander to
devote his life to "official chairmanships and
charitable committees," as well as the accumula-
tion of considerable material possessions.[28]

The Alexander Telfair House was originally a two-story stucco structure on a high
basement. Its tetrastyle Corinthian entrance
porch has intricate coade stone capitals, and the
modified entablature extends around the building
as a string course. As with the Scarbrough
House, a segmental arch under the porch is
repeated in the second-floor Diocletian window.
The two large French windows flanking the portico are ornamented with grilles of Greek fret-
work. Although the structure was extensively
remodeled in the 1880s by New York architect
Detlef Lienau (1818-1887), the interior still
reflects the central hall plan.[29] The carefully
restored Octagon Room and dining room are to
the left of the stair hall, and to the right is an
altered lozenge-shaped double drawing room
which once had separating pocket doors.[30]

Among the few original architectural elements in the house are the marble mantelpieces
from these principal downstairs rooms (**46 a,b;
47**). Also remaining of the original household
fixtures are the chandelier in the Octagon Room
(**48**) and a set of arrow-end curtain poles (**49**).
Fortunately Alexander Telfair's inventory survives, as do many of the original furnishings of
the house, so it is today possible to re-create the
ambience of the early nineteenth century interior, if not all of the precise decorative features.

70

45
George Lethbridge Saunders
(1807-1863)
English
Alexander Telfair
1848
Watercolor on ivory

46 a,b
William and John Frazee
(1790-1852)
American (New York)
Mantels, pair
c. 1818
White marble

47
Unknown maker
Probably English
Mantels, pair
c. 1819
Carved marble, white and
mottled gray

72

49
Unknown maker
American
Curtain rod ends and gilt rings
c. 1820-40
White pine; gesso; gilt

48
Unknown maker
English (probably Birmingham)
Oil chandelier
c. 1819
Gilt bronze; glass; cast brass

Jay's Public Buildings

In addition to houses, Jay designed three important public structures in Savannah: a theater, a bank, and a customs house. Each of these played important civic and aesthetic roles in the burgeoning city. None survive today in their original state; the customs house burned in the great fire of 1820, the bank was torn down in 1924, and the theater was destroyed by fire in 1948.[31]

The first of these to be built was the Savannah Theater on the northeast trust lots of Chippewa Square. Completed in 1818, the interior of this extraordinary building was described in detail by someone signing his name "Peregrinus" to a florid letter to the editor of the *Savannah Georgian*. All evidence points to William Jay, himself, as the author.

The plan of the interior of the building is semicircular, following the choice of the ancient Grecian and Roman theaters in particular, being not only better adapted to the climate but also better calculated for seeing and hearing than the elliptical form used in modern hearing....There are two rows of boxes, supported by sixteen cast-iron columns, fluted, with gilt capitals and bases, uniting an air of great lightness with strength. The panels of the lower tier of boxes are adorned by golden eagles, with a wreath of green foliage, relieved on a white ground. Between each box is a pilastered panel, laid on crimson, and enriched with a Grecian scroll. The second tier is ornamented by the following basso-relievos, painted by Mr. [William] Etty of London.[32]

Like most of Jay's buildings in Savannah, the theater was touched by financial difficulties and was a failed venture for its investors. In its earliest days, however, the Savannah Theater was a neoclassical masterpiece on the inside, and a restrained, monumental edifice on the exterior.[33]

Perhaps most widely known of Jay's Savannah buildings was the Branch Bank of the United States. Founded by Richard Richardson in 1816, it was located on the east corner of Drayton and St. Julian Streets. The cornerstone of the single-story stucco structure was laid on May 8, 1820, inscribed with the names of Richard Richardson, William Jay, builder John Retan, and others.[34] The building was completed by April 1821, when it was reviewed by a local critic:

New United States Bank. — The principal front of this elegant structure is viewed from the south, and finished with a symmetrical portion sustained by six massive columns, in the Grecian Dorrick [sic] order; a double range of stone steps leads up to the grand entrance, at the extremity of which are placed broad pedestals for statuary.[35]

Two early engravings of the bank survive, one by W. G. Mason of Philadelphia which appeared in an 1823 commercial directory of the United States (**50**), the second by William B. Goodacre of New York (**51**), published in Hinton's *History and Topography of the United States* (1830-1832). With its monumental hexastyle porch, simplified entablature, and pilasters articulating the round-headed windows and the corners of the building,

74

50
Drawn by Joshua Shaw
(1777-1866)
American (Philadelphia)
Engraved by W. G. Mason
(active 1822-1860)
American (Philadelphia)
*Branch Bank of the United States,
Savannah*
1823
Steel engraving

51
Drawn by William Goodacre
(active 1829-1835)
American (New York)
Engraved by Fenner, Sears & Co.
English (London)
*Branch of the United States Bank,
Savannah*
c. 1830-1832

the Branch Bank as executed resembled the Goodacre engraving more closely than that of Mason.[36] Yet it was Mason's engraving after the drawing by Joshua Shaw that became a transfer print for a series of Staffordshire dishes, widely exported from England and clearly popular in Savannah in the 1820s and 1830s (**52 a,b,c,d**).

A third public commission was "a brick building intended to be used as a Custom House according to the plans...by William Jay."[37] Archibald Bulloch, as a customs official in 1817, helped choose the site for the two-story structure on Bryan Street east of Bull Street between Bull and Drayton Streets (lot number nine Jekyl Tything),[38] Jay's new custom house was nearly complete when it was destroyed in the great fire of January 1820. Its ruins are visible in the 1837 panorama of Savannah painted by Joseph Louis Firmin Cerveau.[39]

Another public building in Savannah attributed by some to William Jay is the City Hotel, which reopened for business on East Bay Street in 1821.[40] Its simple exterior can be seen on the extreme right of Cerveau's panorama. The interior of the hotel was far grander with "thirty-three rooms, exclusive of the bar, reading, dining and sitting rooms, in the latter of which there are four superb mantelpieces, grates, etc."[41] The proud proprietor, Oran Byrd, inserted a classically bordered advertisement in Shaw's *United States Directory* of 1823:

This Elegant Establishment which is entirely new with all its Furniture and other arrangements is in the centre of Business and contiguous to the Banks &c —The Post Office is attached to the Premises— all the Stages start from the door. (**53**)

Other Savannah Houses

While Jay's buildings in Savannah were the most innovative, other fine and important houses were constructed during the late teens and twenties by citizens of great wealth and prominence.[42] Among these were the town and country houses of Scottish builder Henry McAlpin (1780-1851) and his wife Ellen McInnis (c. 1799-1831) (**54, 55**). McAlpin's plantation, the Hermitage (**56**), situated three miles west of Savannah, was the only Savannah River plantation dedicated to industry rather than agriculture. The Hermitage manufactured the bulk of the "Savannah Grey" bricks used during the reconstruction following the great fire of 1820.[43] McAlpin also had an iron foundry on the plantation, thereby providing both brick and cast-iron work to his fellow architect, associate, and friend William Jay.[44]

It is no surprise that the houses McAlpin built for his family had many neoclassical elements. Both the Hermitage and the townhouse on Orleans Square had classical porticos.[45] The single-story plantation house on a raised basement had two porches based on the Tower of the Winds in Athens and double curving steps like those of the Richardson House.[46]

The distinguished Jones family owned a number of city houses during the eighteenth and early nineteenth centuries, but they concentrated their country holdings at Wormsloe on the Isle of Hope, ten miles southeast of Savannah. The present house was probably built around 1828 as the principal residence of George Jones (1766-1838), mayor of Savannah, physician, and United States Senator (**57**).[47] Originally a two-story house with columned portico, Wormsloe was fitted with superior household furnishings including elegant mahogany furniture, Brussels carpets, handsome lighting fixtures, white and gold porcelain, and paintings executed by prominent American artists (**58**).[48]

53
Cephas Grier Childs & J. W.
Carpenter (active 1822) engravers
American (Philadelphia)
*Advertisement for Oran Byrd's City
Hotel*
1822
Paper; leather binding

52 a, b, c, d
a
J. and W. Ridgway Factory
England (Hanley)
c. 1814–1830
Covered gravy tureen and stand
c. 1820–1830
Transfer printed creamware
Gravy tureen: on one side,
*Branch Bank of the United States,
Savannah*; on opposite side and
on saucer, *Exchange, Charleston
Charleston*

Cover: *Insane Hospital, Boston*
Stand: *Exchange Bank,
Charleston*

b
Relish dish with handles
c
Small Saucer (rectangular)
d
Saucer (of tureen)

Branch Bank of the United States
Savannah
c. 1820–1830

78

54
Unknown artist [possibly John
Wesley Jarvis (1780-1840)]
American
Mr. Henry McAlpin
c. 1820-1831
Oil on canvas

55
Unknown artist [possibly by
John Wesley Jarvis (1780-1840)]
American
*Mrs. Henry McAlpin (Ellen
McInnis McAlpin)*
c. 1820-1831
Oil on canvas

80

57
Rembrandt Peale (1778-1860)
American (Philadelphia)
Dr. George Jones
c. 1838
Oil on canvas

56
Edgerton Chester Garvin
(1881-1950)
American (Georgia)
*The Hermitage, Savannah,
Georgia (June 1915)*
Platinum print

58
Attributed to Raphaelle Peale
(1774-1825)
American
Senator George Jones
1822
Watercolor on ivory

Coastwise Trade

In these finest of Savannah houses could be found furnishings imported from a variety of locations, both in the United States and abroad. In America, New York was the primary point of origin of furniture, followed by Philadelphia, Providence, and Boston. Relatively little furniture was imported into Savannah from England or France during the period from 1800 to 1840. However, the bulk of the earthenwares came from England, and porcelains were imported from England, France, and China. Lighting fixtures were chiefly made in England, although many were retailed and purchased through dealers in Boston and New York. Glass came from England and from New England, the majority from the New England Glass Company. Silver was sold by a number of jewelers and silversmiths in Savannah, but most was made in the Northern cities of New York and Philadelphia, and in England.

An abundance of written sources documents this wealth of imported goods available on a weekly basis via schooners and brigs arriving in Savannah's busy port. Newspapers printed advertisements of local merchants wishing to sell their recently received shipments. Regular notices in the newspapers also announced the arrival of ships and listed their passengers and cargoes. In addition, ship captains were required to write a manifest of all the goods on board, with both the shipper and consignee listed.

Relatively few bills and receipts for purchases have survived, but a few detailed letters exist documenting the placement and expediting of orders in Northern cities. This correspondence was often between family members or close friends, with the person in the North acting as agent, formally or informally, for the one back home in Savannah. These letters prove that the interchange of goods and styles was fast and frequent in the early nineteenth century. If a cousin in Philadelphia could own an elegant classical sofa or table, so too could his relative in the South, within a matter of weeks in fact. There were hazards in shipping these goods to so distant a destination, but perhaps no greater than those we encounter today.

While the public face of Savannah changed considerably from 1810 to 1830, due in large part to the contributions of William Jay and other builders, the twenties was a decade of struggle. The fire, the epidemic, and the depression of 1820 "plunged the city into gloom." This state of affairs was slow to improve. However, by the 1830s greater optimism was in the air.[49]

1

Charles S. H. Hardee, *Reminiscences and Recollections of Old Savannah* (Savannah, GA: Privately Printed, 1928), p. 61.

2

Lynn Harvey, "King Cotton and Its Effect on the Savannah, Georgia of William Jay 1816-1821" (Unpublished manuscript, Chicago, 1994), p. 9.

3

James Silk Buckingham, *The Slave States of America* (London: Fisher, Son & Co., 1842), pp. 119-120; quoted in Shellman, 1982, p. 9.

4

Henry Carrington Bolton and Reginald Pelham Bolton, *The Family of Bolton in England and America, 1100-1894* (New York: Privately Printed, 1895), p. 330, states that Anne Jay and Robert Bolton married in May 1810; however, the Chatham County Superior Court deed book 2D, p. 275, has a date of April 15, 1811.

5

Hanna H. Lerski, *William Jay, Itinerant English Architect, 1792-1837* (Lanham, MD: University Press of America, Inc., 1983), pp. 37-40. For discussion of Jay's possible involvement with IPC see James V. McDonough, "William Jay, Regency Architect in Georgia and South Carolina" (Ph.d. Dissertation, Princeton University, 1950), p. 26 and Lerski, 1983, pp. 37-39.

6

An inscription beneath the entrance porch reads, "John/Retan/Began Nov AD 1816/Finished Jan AD 1819". Inaccurate interpretations of the inscription have been published earlier. See Lerski, p. 63 and McDonough, p. 29. It has been suggested that the basement was begun by Retan, a master mason, before Jay's arrival. [Lerski, 1983, p. 63]

7

Because the Richardson House was designed by a British architect in the contemporary neoclassical fashion of London it is referred to as a Regency-style structure (For more on the Regency style, see Chpt. 1, note 11). Today, American architecture styles of that period are referred to as Federal (Early Neoclassical) or later Greek Revival (Late Neoclassical). The sophisticated plumbing system original to the 1819 Richardson House included at least four rain-fed cisterns which serviced lavatories, sinks, a marble bath, a shower, and two flushing water closets. [George T. Fore and Associates, *Architectural Investigations of the Owens-Thomas House, Savannah, Georgia* (Raleigh, NC, for the Telfair Museum of Art, 1995)]

8

For information on this artificial stone see Alison Kelly, *Mrs. Coade's Stone* (Upton-upon-Severn, GB: The Self-Publishing Association Ltd., 1990).

9

The Corinthian capitals are based on those of the Choralgic Monument of Lysicrates in Athens. Finishes in the entry/stair hall are documented in George T. Fore and Associates, *The Owens-Thomas House, Savannah, Georgia, Conservation Studies, Finishes Analysis* (Raleigh, NC, for the Telfair Museum of Art, 1991), pp. 36-42.

10

The nomenclature used here for the rooms in the Richardson House is based on a bill of sale recorded October 5, 1822, between Richard Richardson and his business partner Durham Hall (Chatham County Superior Court Deed Book 2L-400).

11

This effect resembles the pendentive dome ceiling in the front parlour of Pitzhanger Manor outside of London by Sir John Soane. See Frank Russell, ed., *Architectural Monographs: John Soane* (New York: St. Martin's Press, 1983), p. 17, for illustration. The circular drawing room of Jay's Bulloch House had an actual domed ceiling. See Cordray-Foltz Collection, Georgia Historical Society.

12

According to Lerski, the younger Westmacott was one of the members of the hanging committee for the Royal Academy exhibition in which Jay was exhibiting (Lerski, 1983, p. 74). The signed drawing is currently in a private collection in Savannah. For illustration of this drawing see McDonough, 1950, figs. 41 and 147.

13

See note 10.

14

Lerski, 1983, p. 78.

15

According to an article in the *Savannah Georgian* (March 22, 1825), the Marquis stayed in the large first-floor bedchamber adjacent to the cast-iron balcony.

16

Account of the Reception of General Lafayette, 1825, p. 18.

17

Cooper, 1993, p. 236. According to Cooper, there were two main reasons for creating heroes for the new nation: "to recognize past deeds performed for the good of all men, and, thus to promote virtuous behavior and inspire future good works by others" (p. 237).

18

A third story was added to the building in the 1830s, and further alterations followed when the house became in 1878 the first public school for African Americans in the city. The additions were removed in 1976, but the present restoration of the space is conjectural. See Mills Lane, *Architecture of the Old South, Georgia* (New York: Abbeville Press, 1990), pp. 121-126.

19

Frank O. Braynard, *S.S. Savannah: The Elegant Steam Ship* (Athens, GA: University of Georgia Press, 1963), pp. 30-31.

20

Coulter, 1971, p. 341.

21

Savannah Georgian (May 14, 1819).

22

The sale took place May 13, 1820. Isaac purchased the house for the express purpose of allowing the Scarbrough family to continue as residents. [Raymond Earle Davis, Jr., "Scarbrough House Hosted Fancy Ball" (Unpublished manuscript, Savannah, GA: 1976), n.p.; a published version of this article appeared in the *Savannah Morning News* (November 19, 1976), p. 4B.]

23

Jan Flores, "Archibald Stobo Bulloch" (Typed Manuscript, History 500, Armstrong State University, Savannah, GA, 1990), p. 9. Bulloch's house suffered the same ignominy as Richardson's; it too served as a boarding house, run by the ubiquitous Mrs. Mary Maxwell. [Lerski, 1983, p. 109]

24
Ten cases of furniture, marked "A.S.B." arrived in Savannah aboard the brig *Levant* on October 5, 1819. They had been consigned by "Honore Lannuier" of New York. [NA/ICM 36, Box 13] Shortly thereafter Bulloch sold a quantity of "elegant furniture," assumedly to make room for the new shipment recently arrived. [*Savannah Georgian* (October 14, 1819)] The announcement of the Sheriff's sale on the first Tuesday in September, 1822, lists furniture that may have been part of the Lannuier shipment: "2 mahogany couches, 2 do. ottomans, 2 do. screens, 2 do. foot benches, 1 set mahogany tables, 1 do. sideboard with marble tops, [and] 1 do. celeret [*sic*]." [*Savannah Georgian* (August 6, 1822)]

25
See Lynn Harvey, "William Jay: A Conjectural Reconstruction of The Archibald Stobo Bulloch House, Savannah, Georgia" (Unpublished manuscript, Chicago, 1994).

26
The architectural fragments from the Bulloch House include a piece of mahogany handrail that was among the contents of the cornerstone box (currently lost) for the Municipal Auditorium which occupied the site from 1916-1971, a pair of coade stone capitals (**43**), a portion of iron fence now installed in the 100 block of East 34th Street, and two marble mantlepieces now in a house at 138 East 46th Street. Photographs taken in 1916 before and during demolition are in the Cordray-Foltz Collection of the Georgia Historical Society.

27
Other area houses have been attributed to Jay, although sufficient proof is lacking. These include the residence of James Moore Wayne (1790-1867), today known as the Juliette Gordon Low Birthplace and operated as a museum by Girl Scouts USA; the home of shipbroker Hazen Kimball (1767-1819) on Bryan Street (destroyed); and the house at Hofwyl Plantation in Darien, GA of Dr. James McGillivray Troup (1784-1849) (destroyed). [Lerski, 1983, pp. 169-173] The construction date of Telfair's residence is based on property valuation listings in the 1817, 1819, and

1820 tax digests. [City of Savannah, Savannah City Treasurer, *Tax Digests 1817, 1819, and 1820*]

28
Lerski, 1983, p. 119. Alexander Telfair was also a shipowner and landowner. For six years near the end of his life, Telfair was active in the development of the Savannah-Ogeechee-Altamaha Canal, in addition to being involved in Georgia's political affairs. [see Feay Shellman, *The Octagon Room* (Savannah: Telfair Academy of Arts and Sciences, Inc., 1982), pp. 13-15]

29
It was Lienau's mission to "remodel and extend the original dwelling so that it could function as an art museum." [Feay Shellman Coleman, *Nostrums for Fashionable Entertainments: Dining in Georgia, 1800-1850* (Savannah: Telfair Academy of Arts and Sciences, Inc., 1992), p.6] Fortunately his drawings of the house prior to renovation still exist in the Detlef Lienau Collection, Drawings and Archives, Avery Architecture and Fine Arts Library, Columbia University.

30
A team of archaeologists, historians, and preservationists was involved in the restoration of two of the principal, public rooms on the first floor of the original Telfair Mansion. These rooms were carefully restored using physical evidence, contemporary documents, and other Jay buildings as their guides. The restoration of the Octagon Room is described in Shellman, 1982, and the entire project is discussed in Coleman, 1992, pp. 4-12.

31
McDonough, pp. 58, 65, and William R. Mitchell, *Classic Savannah* (Savannah, GA: Golden Coast Publishing Co., 1991), p. 21.

32
The Georgian (December 9, 1818). Etty, who painted the portraits of Reverend Robert and Anne Jay Bolton (**23,24**), executed a group of allegorical frescoes for the theater, including *The Descent of the Genius of Drama, Comedy, Tragedy, and their Attributes*; *Jove, when an Infant*; *The Passions of Rage, Fear and Pity, accompanied by Hope and Revenge*; and *Hesperus and his Daughters*. These and five other scenes were all taken from classical mythology.

33
McDonough, 1950, p. 58. By 1854 extensive changes had been made to the theater's interior, including adding a third tier with partitioned space for African American patrons. By the 1890s the stage had been moved, a heating system installed, the decoration altered, and the theater enlarged to accommodate 400 people. [Lerksi, 1983, p. 147] For reconstructed plans and elevations of the theater see McDonough, figs. 100-104.

34
For a discussion of this cornerstone plate (now lost) and its inscription see McDonough, 1950, p. 104.

35
The Georgian and Evening Advertiser (April 19, 1821). No representation of the bank interior is known, although the following description appeared in *The Daily Georgian* (September 10, 1847): "We had the pleasure yesterday of examining its spacious halls and appurtenances, which show to great advantage in the new and very superior coat of painting which has been put upon the walls and woodwork. The imitation of oak on the doors is exquisite."

36
McDonough, 1950, pp. 66-67.

37
The contract dated May 27, 1819, survives in the National Archives. [Records of General Acounting Office, R.G. 217, No. 44488; quoted in Mitchell, 1991, p. 21]

38
Letter from Archibald Bulloch to William H. Crawford, May 20, 1817 [National Archives, General Records of the Treasury Department, R.G. 56; quoted in Mitchell, 1991, p. 138]

39
Cerveau's painting is on view at the Georgia Historical Society. A fold-out reproduction can be found in Waring, 1973, end page.

84

40

Compared to other documented Jay buildings in Savannah, the City Hotel attribution is less decisive. An explanation of the attribution is offered in Lerski, 1983, pp. 158-168. See also Malcolm Bell, "Ease and Elegance, Madeira and Murder: the Social Life of Savannah's City Hotel," *Georgia Historical Quarterly*, v. 76, # 3 (Fall, 1992), pp. 551-76. The building still stands, vacant, with most of its interior framework stripped bare.

41

The Georgian (August 28, 1828); *The Georgian* (July 6, 1829).

42

William Jay's modern designs were not embraced by all of Savannah's elite. Conservative residents such as builder Isaiah Davenport continued to build in the Federal idiom. Davenport's own house on Columbia Square (now operated as a museum by Historic Savannah Foundation) was completed in 1820, a year after most of Jay's domestic commissions, yet it resembles a Federal house of 1800. See Nichols, 1976, pp. 43-4.

43

After "the destructive fire in January 1820 reduced nearly half of the best built part of the city to ashes," others followed Jay's lead in using fireproof materials. Consequently it was reported that "the buildings since erected are generally of brick, and much better than they were before." [Kayser, 1823, p. 37]

44

Granger, 1947, pp. 422, 437.

45

The McAlpin's city residence is illustrated in J. Robie Kennedy, "Examples of Georgian and Greek Revival Work in the Far South," *Architectural Record*, 21, # 3 (March 1907), p. 222.

46

The date of construction of the brick mansion at the Hermitage has been variously listed as 1808, 1820, and 1840. Frederick Nichols, who has assigned the latest date, bases his conclusion on the asymmetrical plan of the house (see Nichols, 1976, p. 58, for illustration of the plan). The design of the Hermitage is attributed to architect Charles B. Cluskey, whose greatest houses were built in Georgia from 1830 to 1847.

47

On July 25, 1828, George Jones entered into contract with Alexander J. C. Shaw "to erect…a two story Timber and shingled building at Wormsloe…said building to be completed on or before the first day of December next." [William M. Kelso. *Captain Jones' Wormsloe: A Historical, Archaeological and Architectural Story of an 18th century Plantation Site Near Savannah Georgia* (Athens, GA: University of Georgia Press, 1979), p. 15]

48

George Jones' inventory is on file at the Chatham Country Courthouse, File Box I, Folio 74 (1838).

49

While in the 1820s Savannah's population had grown only by 200 to a total of 7,723 in 1830, during the following decade the city saw a 33% increase in population, to 11,214 in 1840. [Waring, 1973, p. 5]

23
William Etty, R.A. (1787-1849)
English
Reverend Robert Bolton
1818
Oil on canvas
**50 3/4 x 41 1/4 in. (128.9 x
104.8 cm.)**

*Inscription: verso, on canvas "Miss
Adele Bolton"*

*Provenance: Robert Bolton; to his
son James Bolton (1824-1863); to his
son Reginald Pelham Bolton (1856-
1942); The New-York Historical
Society.*
*Loan from The New-York Historical
Society, OT 1.1975*

86

The life stories of William Etty,
William Jay, and Robert and
Anne Jay Bolton are inextricably
intertwined. Etty, the British
painter, was architect Jay's best
friend. Both knew each other's
families, and Etty painted a particularly fine portrait of Jay's evan-
gelistic father, Reverend William
Jay of Bath. This, and a painting
of the younger Jay's sister
Arabella, were exhibited at the
Royal Academy in 1818.[1] A native
of York, England, Etty was one of
the most prominent English acad-
emic painters in the first half of
the nineteenth century.[2]

Robert Bolton (1788-1857) met
Etty through William Jay, his
wife's brother. He had traveled in
1807 to England where he met
Reverend Jay, who inspired him to
study for the ministry. Upon arriving in Bath, Bolton wrote his

family in Savannah: "Every thing
in Mr. Jay's family pleased, and
profited me. I saw religion in its
loveliest form; and my mind
already tending towards the ministry, it seemed to me what I
should desire above all things."[3]
Bolton returned to the United
States in 1807, but he later
returned to England in 1810 to
pursue religious studies. Despite
his clerical training, however,
Bolton set aside his calling to
manage his family's mercantile
business, R. and J. Bolton, from
an office in Liverpool (**19**).

It is as a wealthy merchant, then,
that Bolton is portrayed in this
grand, almost life-size portrait.
Standing relaxed against a para-
pet, with an Ionic column at his
back and a distant ship in the harbor beyond, the sitter is pictured
with all the trappings of grand
manner portraits. Included is the
primary symbol of his material
circumstance, the schooner in full-
sail, as is the less specific convention of the column, acknowledg-
ing the artist's debt to the long
tradition of formal portraiture.[4]

Bolton was so enthusiastic about
this portrait that he wrote a poem
to the artist: "Etty, `tis done! the
very man breathes now. I feel the
likeness,…"[5] The majority of the
poem deals with Bolton's family,
career, and calling, but its essence
is an exhortation to the clergyman
to live up to the ideal suggested in
the portrait, that is to live up to
his "'Type,' to assume a benevo-
lent aspect, to impart sundry

sound moral precepts, and say a
good word for the defunct original,—to do, in fact, more than a
poor picture well can."[6]

Ultimately Reverend Bolton relin-
quished his business responsibili-
ties, returned to America with his
wife and fourteen children, and
built Pelham Priory and Christ
Church in Pelham, New York. He
remained pastor there for thirteen
years until 1850, when he returned
to England and was chaplain
to the Earl of Ducie in
Gloucestershire until his death
in 1857.[7]

1
Lerski, 1983, pp. 26-7.
2
The New-York Historical Society,
*Catalogue of American Portraits in The New-
York Historical Society*, v. 2 (New Haven
and London: Yale University Press, for the
Society, 1974), p. 85.
3
Robert T. Bolton, *Genealogical and
Biographical Account of the Family Bolton in
England and America* (New York: A. Gray,
1862), p. 329.
4
Ann M. Hope, *The Theory and Practice of
Neoclassicism in English Painting: Origins,
Development, and Decline of an Ideal* (New
York and London: Garland Publishing,
Inc., 1988), pp. 120, 123.
5
Alexander Gilchrist, *Life of William Etty,
R.A.* (London: David Boque, 1855), p. 78.
6
Ibid.
7
The New-York Historical Society, 1974, p.
84.

24
William Etty, R.A. (1787-1849)
English
Anne Jay Bolton and children,
William and Anne
1818
Oil on canvas
51 x 41 ¼ in. (129.5 x 104.8 cm.)

Inscriptions: on back of canvas "Miss Adele Bolton"

Provenance: Anne Jay Bolton; to her son James Bolton (1824-1863); to his son Reginald Pelham Bolton (1856-1942); The New-York Historical Society.
Loan from The New-York Historical Society, OT 2.1975

Through the generosity of his uncle, William Etty was able to study with Sir Thomas Lawrence, the British academician whose distinctive style inspired many copyists in early nineteenth-century England.[1] The influence of Lawrence is readily apparent in this portrait of Anne Jay Bolton (1793-1859) and her two oldest children, Anne (1815-1884) and William (1816-1884), painted seven years after her marriage to Reverend Robert Bolton.

Anne Jay met Robert Bolton when she was only seventeen years old, soon after his arrival in Bath in 1807. His stay was short-lived; he returned to Savannah due to the threat of war between England and France. Bolton soon corresponded with the Reverend Jay from the United States about his wishes to join the ministry, and about his daughter with

whom he had fallen in love. Wrote Bolton, "I laid my heart entirely open to him. His answer came to me at Savannah. He replied encouragingly, stating that, if I were fixed in England, there was no one whom he would so gladly intrust his daughter to."[2] Returning to Bath, Bolton married Anne Jay in May 1810. She was a woman "exactly suited to him, not by resembling him in character, but by being just the complement he needed, meeting his wants, sharing his burdens, and encouraging him in every good and holy enterprise."[3]

In Etty's portrait Anne Bolton is stylishly dressed in the diaphanous Empire-style gown, but on her knee is draped a Turkish shawl, suggesting the modesty of the young matron who later became the mother of nine girls and five boys. Like her husband, Anne Bolton is posed among the accoutrements of wealth and privilege, including an elaborate marbletop table, on which rests a large vase of flowers. The rich red curtain to her right frames the sitters and acts as a backdrop to Anne, called Nanette, the eldest Bolton girl, who is standing on her mother's lap.

Never married, Nanette taught for many years at the parish school that her parents founded in Pelham, New York, and died in Switzerland. William Jay Bolton began his career as an artist, designer, and stained-glass maker.[4] Like his father, he entered the ministry late in life, becoming

a priest in 1854 and serving as minister to parishes in Stratford, Essex, and finally, in Bath.[5]

---

[1]
Michael Bryan, *Dictionary of Painters and Engravers, Biographical and Critical*. Robert Edmund Graves and George C. Williamson, eds., 5 vols. (London: George Bell, 1903), p. 468.
[2]
Bolton, 1862, p. 329.
[3]
Ibid., p. 330.
[4]
See Willene B. Clark, *The Stained Glass Art of William Jay Bolton* (Syracuse, NY: Syracuse University Press, 1992).
[5]
The New-York Historical Society, 1974, p. 85.

25
Drawn by William Goodacre
(active 1820-1835)
American (New York)
Engraved by Fenner, Sears and Co.
English (London)
Interior of William Holden Green's Savannah Independent Presbyterian Church
c. 1831
Published in: John Howard Hinton, ed., *History and Topography of the United States* **v. 2 (London: I. T. Hinton, Simpkin, & Marshall, 1830-1832), pl. 73.**
Steel engraving
Sheet: 7 ½ x 10 ⅜ in. (19.1 x 26.4 cm.); matted: 12 ¼ x 13 ⅜ in. (31.1 x 33.9 cm.)

Inscriptions: l.l. "Drawn by W. Goodacre Junr. N.Y."; l.r. "Engraved & printed by Fenner Sears & Co.";

l.c. "INTERIOR OF THE PRESBYTER-
IAN CHURCH, SAVANNAH/*London
Published. Nov. 1 1831. by I. T.
Hinton & Simpkin & Marshall"
Loan from V & J Duncan*

The Independent Presbyterian
Church of Savannah looks very
much as it did when completed in
1819, although none of the original
structure remains, having been
destroyed by fire in 1899.[1] The
architect, William Holden Green
(1777-1850) of Rhode Island, is
said to have based his design on
St. Martin's-in-the-Fields, the
London masterpiece of James
Gibbs. Considered to be showy
and costly, the church was
described in 1828 as:

*a house of public worship equal to
any in the United States. It is built
of rough stone covered with slate.
The steeple is supported by large
carved pillars, which may be seen at
a distance. The inside is of elegant
carved work, the pulpit is mahogany,
and supported with pillars of carved
work. The main pillars that support
galleries are also elegantly carved.
The floor is of blue and white marble, laid in checkers and diamonds.[2]*

Green has been described as an
"essentially conservative designer,"
having seldom used Greek forms,
but the interior of the
Independent Presbyterian
Church, as drawn for this engraving,
appears to have been a grand and
innovative classical space.[3] For
Savannahians, there was cause for
celebration upon its completion,
for they declared that "this church

is not surpassed by any in the
United States."[4] That the church
was reconstructed after the fire to
duplicate the original is testimony
to the long-lived appreciation of
its design.

1
Walter C. Hartridge, "Architectural Trends
in Savannah," *The Magazine Antiques*, v.91,
#3 (March, 1967), p. 6.
2
Eleazar Sherman, quoted in Lane, 1969, p.
56.
3
Talbot Hamlin, *Greek Revival Architecture
in America* (London: Oxford University
Press; reprinted, New York: Dover
Publications, Inc., 1944), p. 181.
4
*Columbian Museum and Savannah Daily
Gazette* (May 10, 1819).

26

Photograph, cast-iron balcony
Richardson-Owens-Thomas
House, c. 1819

Ornamental ironwork was an inte-
gral part of William Jay's residential as well as commercial designs.
In his commissions completed
before the great fire of 1820, as
well as through advertisements
published after this tragic event,
Jay enthusiastically espoused ironwork as a valuable building element. Shortly after the devasta-
tion, Jay suggested "a plan to erect
fire-proof stores…to use Iron
instead of timber, to make the
floor joists of cast iron,…the roof
to have iron rafters…,The shut-
ters and sash frames to be of
iron,…" Furthermore he had
"made arrangements with Mr.
McAlpin who lately has erected
a foundry for cast iron…."[1]

The cast-iron balcony for Richard
Richardson's house was probably
imported from England.[2] It rests
on huge inverted scrolls decorated
with acanthus foliage, a classical
element that can be found as
ornament on Regency-style furniture and architecture, and the
Corinthian capitals are identical
to those Jay used on the south
piazza of the Scarbrough House.
The balcony is attached to the
side of the house with a steeply
sloping copper roof, crowned with
a band of anthemia, a motif which
Jay used repeatedly in his
Savannah houses. Legend has it
that Lafayette greeted the people
of the city from this balcony.[3]

1
Daily Georgian (January 2, 1820), quoted
in Granger, 1947, pp. 436-7 (see 56, 57).
2
Hartridge, 1967, p. 9, suggests that the balcony is English. McDonough, 1950, p. 34,
note 9, writes of Jay's importing building
materials from New York. It is probable
that some of the goods shipped from New
York were manufactured abroad, but a
Savannah provenance for the balcony is
unlikely in that McAlpin's foundry, the
first iron manufactory in the area, was not
begun until 1820. Richardson's house is
thought to have been completed by that
date.
3
Lerski, 1983, p. 80. According to an
account in the *Savannah Morning News*
(May 16, 1897), "Lafayette was given a suite
of rooms in the house….The rooms were
on the first floor by President Street." It
has been suggested that the hero stayed in
the chamber adjacent to the balcony, but
there is no written account that gives the
precise location for Lafayette's two speech-
es at the House.

27
Unknown maker
English
Consoles (pair), **c. 1819**
White pine; marble (mahogany
replacement element on
1951.152.2)
19 x 49 ½ x 30 in. (48.3 x 125.7 x
76.2 cm.)

*Provenance: installed by Richard
Richardson; to Durham Hall; to the
Bank of the United States; to George
Welshman Owens (1786-1856); to his
daughter Margaret Wallace Owens
Thomas (1829-1915); to her daughter
Margaret Gray Thomas (1871-1951);
Telfair Museum of Art.*
*Bequest of Margaret Thomas,
1951.152.1-2*

Viewed vertically, the brackets for
these console tables resemble the
consoles that support the
Richardson House iron balcony.
While the simple S-shaped brackets of the balcony are most typical
in neoclassical designs, the
rosettes, leafage, and scrolls intertwined in the elaborate carved
supports installed in the
Richardson entrance hall were all
popular decorative elements in the
first three decades of the nineteenth century. Each of these
motifs can be found in George
Smith's *A Collection of Ornamental
Designs after the Manner of the
Antique* (1812); a similar bracket
incorporating these elements is
illustrated as Pl. 24 in that publication. Brackets were a popular
furnishing item in houses of the
period, supporting all manner of
decorative objects, from clocks to
sculpture to lighting devices.
Smith described a related bracket

illustrated in his 1808 *Collection of
Designs for Household Furniture* as
"intended to support lights,
clocks, & c. to be executed in
gold, or bronze and gold, as may
suit best the rooms."[1]

In their original state, the consoles
in the Richardson House were
polychromed with antique verte
and gilt finishes. When the house
was completed, the console tables
complemented the original verdigris and bronze gilt balusters of
the staircase and the Corinthian
columns with gilded capitals and
marbleized plinths.[2] They were
described in an 1822 inventory of
the house as "2 marble slabs," and
were valued at £26.[3]

1
George Smith, 1808, p. 21.
2
A 1994 microscopy report by Robert
Mussey [Owens-Thomas House files]
confirmed the finishes of the brackets.
*The Owens-Thomas House...Finishes
Analysis,* 1991, pp.36-42, documents the
original finishes of the Richardson-
Owens-Thomas House staircase.
3
Chatham County Courthouse, Deed Book
2L-400, p. 43. This is the list of household
contents sold by Richardson to Durham
Hall, October 5, 1822.

28
After Bertel Thorvaldsen
(1770-1841)
Danish
Lord Byron
after 1817
Plaster, painted to simulate
bronze
32 x 24 x 16 in. (81.3 x 61 x
40.6 cm.)

*Provenance: George Welshman
Owens (1786-1856); to his daughter
Margaret Wallace Owens Thomas
(1829-1915); to her daughter
Margaret Gray Thomas (1871-1951);
Telfair Museum of Art.*
Bequest of Margaret Thomas,
1951.101.2

George Gordon, Lord Byron
(1788-1824), was a romantic hero
of proportions that matched his
epic poetry. His tempestuous love
life, his acerbic manner, his
inspired literary career—all were
climaxed by his tragic premature
death in Greece, struck down by
illness during the War of Greek
Independence against the Turks.[1]
Byron was one of many
Englishmen who were interested
in the Greeks' fight to overthrow
Turkish rule, yet his journey to the
scene of revolt and his direct
involvement with the conflict
made him legendary. To those in
democratic societies, the struggle
for independence recalled the
ancient grandeur of Classical
Greece, sparking renewed and
intense interest in the Greek civilization.

Thorvaldsen's bust of Byron was begun in April/May 1817, but it was Byron's fame and the circumstances surrounding his death that brought about numerous requests for marble replicas.[2] The figure is draped in classical dress and is restrained in pose, drawing a "parallel between the world of the moderns and the ancients."[3] Thorvaldsen, a Dane who was one of the most famous sculptors of the day, spent much of his career in Italy, where he executed Byron's bust.[4] He modeled a second statue of a seated Byron in 1831-1834. The bust from the Richardson House is a plaster replica painted to look like bronze after a marble original. While the sculpture may have been owned by Richardson, it is more likely that the portrait bust was purchased by the next owner, George Welshman Owens, when he moved into the house in 1830.

1
Dictionary of National Biography (London: Oxford University Press, 1937-8), v. III, p. 604.
2
Bertel Thorvaldsen: Skulpturen, Modelle, Bozzetti, Handzeichnungen (Köln: Museen der Stadt Köln, 1977), p. 124.
3
Cooper, 1993, p. 65.
4
Hawley, 1964, n.p. (#173).

29
After Sir Francis Legatt Chantrey (1781-1841)
English
***Sir Walter Scott*, after 1821**
Plaster, painted to simulate bronze
30 x 26 ½ x 16 in. (76.2 x 67.3 x 40.6 cm.)

Provenance: George Welshman Owens (1786-1856); to his daughter Margaret Wallace Owens Thomas (1829-1915); to her daughter Margaret Gray Thomas (1871-1951); Telfair Museum of Art.
Bequest of Margaret Thomas, 1951.101.1

The bust of another famous British literary figure shared the Richardson House entry in the early nineteenth century, that of the Scottish author and poet Sir Walter Scott (1771-1832). A prolific writer, Scott's most famous works include *Waverley Novels* and *Ivanhoe*, and the poem *The Lady of the Lake*. Among his many admirers was Sir Francis Legatt Chantrey, an English sculptor and painter whose career represented to some "the summit of the British School of Sculpture."[1] His greatest strength was in the modeling of portrait busts, such as the one of Scott, commissioned by the first Duke of Wellington in 1821.[2]

According to his biographer, Chantrey's admiration for Scott was so great that he personally invited the writer to sit for him, the only time he had ever made such a request. In fact Chantrey completed two identical busts of Scott, one which he presented to the author, the second for his patron, the Duke of Wellington. It was widely thought to be the finest portrait of Scott, a man whose likeness was not easy to capture.[3] The portrait bust was inspired by Roman antique portraiture, with its simple naturalistic pose. Many copies were made of this famous bust, including this one of plaster painted to simulate bronze.[4] The standard antique drapery is modified to suggest plaid fabric of the author's native Scotland.

1
Col. Maurice Harold Grant, *A Dictionary of British Sculptors* (London: Rockliff, 1953), p. 56.
2
Alex Potts, *Sir Francis Chantrey 1781-1841* (London: National Portrait Gallery, 1981), p. 21. Chantrey exhibited 125 busts at the Royal Academy in London. It has been noted that "everyone who was anybody" sat for him, and that "the nobodies were immortalized by as much consummate skill…as the kings, noblemen and statesmen themselves." [Ibid., p. 57] So prolific was Chantrey that he ran his own foundry at Pimlico where he employed many assistants, and at his death in 1841 the sculptor's estate was valued at £105,000. [*The Connoisseur's Complete Period Guide to the Houses, Decoration, Furnishing and Chattels of the Classic Periods* (New York: Bonanza Books, 1968), p. 1099]
3
Potts, 1981, p. 21.
4
According to a letter from M. Keith Kapp, President, Dialectic and Philanthropic Societies Foundation Inc. in 1979 to the Curator of the Richardson-Owens-Thomas House, the replica of the Chantrey bust of Sir Walter Scott was one of thousands of pirated copies made. [Richardson-Owens-Thomas House files]

30

Anthemia, cornice frieze
dining room, Richardson-Owens-Thomas House
c. 1819

The anthemion design was a common Greek ornament based upon a honeysuckle flower. In the late eighteenth and early nineteenth centuries, the anthemion, also called a palmette, was used abundantly in interior decoration and as a motif on furniture, silver, and ceramics. As such, it is seen as a hallmark of the Neoclassical style.

For William Jay, the anthemion was a favorite device which he used abundantly in both the interiors and exteriors of his Savannah buildings. The anthemia in the large "Dining Room or Large Parlour" in the Richardson House are made of plaster, while those crowning the balcony are of cast-iron. All were derived from the Choralgic Monument of Lysicrates, as illustrated in Stuart and Revett's *Antiquities of Athens*.[1]

1
Lerski, 1983, p. 73. The four volumes of *Antiquities of Athens* were published between 1762 and 1816.

31

Unknown maker
English
Built-in marbletop sideboard
c. 1819
Mahogany; white pine; brass; marble
39 ½ x 72 x 30 in. (100.3 x 182.8 x 76.2 cm.)

Provenance: originally installed by Richard Richardson; to Durham Hall; to the Bank of the United States; to George Welshman Owens (1786-1856); to his daughter Margaret Wallace Owens Thomas (1829-1915); to her daughter Margaret Gray Thomas (1871-1951); Telfair Museum of Art.
Bequest of Margaret Thomas, 1951.3

In 1822 when Richard Richardson's household effects were sold to Durham Hall, the "marble slab or side board" in the "Dining Room or Large Parlour" was valued at £48.[1] This extraordinary survival is an important document of the high-style Regency interior that Jay achieved in this, his first Savannah house. Taken out of this context, this sideboard might well be considered to have been made in the 1830s, but paint and structural analysis have demonstrated that this table dates from the construction of the house, between 1816 and 1819. The original finish of the apron was antique verte, highlighted by gilding. The mahogany monopodia support has been blackened over the years by linseed oil, but was originally bright-red, shiny mahogany.

Related to elements in George Smith's design books, the carving on this sideboard can be said to "exemplify the mainstream quintessential high Regency style, a fusion of antique and Empire motifs."[2] Animal monopodia were one of Smith's most frequently used features as were oversized lion's feet with exaggerated claws. No precise model for this sideboard is known in England, but given the similarities between the sideboard and the consoles in the entry (**27**) and plates in Smith's publication, Jay may well have ordered these pieces from one of the furniture-makers in London. The brass gallery at the rear of the table is part of the original design, which was adapted to the curved niche below the amber wall light.

1
Richard Richardson's household inventory, 1822 (Chatham County Courthouse, Deed Book 2L-400, p. 43).
2
John Morley, *Regency Design: Gardens, Buildings, Interiors, and Furniture* (London: A. Zwemmer Ltd., 1993), p. 391.

32
Unknown maker
English
Door push plates in the Egyptian style (one of three)
c. 1818
Brass
12 ½ x 3 ¼ x ⅛ in. (31.8 x 8.3 x .33 cm.)

Provenance: originally installed by Richard Richardson; Durham Hall; the Bank of United States; George Welshman Owens (1786-1856); to his daughter Margaret Wallace Owens Thomas (1829-1915); to her daughter Margaret Gray Thomas (1871-1951); Telfair Museum of Art.
Bequest of Margaret Thomas, 1951

One of the earliest neoclassical volumes to introduce the Egyptian style to Europe was published by G. B. Piranesi in 1769, followed by numerous other books that documented this rich and exotic decorative tradition.[1] Subsequently the English, Italians, and French all took up this style with enthusiasm, creating entire Egyptian rooms. The rise of "Egyptomania" in France coincided with Napoleon's invasion of Egypt in 1798. Accompanying him was an "army of scholars" who documented and later published numerous volumes on Egypt and its antiquities.[2]

Many of the more familiar Egyptian motifs had been adopted by the Romans, so were associated with the Classical tradition as well as with the earlier culture.

Sphinxes, pyramids, such as those on these push plates, and obelisks could be found in ancient Roman decoration, as well as in the art of Renaissance and Baroque Italy. The other design elements on the push plates are all familiar classical motifs: the acanthus leaf, the double wreaths, and the vase under the sphinxes' paw.

[1]
In publishing his designs, Piranesi cautioned: "No one, I believe, will imagine that these designs, which I give to the public, are really taken from chimneys, which were in use among the Egyptians, the Tuscans, the Greeks, and Romans....What I pretend by the present designs is to shew [sic] what use an able architect may make of the ancient monuments by properly adapting them to our own manners and customs." [Diverse maniere d'adornare i cammini ed ogni altra parte degli edifici (Rome, 1769), quoted in Donald Fennimore "Egyptian influence in early nineteenth century American furniture," *The Magazine Antiques*, v. 137, # 5 (May 1990), p. 1191] The profusion of decorative elements included in Piranesi's designs inspired a variety of artists to incorporate individual motifs in the Egyptian taste into their own work.
[2]
Fennimore,1990, p. 1196. Best known of these was *Voyage dans la Basse et la Haute Egypte*, published by Baron Dominique Vivant Denon in Paris (1802).

33
Photograph, white marble figural fireplace
front parlour/drawing room
Richardson-Owens-Thomas House
c. 1819

The small front room to the right of the entry of the Richardson House originally served as the "Front Parlour or Drawing Room".[1] The room features a number of fine architectural features, including a continuous Greek fret ringing the ceiling, a central plaster medallion, sunburst spandrels in the corners that diminish to leaf-ornamented brackets, and a handsome white marble mantelpiece embellished with a pair of female figures.[2] The central plaque of the mantelpiece is also adorned with a high relief of the mythological Hebe, cupbearer of the gods who was seduced by Zeus in the form of an eagle. The mantels may have been executed by British sculptor Richard Westmacott, Jr. (see **34**).

[1]
Room designation is from the 1822 Bill of Sale from Richard Richardson to Durham Hall (Chatham County Courthouse, Deed Book 2L-400).
[2]
Lerski suggests an association of the design of the plaster spandrels with the designs of French architects Percier and Fontaine for the "imperial tent" at Malmaison where plaster was substituted for silk (p. 75). See also Chpt. 2, 1820 essay, note 11.

34
Sir Richard Westmacott (1775-1856) or his son Richard Westmacott (1799-1872)
English
Drawing of chimney surround
c. 1820
Pen and ink on paper
16 3/16 x 11 1/4 in. (41.1 x 28.6 cm.)

*Inscription: on recto, l.l., signature in script "Richd Westmacott Junior.";
verso, in ink "W. Wyatt"*

Provenance: found in Savannah in a washstand by Will Theus (Mrs. Charlton Theus) in 1940s.
Loan from Will Theus

Found rolled with a signed elevation drawing by William Jay, this Westmacott drawing may well have been sent on approval to the architect by Richard Westmacott, a British sculptor.[1] Comparison of the drawing to the mantel at the Richardson House (**33**) and with photographs of two mantels in the now-destroyed Bulloch House strongly suggests that Westmacott may have been supplying mantels for Jay's Savannah houses.[2]

The Westmacott family consisted of a group of artists, many of whom were decorative sculptors. The most famous of these was Sir Richard Westmacott, who is best known for his statue of Achilles in Hyde Park (London). Commissioned in 1826 to commemorate the achievements of the Duke of Wellington, the sculpture was made from French guns captured at Waterloo.[3] The sculptor's eldest son, also named Richard (1799-1872), would have been a

contemporary of William Jay. Both Richard Westmacotts studied at the Royal Academy during the tenure of John Flaxman (1755-1826) as professor of sculpture; Flaxman's influence can be seen in this drawing.[4]

Most likely this drawing is by the younger Westmacott, whose father would probably have been busy with more important commissions when Jay was working in America. In this drawing, Westmacott chose the images of two famous classical women: the biblical heroine Judith, shown holding the head of Holofernes, and the classical poetess Sappho, with her lyre. Judith was the Israeli woman who decapitated Holofernes, chief captain of the marauding Assyrian army who threatened to starve the Israelites and destroy their temples. She became the savior of the people of Israel.[5] Sappho (c. 620-c. 565 B.C.E.), born on the island of Lesbos, was the most famous Greek poetess. As Plato's "tenth muse" and as a bard whose verses were delivered as songs, she is shown with a lyre.

[1]
McDonough, 1950, pp. 37-8. The Jay drawing is in a private collection in Savannah. See McDonough, figs. 41 & 147.

[2]
Rolled with the signed Jay elevation drawing and the Westmacott mantel drawing was a third sketch, which has long been associated with the William Mason Smith House in Charleston, SC, based on its similarity to the three-bay facade of the Smith house at 26 Meeting Street. See McDonough, fig. 156. Recently, a receipt has been discovered in the papers of William Mason Smith at Middleton Place showing that Jay was involved with the construction of this house. Also in the Smith papers is an unidentified drawing of classical figures to be "put in niches... to hold lamps to light part of a Staircase." [*The Vernacular Architecture of Charleston 1670-1990, A Field Guide* (Charleston, SC: Historic Charleston Foundation, 1994), pp. 170, 171] The design of these figures is remarkably similar to those in the Westmacott mantel drawing.

[3]
The *Connoisseur's Complete Period Guide*, 1962, p. 1099.

[4]
McDonough, 1950, p. 38.

[5]
Judith, 1-16, *New Oxford Annotated Bible, New Revised Standard Version with Apocrypha* (Oxford: University of Oxford Press, 1991). The rendering of Judith relates to the painting by Andrea Mantegna, one of the many painters of the Italian Renaissance who chose biblical subject matter as a way of interpreting classical civilization. The head of Holofernes is modeled after a Greek tragic mask.

35
John Crawford (active in New York 1815-1836 and Philadelphia 1837-1843)
American (New York)
Tea service (4 pieces)
c. 1815-1820
Sterling silver
Teapot: 9 1/2 x 12 x 4 5/8 in. (24.1 x 30.5 x 11.7 cm.); sugar bowl and lid: 9 x 8 x 6 1/2 in. (22.8 x 20.3 x 16.5 cm.); waste bowl: 6 x 6 1/2 in. (15.2 x 16.5 cm.); cream pitcher: 7 5/8 x 6 1/4 x 3 1/4 in. (19.3 x 15.9 x 8.3 cm.)

Marks: verso, on all four pieces in rectangle in Roman capitals "J. CRAWFORD"; verso, punch engraved inside foot ring of teapot "F.L.B. Richardson"

Inscription: on front of all four pieces, engraved in Old English capital "R"

Provenance: Frances Lewis Bolton Richardson (1794-1822); Schindler's Antique Shop, Charleston, SC; Descombe Wells, 1956; Telfair Museum of Art.
Museum purchase with funds from Mrs. Gordon Carson, Miss Sara Cunningham, Miss Dorothy Farr, Mrs. James Glover, Mrs. Hunter Harris, Mr. Tom Hilton, Mr. Lester Karrow, Mrs. Richard Meyer, Mrs. Henry L. Richmond, Mrs. Fred J. Robinson, Miss Margaret Stiles, Mrs. Rufus Wainwright, and Mr. & Mrs. Descombe Wells, OT 1956.1-5

The Richardson tea service was made by silversmith John Crawford during his years in New York City. Considering the quantity of silver made by him that survives, it is apparent that he was a maker of quality in both design and craftsmanship.[1] Classical references in this service appear in the form of acorn-shaped finials and acanthus and oak leaves. The bulbous curves of the bodies, typical of the Empire style, are highlighted by stamped bands of ornament (frequently provided by specialists, much as specific craftspeople made bands of inlays for furniture-makers).

According to tradition, this tea service was a wedding gift to Frances Lewis Bolton upon her marriage to Richard Richardson on December 10, 1811. Since Crawford is not recorded in business before 1815, however, it is more likely that the tea service was commissioned by the Richardsons for their new house, completed in 1819.[2] Each of the four pieces is engraved "R" and the inside of the teapot footring is punch engraved "F.L.B. Richardson."

[1]
Today Crawford's silver is represented in the collections of the Museum of the City of New York, The New-York Historical Society, the Winterthur Museum, and the Chicago Art Institute, among others. [Naeve, 1986, p. 88]

[2]
Coleman, 1992, p. 96.

36 a, b, c, d
a
Unknown maker
English (Staffordshire)
Pitcher
c. 1825-1835
One side: *Portrait of LaFayette*
Other side: *Cornwallis resigning his sword at Yorktown*
On front under spout: *Cluster of fruit*
Copper lusterware
7 1/4 x 9 x 4 in.(18.4 x 22.9 x 10.2 cm.)

Sources of prints: Two figures of Fame hold laurel wreath above framed bust of Lafayette, taken from portrait and engraving by Amédé Geille, printed by The Elder Chardon; Cornwallis scene from engraving by James Heath of painting by William Smirke, which was based on sketch by Robert Fulton. [Used as illustration of patriotic poem "The Columbiad" by Joel Barlow (Georgetown, DC, 1825).]

Inscriptions: on one side "LAFAYETTE"; on reverse "Cornwallis Resigning his Sword at York Town, Octr. 19th 1781."[1]
Loan from Estate of Anderson C. Bouchelle, OT 1.1962

b
Unknown maker
English (Staffordshire)
Pitcher, smaller version of above
c. 1825-1835
4 3/4 x 6 x 2 1/4 in. (12.1 x 15.2 x 5.7 cm.)
Loan from Daniel Denny

94

c
Richard Hall & Son
English (Staffordshire)
Pitcher
c. 1825-1832
One side: *Portrait of Lafayette*
Other side: *Portrait of*
Washington
Under the spout: *American eagle*
Transfer printed creamware
5 x 5 3/4 in. (12.7 x 14.6 cm.)

Mark: in script under spread eagle,
under spout "Ric^d Hall & Son"
Sources of prints: Gilbert Stuart's
Athenaeum Portrait of Washington
(1796) [inscribed: "WASHING-
TON/HIS COUNTRYS
FATHER"]; Ary Scheffer's portrait of
Lafayette (1822), engraved by
Cyprien Jacquermin [inscribed:
"FAYETTE/THE NATIONS
GUEST"]

Inscriptions: on bands around top of
pitcher "FIRST IN WAR, FIRST IN
PEACE/AND FIRST IN THE
HEARTS OF HIS/FELLOW CITI-
ZENS."; on other side "IN COM-
MEMORATION, OF THE/
VISIT OF GENL LA FAYETTE,
TO/THE U,S, OF AMERICA,
IN THE YEAR/1824."; under spout
around drawing of spread eagle with
shield "REPUBLICANS/ARE NOT
Always UNGRATEFUL/Ric^d Hall
& Son"
Telfair Museum of Art
Museum purchase, OT 1961.26

d
Enoch Wood and Sons (active
1818-1846)
English (Burslem, Staffordshire)
Retailed by Harris & Chauncey
New York
Small Tureen with saucer
c. 1826-1829
On both sides of tureen, on lid
and on saucer: *Lafayette at*
Washington's Tomb
Transfer printed creamware
7 3/4 x 7 1/2 x 6 3/4 in. (19.7 x 19.1
x 17.2 cm.)

Source of print: drawing by D.W.
Jackson

Inscriptions: tomb marked "WASH-
INGTON."; marked in underglaze
enamel on bottom of plate "Harris &
Chauncey, 70 Wall St., New York"

Provenance: descended in the
Stewart family of Savannah; Will
Theus, 1930s; to her daughter
Will Theus Quaile.
Loan from Mrs. George Quaile

Lafayette's military successes and
his triumphal return to the United
States in 1824-1825 were the inspiration for vast quantities of com-
memorative earthenwares, made in
England and retailed in America.
These were typically decorated
with transfer prints, usually copied
from well-known images.[2] Among
the most popular were those seen
on two yellow and bronze luster
pitchers (**36 a, b**), honoring two
famous generals of the American
Revolution—Lafayette and
Cornwallis. Made in a variety of
sizes, these jugs

incorporate two well-known classical motifs, the laurel wreath,
here held aloft by two maidens,
and the eagle. Both were used as
symbols of American patriotism.[3]

Another pitcher linking two
Revolutionary War figures is the
small creamware jug bearing the
portraits of Lafayette and
Washington (**36 c**). Both images
were taken from well-known
paintings: the one of Washington
was based on Gilbert Stuart's
unfinished Athenaeum portrait,
commissioned by Martha
Washington in 1796. Called by
Stuart his "hundred-dollar bills"
because of the number of copies
which he sold (**26**), this image has
become America's "most famous
national image of Washington."[4]
Although not clothed in a Roman
toga, Washington echoes classical
portraits in his nobility and dignity.

On the other side of this pitcher
is Lafayette, "The Nation's
Guest," as portrayed by Ary
Scheffer (see **37 a**). In thanks for
Lafayette's service to the country,
the United States Congress invited him to be a permanent "guest"
with their gift of 240,000 acres of
land.[5] The ubiquitous American
eagle appears under the spout,
with the legend, "Republicans are
not Always ungrateful."

Representing a third popular
image, a Lafayette-related transfer
print is seen three times on the
small covered tureen with saucer
(**36 d**). This design can be found

on teapots, cups and saucers, coffeepots, washbowls, pitchers, etc., with one significant variation: in some cases the tomb to Lafayette's left is identified as that of Washington, and elsewhere as Franklin's![6] The other variable is the proximity of Lafayette to the tomb, depending on the size of the object and how much space is needed for the printed image.

During this period, tombs were an important part of American iconography. Tombs graced with urns figured prominently, in paintings, needlework, jewelry, and ceramics, becoming "objets d'art in the refined American home."[7] Lending respectability and dignity to one's living room, such objects were less tokens of grief than a recognition of civility and patriotism and a symbol of "fashionable classicism."[8]

The largest exporters of earthenwares to America, Enoch Wood & Sons, may have made this small tureen. Although it does not bear their stamp, other marked examples are known.[9] On the bottom of the saucer is the mark of Harris & Chauncey, ceramics importers at 70 Wall Street, New York.

1
According to Larsen, it was General O'Hara, not Cornwallis, who surrendered his sword at Yorktown, to General Lincoln, not to Washington. [Ellouise Baker Larsen, *American Historical Views on Staffordshire China* (New York: Doubleday, Doran and Company, Inc., 1939), p. 263]

2
Transfer printing, popular from the middle of the eighteenth century onwards, required considerable skill. The print was taken from an engraved copper plate to which a heated mixture of coloring oxide and oil was applied and wiped off. This left the engraved lines filled with color. A sheet of wet tissue paper was applied to the plate, a thick piece of flannel placed on top of it, the whole then put in a press. When the paper was peeled off, it bore the engraved design. The paper was then placed on top of the glaze of the ceramic object, face down, and the back rubbed, thereby transferring the design. The paper was washed off and the whole was then fired in the enamelling kiln. The most common transfer color was black, with blue, red, brown, purple, and green having also been used. [Robin Reilly and George Savage, *The Dictionary of Wedgwood* (Suffolk, GB: Antiques Collectors' Club, Ltd., 1980), p. 339]

3
Similar examples are illustrated in W. D. John and Warren Baker, *Old English Lustre Pottery* (Newport, GB: R.H. Johns, Ltd., 1951), pp. 41 E, 44 A and B, and 50 E; *Lafayette: The Nation's Guest: A Picture Book of Mementos which Express the Respect and Affection of the American People for Lafayette* (Winterthur, DE: the Henry Francis Dupont Winterthur Museum, 1957), p. 12; and Sotheby's, *Important Americana: The Bertram K. Little and Nina Fletcher Little Collection, Part I*, Sale # 6526 (January 29, 1994), # 238.

4
John Wilmerding, ed., *The Genius of American Painting* (New York: William Morrow and Company, 1973), p.86.

5
Larsen, 1939, p. 254. Lafayette also received a gift of $20,000 from the U.S. government.

6
Ibid., pp. 28, 29

7
Anita Schorsch, *Mourning Becomes America: Mourning Art in the New Nation* (Harrisburg, PA: William Penn Memorial Museum, 1976), n.p.

8
Ibid.

9
Geoffrey Godden, *An Illustrated Encyclopedia of British Pottery and Porcelain* (New York: Bonanza Books, 1966), p. 358. See, for example, Lafayette: *The Nation's Guest*, 1957, p. 22.

37 a, b, c
a
Ary Scheffer,
(1795-1858) painter
German/French
Jean Marie Leroux,
(1788-1871) engraver
French
General Marquis de Lafayette
1824
Steel engraving
19 x 27 1/2 in. (48.3 x 69.9 cm.)

Inscription: l.l. "A. Scheffer pinxᵗ 1822."; l.c. "Imprimé par Durand & Sauvé"; l.r. "Leroux Sculpᵗ. 1824." Identified as "Lafayette/à Paris, chez l'Auteur, Rue Sᵗ. Victor, Nᵒ. 9, et chez Chaillou, Mᵈ. d'Estampes, Rue St. honoré, Nᵒ. 140." Loan from V & J Duncan

b
Fairman, Draper, Underwood & Co. (active 1823-1827) engravers
American (Philadelphia)
Copper plate, ten and twenty dollars currency
1823-1827
Copper
9 5/8 x 8 x 7/8 in. (24.5 x 20.3 x 2.2 cm.)

Inscription on ten plate: "10 Nᵒ TEN Nᵒ M 10/Marine Fire Insurance Bank/ᵒᶠ ᵗʰᵉ STATE OF GEORGIA/Promise to pay _____ or/bearer on Demand TEN Dollars/at the BRANCH in

96

*MACON. Savannah _____ 18 __/
_____CASH.ᴿ _____ PRES.ᵀ
/Fairman Draper Underwood
& Co."*

*On left side: "10" over Lafayette
over "X" on; on right side: "10"
over unknown person over "X";
center: a woman holding a scale
and a sword*

*Inscription on twenty plate: "L No
TWENTY No/ᵀʰᵉ Marine Fire
Insurance Bank/of the STATE OF
GEORGIA promise to pay _____ or
Bearer on/Demand TWENTY
Dollars, at the BRANCH in
MACON./Savannah _____ 18 __ /
_____CaSh.ᵀ _____ PreS.ᵗ
/Fairman Draper Underwood
& Cᵒ."*

*On left side: "XX" over Franklin
over "20"; on right side: "20" over
Jefferson over "XX"; center: woman
holding scale above her head leaning
on a plinth with image of George
Washington*
Loan from H. Paul Blatner

c
Anker Smith (1759-1819)
painter and engraver
English
General Marquis de Lafayette
c. 1790-1810.
Engraving
7 3/4 x 5 in. (19.8 x 12.7 cm.)

*Inscription: under oval of portrait
"Anker Smith Sculp.ᵗ M. de La
Fayette."*
*Provenance: George Welshman
Owens (1786-1856); to his daughter
Margaret Wallace Owens Thomas*

(1829-1915); to her daughter
*Margaret Gray Thomas (1871-1951);
Telfair Museum of Art.
Bequest of Margaret Thomas,
1951.86*

Elizabeth Peabody described in
her letters to Maria Chase of
Salem, Massachusetts, the
moment she laid eyes on Lafayette
in Boston: "When [Daniel
Webster] addressed La Fayette-
the hero rose and I saw him. I was
astonished at this gigantic figure
and strongly marked
countenance."[1] Lafayette's size
and strength seem aptly captured
in the life-size portrait by French-
born German painter Ary
Scheffer (**37 a**). According to one
source, "Of the countless portraits
made during his lifetime it is said
to have been the likeness that
Lafayette himself preferred."[2]
Shown in a great coat carrying a
hat and cane, the Marquis is here
portrayed as a simple citizen.
Lafayette was similarly dressed
during many of his public appearances in Savannah, as described in
a contemporary newspaper
account: "The General was
dressed in a plain black suit and in
his deportment he is dignified and
truly republican, presenting an
example of that general demeanor
which is the delight of our
citizens."[3]

Scheffer painted three portraits of
Lafayette, all more or less the
same likeness. The first, painted in
1818, was Lafayette's favorite; the
second hangs in the United States
House of Representatives, a gift of
the artist in 1825; and a third,

smaller version, which was the
model for this engraving, was
painted in 1822.[4] That Scheffer
should have repainted his portrait
of Lafayette exactly the same size
as the Leroux engraving suggests
that it was made precisely for the
reproduction. Perhaps he recog-
nized the immense popularity of
Lafayette and the market for his
images on both sides of the
Atlantic.[5] The engraver Leroux
was a student of Jacques Louis
David, the famed neoclassical
painter. The majority of Leroux's
work was of a religious and/or
historical nature.[6]

Proof of the popularity of the
Scheffer image of Lafayette is the
appearance of it in bust format on
a $10 Marine Fire Insurance Bank
note (**37 b**). This institution,
which was the principal bank in
Savannah in the 1830s, issued currency in a variety of denomina-
tions, featuring numerous
engraved images. Portraits of such
famous Americans as Jefferson,
Franklin, and Washington are
found on these bank notes, as well
as allegorical and mythological
scenes.[7]

In contrast to the Scheffer portrait
of Citizen Lafayette is the oval
engraving by Anker Smith depicting the young general (**37 c**).
With wig and full military uni-
form, this image shows the profile
of a much younger Lafayette, at
barely age twenty when he arrived
in America for the first time. A
contemporary of Lafayette, Anker
Smith was considered to be one of
England's ablest engravers,

"his small plates being specially distinguished for correctness of drawing and beauty of finish."[8] The source for Smith's engraving is not known.

1
Elizabeth Peabody, "Elizabeth Peabody's Letters to Maria Chase of Salem, Relating to Lafayette's Visit in 1824," *Essex Institute Historical Collections*, v. 85 (October 1949), p. 363.
2
Agnes Mongan, *Harvard Honors Lafayette* (Cambridge: Fogg Art Museum, Harvard University, 1976), p. 120.
3
The Georgian (March 22, 1825).
4
Treasures of State, 1991, p. 290. The earliest portrait hangs at La Grange, Lafayette's own home. Scheffer was a friend and frequent guest of Lafayette. [Mongon, 1976, p. 122]
5
Mongan, 1976, p. 122.
6
Bryan, 1910, v. 3, p. 45.
7
The twenty dollar note included portraits of Franklin, Jefferson, and Washington. The $50 and $100 currency showed a woman holding a caduceus, sitting on barrels near the waterfront, symbolizing commerce. For a discussion of the iconography of engravings on early nineteenth-century paper currency, see V. H. Hewitt and J. M. Keyworth, *As Good as Gold: 300 Years of British Bank Note Design* (London: Published for the Trustees of the British Museum by British Museum Publications, 1987), pp. 82–105. Gideon Fairman (1774-1827) and John Draper (b. 1770), two of the engravers of this bank note, were long associated with bank note engraving, being original members of the firm that became in 1858 the American Bank Note Co. and remained in business for over 100 years. [William Griffiths, *The Story of the American Bank Note Company* (New York: the company, 1959), pp. 19-31]

Fairman, with fellow American Jacob Perkins, succeeded in developing a process of reproduction called "siderography" which "ensured identity of the notes through the plate transfer press, longevity of the plates because they were of hardened steel, and security through intricate machine-engraving." [Keyworth, 1987, pp. 57-58] Bills printed with this process were more difficult to counterfeit.

8
Dictionary of National Biography, 1937-8, v. 18, p. 424.

38 a, b, c
a
Unknown maker
English or American
Miniature bird, **c. 1825**
White opaque glass
H: 3/4 in. (1.9 cm.)

Inscription: on paper accompanying gift "This bird was an ornament on Gen. Lafayette's cake at the grand ball given in honor of his visit to Savannah many years ago. When the cake was cut this was handed to Gen. Lafayette, he presented it to my grandmother Mrs. Col. Steele White. This [bird] with the diamond ring of my great grandmother Anne Matthews Guerard are for my marriage. M. A. I. [or J]"

Provenance: descended in the Steele White/Jackson family; Telfair Museum of Art.
Bequest of Mary White Jackson, 1951, OT 1962.3.1

b
Unknown maker
American or English
Cockade, **1825**
Silk taffeta, mounted on paper
Dia.: 3 in. (7.6 cm.)

Inscription: verso, on paper "This cockade was worn by Charles H. Ha[rden?]/ during the visit of General La Fayette/in Savannah in March 1825 in/ imitation of that worn by the old revolutionary/soldiers."

Provenance: descended in the Harden family; to Mrs. C.M. Strahan; to Mrs. E. P. Lawton; Telfair Museum of Art.
Gift of Mrs. E. P. Lawton, 1959

c
Unknown maker
English or French
Fabric swatches (two)
c. 1825
Silk brocade
9 1/4 x 7/8 in. (23.5 x 2.2 cm.);
8 1/4 x 1 1/2 in. (20.9 x 3.8 cm.)

Inscriptions: on paper accompanying gift "This is a small piece of the dress worn by Mrs. Harden, wife of Gen. Harden, at the ball given to Lafayette when he was in Savannah, 1825/Gift of Miss Elizabeth Carithers/of Athens"

Provenance: descended in the Harden family; Telfair Museum of Art.
Gift of Miss Elizabeth Carithers

Lafayette's visit to Savannah was anticipated for months. The returning hero had initially been invited before he had left France in 1824, and the invitation was reiterated in February 1825, when it was learned that Lafayette was planning a trip to the South.[1]

Therefore, the people of Savannah had plenty of time to prepare their wardrobes for the coming, resulting in a great display of finery during the hero's three-day stay. Children and adults alike looked their best for this momentous occasion, and the historical nature of the visit caused many to save personal mementoes as souvenirs.

Three such souvenirs are in the Telfair collection; attached to each is a unique and very personal history. According to the note affixed to the box in which the tiny glass bird (**38 a**) arrived at the museum, it was an ornament on Lafayette's cake at the grand ball on Saturday, March 19, 1825. The ball followed a dinner for 300 guests held in the Council Chamber, which was decorated with arches, greenery, banners, and large lighted transparencies in the windows, one with a monument surmounted by the bust of Lafayette, two others with portraits of Washington and Lafayette.[2] As the recently widowed wife of Col. Steele White, officer of the Savannah Volunteer Guards, Ann Matthews Guerard White was the fitting recipient of this token of esteem (see **14**).

Another lady attending the ball was Mrs. Charles H. Harden. Two small pieces of her elegant green silk embroidered brocade dress (**38 b**) descended in her family, as did a cockade (**38 c**) worn by her husband, in imitation of ones worn during the Revolutionary War. That each of these items was so lovingly preserved by those

who attended the festivities, as well as by their descendants, speaks of the powerful impact of this event and the memories it created.[3]

1
Marian Klamkin, *American Patriotic and Political China* (New York: Charles Scribner's Sons, 1975), p. 131.
2
Ibid., p. 134.
3
Writing in 1889, Adelaide Wilson wrote about the powerful nostalgia surrounding Lafayette's visit: "One now hoary with age, then a bright blue-eyed boy, took the hand of his little granddaughter not long since, saying, 'Remember, my child, this hand that holds yours was once held in the hand of Lafayette.'" [Wilson, 1889, p.145]

39
Unknown maker
American or English
Engraved invitation with classical border
c. 1834
Paper
folded: 8 3/4 x 4 7/8 in. (22.2 x 12.4 cm.); unfolded: 8 3/4 x 9 5/8 in. (22.2 x 24.5 cm.)

Mark: watermark, l.c., when unfolded "J KooL"

Inscriptions: "COUNCIL CHAMBER,/SAVANNAH, July 7, 1834./The undersigned respectfully invite/William Taylor Esq President/of the St. Andrews Society/to join the Civic and Military Procession to be formed at/10 o'clock, A.M. on Thursday, the 17th instant, in front/of the Exchange, to proceed from thence to the Indepen/dent Presbyterian Church, where an Address will

be de-/livered by the Reverend Dr. W.M. CAPERS, in honour of/the memory of GENERAL LAFAYETTE./Committee of Council.[:] WM. THORNE WILLIAMS,/Mayor./WM. H. CUYLER,/GEO. A. ASH,/JACOB SHAFFER,/THOMAS CLARK,"; *verso, in ink, in script "Wm T. Williams + Others/Invitation to La Fayette Funeral/Honors. 7th July 1834."; verso when unfolded, in ink, in script "Wm Taylor Esqr/Pres + St Andrews Society"*
Provenance: from Chatham County Ordinary Court Estate vouchers, being disposed of in 1966, salvaged by Charlton Theus, Jr.
Loan from Mr. Charlton Theus, Jr.

The citizens of Savannah were deeply saddened by the death of their adopted hero, the Marquis de Lafayette, who had visited the city in 1825. The inhabitants turned out in great numbers for the ceremonies surrounding his memorial. As was typical of Savannah, the occasion was marked by a large parade with participants from all the civic and military organizations, including the St. Andrews Society, whose president, William Taylor, received this invitation. "Composed of the sons of old Scotia," the Society was founded about 1790. During the War of 1812 the organization appears to have died out, but it was revitalized in 1819.[1]

The handsome engraved border on this invitation includes a veritable encyclopedia of neoclassical ornament: urns, swags, capitals, rosettes, scythes, classically garbed maidens, palmettes, etc. Restrained and elegant, the document pays homage to a great republican and a man of virtue.

1
Lee and Agnew, 1869, p. 185.

40
Attributed to Samuel John Stump (d. 1863)
English
William Scarbrough
c. 1800–1810
Watercolor (gouache?) on ivory; silver gilt brass case; clear and blue glass; hair
Locket with chain ring: 3 7/8 x 2 7/8 in. (9.9 x 7.3 cm.); image: 2 7/8 x 2 1/4 in. (7.3 x 5.7 cm.)

Provenance: Mrs. Leslie Taylor Cummins, Reform, Alabama; The Colonial Dames of America, Atlanta Town Committee; Georgia Department of History, 1946. Photograph courtesy of the Georgia Department of Archives and History

A dashing, young William Scarbrough (1776-1838), wearing a dark blue coat with silver buttons and high white collar, appears in this miniature by Samuel John Stump, probably painted between 1800 and 1810.[1] Raised in South Carolina on a plantation in Allendale County, Scarbrough moved to Savannah in 1802 after two years in Europe as a commercial apprentice to Danish merchant Severin Erichson. Here he joined such established merchants as William Taylor, Robert

MacKay (1772-1816), Andrew Low, and Robert Isaac, becoming one of Savannah's merchant princes and an outstanding civic leader.[2] His business partnership, called Scarbrough and McKinne, was one of the largest and most successful merchant houses in the city. They served as ship agents and importers for endless quantities of merchandise during the first two decades of the nineteenth century.[3]

According to a handwritten note attached to the miniature, the artist was "Pinky Stump," a London portraitist and miniaturist of great repute. While Scarbrough was often in London as a young man, it has been suggested that the painting may also have been executed in Savannah by Edward Greene Malbone, uncle of Robert MacKay, who was Scarbrough's great personal friend.[4]

During the decade of 1810 to 1820, Scarbrough prospered and his business enterprises expanded to include partners in Augusta, Georgia; New York City; and Liverpool, England.[5] The year 1818 was a particularly important one for Scarbrough and his beautiful wife, Julia, whose lifestyle was described by one who knew them:

Luxury and extravagance is carried to a greater excess than I ever expected it could have arrived at in America. We hear ladies with families of small children boast of having been out to parties 10 nights in succession until after midnight, and

sometimes until 3 o'clock in the morning; and that they had not seen their husbands for a week. You must know that it is not the ton *for husband and wife to go to the same party; the husband toils through the day to raise money for his wife to spend at night, when he takes charge of the nursery. Mrs. Scarbrough lately sent out cards of invitation to five hundred persons. Three hundred attended. Every room in a large house was newly furnished for the occasion, the beds, etc. sent out; refreshments handed round from garret to cellar through the night to guests who were mostly standing and "delightfully squeezed to death."*[6]

Later that year William Jay began to build a new house for Scarbrough which was completed in 1819, in time for the visit of President James Monroe. Also in 1818, Scarbrough formed the Savannah Steam Ship Company, an undertaking that proved financially devastating for all concerned.

1
J.J. Foster, *A Dictionary of Painters of Miniatures 1525-1850* (1926; reprinted New York: Burt Franklin, 1968), p. 28.
2
Kenneth Coleman and Charles Stephen Gurr, eds., *Dictionary of Georgia Biography*, v. 2 (Athens, GA: University of Georgia Press, 1983), p. 869. The entry on William Scarbrough was written by Reverend Raymond E. Davis, Jr., whose inexhaustible knowledge about Scarbrough and his family was generously shared with the author.
3
Lerski, 1980, p. 85.

100

4

Raymond Earle Davis, Jr., "Scarbrough House Hosted Fancy Ball" [Unpublished typed manuscript, 1976, n.p., # 2, annotated list of photographs: a published version of this article appeared in the *Savannah Morning News* (November 19, 1976), p. 4B].

5

Coleman and Gurr, 1983, p. 869.

6

Marion Alexander Boggs, ed., "Savannah Society in 1818: Mrs. David Hillhouse to her Son, David (April 25, 1818)", *The Alexander Letters 1787-1900* (Athens, GA: University of Georgia Press, 1980), pp. 49-50.

41

Attributed to Nathaniel Jocelyn (1796-1881)
American (in Savannah 1820-1822)
Joseph Habersham II
c.1820-1822
Oil on canvas
25 1/2 x 30 3/8 in. (64.7 x 77.2 cm.)

Provenance: Joseph Habersham II; to his nephew William Neyle Habersham (1817-1899); to his daughter Anna Wylly Habersham Jones (1849-1888); to her son George Noble Jones (1874-1955); to his daughter Caroline Wallace Noble Jones Wright (b. 1911); to her daughter Anna Habersham Wright (b. 1950).

Loan from Anna Habersham Wright

Merchant Joseph Habersham II (1785-1831), seen here in a dark suit with white stock and ruffled jabot, came from one of Savannah's finest and wealthiest families, "whose annals from the earliest colonial days, when James Habersham was the friend of

Oglethorpe, to the present time, have been alike honorable to nation and State. One of the best governors of Georgia, and an able postmaster-general to President Washington, were members of this sterling family."[1] Married to his first cousin, Susan Dorothy Habersham (b. 1798), Joseph Habersham died childless at the relatively young age of 46.[2] By then he had accumulated such a substantial estate that it continued in execution for more than 30 years, left in the able hands of his brother and business partner, Robert (1783-1870).[3]

It was through Joseph Habersham that William Scarbrough met Captain Moses Rogers, the man who conceived of converting a ship to steam for transatlantic travel. Habersham met Rogers on board the SS *Charleston*, the first steamboat to travel between Charleston and Savannah on December 10, 1817.[4] In less than six months, a subscription for investment in the Savannah Steam Ship Company was offered and closed within hours of the offering, launching this venture that unfortunately ended in financial failure by 1820.[5] Habersham was one of five elected directors of the company, along with William Scarbrough, Robert Isaac, S. C. Dunning, and James S. Bulloch.[6]

According to family tradition this painting is attributed to Nathaniel Jocelyn, an important American artist whose career spanned 65 years.[7] While most of his career was spent in New York and New

Haven, Connecticut, Jocelyn painted in Savannah from 1820-1822. During this time he kept a list of portraits painted, including those of Dr. George Jones and Judge John McPherson Berrien. The portrait of Joseph Habersham II is not included on this list, but those familiar with Jocelyn's work feel that this attribution is sound.[8]

1

Wilson, 1889, p. 146. Joseph Habersham II was the son of Colonel Joseph Habersham and Isabella Rae Habersham.

2

Susan Habersham was the daughter of Major John and Mary Bolton Habersham.

3

Estate records, Joseph Habersham, R. Habersham executor, Microfiche H.2, pp. 718-813 (1832-1864). Chatham County Courthouse. Robert Habersham's son William inherited this portrait of his uncle. It has descended in his family. A notice of the sale of Joseph Habersham's household effects was advertised in *The Georgian* (January 9, 1832): "Executor's Sale: On Monday the 20th February, Will be sold at the residence of the late Mr. Joseph Habersham, Jefferson St., a variety of furniture and other household goods; a carriage, horse, etc., and some very superior old wine." Another sale notice, this time advertised by auctioneer J.B. Herbert and Co., appeared on February 20, 1832.

4

Braynard, 1963, p. 23, 28.

5

The offering was made on May 7, 1818, in the *Savannah Gazette*, and raised $600,000 in one day. This historic advertisement is quoted in full in Braynard, 1963. p. 28-30.

6

Ibid., p. 71.

7

The Habersham portrait was attributed to Jocelyn by George Noble Jones, great grandnephew of the sitter.

8

This painting was also not included by Foster W. Rice in his "Checklist of paintings, miniatures and drawings by Nathaniel Jocelyn 1796-1881," *Bulletin of the Connecticut Historical Society*, v. 31, # 4 (October 1966), pp. 97-145, but based on its stylistic resemblance to several of Jocelyn's portraits in their files, the Frick Art Reference Library accepts the attribution. [see letter to Caroline N. J. Daniel from Mildred Steinbach, FARL, 1972, p. 3]

42

Joseph-Pierre Picot de Limoëlin de Clorivière (1786-1826)
French
Oliver Sturges
c. 1805
Watercolor on ivory; brass
Image: 2 3/4 x 2 1/8 in. (6.9 x 5.4 cm.); locket: 3 1/2 x 2 1/2 in. (8.9 x 6.4 cm.)

Signed: l.r. "Picot 1805"

Provenance: Eliza Nail Sturges (Mrs. Oliver) (1783-1841); to her daughter Elizabeth Sturges Hunter (1803-1872); to her daughter Sarah Campbell Hunter Claghorn (1828-1886); to her son Rufus Samuel Claghorn (1849-1916); to his daughter Marguerite Claghorn Gilchrist (1889-1952); to her daughter Margaret Claghorn Gilchrist Livingston (b. 1919).
Loan from Mrs. Lorton Stoy Livingston

This exquisite miniature depicting a young Oliver Sturges (1777-1824) shortly after he moved to Savannah was painted by the itinerant French immigrant artist, Picot de Clorivière (see **14**). Sturges was born in Fairfield, Connecticut, and in 1803 moved

to Savannah where he joined in partnership with Benjamin Burroughs as a merchant and shipper. A prominent member of the community, being director of the Branch Bank of the United States and chairman of the Board of Trustees of the Independent Presbyterian Church, Sturges was also a major owner of the SS *Savannah*.[1]

After the steamship company failed, the SS *Savannah* was converted to a sailing ship, captained by N. H. Holdridge. Sometime in late 1820, Sturges and Burroughs bought into this enterprise, becoming two-thirds owners of the vessel.[2] On November 5, 1821, the ship struck a sandbar, drifted, and wrecked on the shores of Fire Island, off the coast of Rhode Island. Sturges lost nearly everything, and he died a broken man only a few years later.[3]

1
Bright, 1975, p. 296.
2
Braynard, 1963, p. 199.
3
Sturges's brick house built in 1813 is still standing at 27 Abercorn Street. His partner, Benjamin Burroughs, lived in the adjoining house (now demolished).

43

Unknown maker, possibly by George James Bubb (1782-1853)
English
Ionic capitals (pair), **c. 1818**
Coade stone
8 7/8 x 20 1/8 x 14 3/4 in. (22.6 x 51.1 x 37.5 cm.)

Provenance: originally on outside rear porch of Bulloch/Habersham house, built by William Jay c. 1818-1819; sold at 1916 sale of Habersham materials and contents; Mr. Shevy for use on a warehouse on River Street; Jim Richmond; John D. Duncan
Loan from V & J Duncan

While no documents survive that can substantiate the assertion that these capitals were once a part of the Bulloch-Habersham House, their provenance is believable for several reasons. The capitals are made of an artificial limestone made of a ceramic compound, called coade stone for the inventor of the process, Eleanor Coade (1742-1821) of Lyme Regis, England. She established a factory at Narrow Wall, Lambeth, in 1769, making a variety of architectural elements—capitals, plaques, friezes, and chimney-pieces, in addition to statues, portrait busts, and vases.[1] William Jay used capitals of this material on his Savannah houses, including the Richardson and Telfair Houses. The coade stone columns on the balustrade in the Richardson House front garden are marked "BUBB," the name of an English manufacturer of this artificial stone who went bankrupt in 1818.[2]

102

Photographs of the interior of the Bulloch House show a pair of unfluted columns with Ionic capitals similar to these. It has been proposed that these capitals originally topped the four columns supporting the rear porch of the house. The *Savannah Press* advertisement of February 9, 1916, itemizes a number of architectural elements from the house to be sold. About this same time, the Habershams' household furnishings were also disposed of at a sale attended, it would seem, by most of Savannah. Today, items bought at this sale belong to many Savannah families, having been cherished during the intervening eight decades for their historic connection to one of Savannah's finest homes.

1
Geoffrey Beard, *Craftsmen and Interior Decoration in England* 1660-1820 (London: Bloomsbury Books, 1980), p. 252.
2
Alison Kelly, *Mrs. Coade's Stone* (Upton-upon-Severn, GB: The Self-Publishing Association Ltd., 1990), pp. 225-6. Bubb's decorations seem to have been noticeably red, a result which was deemed unpleasant and which may have contributed to his business failure. According to a reference in the *New Monthly Magazine* (1818, p. 154), "the process of baking which it undergoes frequently distorts and injures the work, it is of a brick-like ferruginous colour and the general effect is very unpleasing." [Quoted in Kelly, p. 226] The balustrade marked "BUBB" at the Richardson-Owens-Thomas House is not red but a warm tan color.

44
Unknown maker
English or American
***Curtain rod*, c. 1819**
White pine, gesso; gilt
O.l.: 67 1/8 x 2 in. (170.5 x 5 cm.);
the original rod was in two
pieces 41 x 2 in. (104.1 x 5.1 cm.)

Provenance: from the Bulloch-Habersham house, completed by William Jay in 1819. While this rod may date from the Bulloch ownership of the house, it more likely was installed by Robert Habersham who purchased the house in 1834; by descent in the Habersham family to Mr. Reuben Clark; Juliette Gordon Low Birthplace; John D. Duncan; Telfair Museum of Art.
Gift of V & J Duncan, 1981.17

When the furnishings belonging to Archibald Stobo Bulloch and his wife were sold in August 1822, two sets of gilt window cornices and "curtains to suit" were included. It is possible this reference applies to this handsome gilt rod, of carved pine decorated with shells and leafage.[1] Although this particular rod does not appear in any of the early photographs of the interior of the Bulloch House, stylistically similar curtain rods can be seen.[2]

Perhaps English in origin, the rod resembles one illustrated in a popular upholsterer's guide, James Arrowsmith's *An Analysis of Drapery, or the Upholsterer's Assistant* (London, 1819), pl. 20. According to the accompanying narrative, the plate was derived from one of the "most modern Parisian Designs for window

curtains."[3] The currency of this design suggests the overall stylishness of Jay's interior for the Bulloch House.

1
Daily Georgian (August 6, 1822).
2
A number of early interior photographs of the Bulloch House are in the Cordray-Foltz Collection of the Georgia Historical Society. They serve as important documentation of this extraordinary interior.
3
The relationship to Arrowsmith's book was suggested to Gregory A. Smith, former director of the Telfair, by Gail Caskey Winkler of Philadelphia.

45
George Lethbridge Saunders
(1807-1863)
English
***Alexander Telfair*, 1848**
Watercolor on ivory
7 x 5 7/8 x 1/2 in. (17.7 x 14.9 x 1.3 cm.)

Signed: verso, l.r., in black ink "G.L. Saunders/Pinx - Savannah - May, 1848"

Provenance: Mary Telfair (1791-1875).
Bequest of Mary Telfair, 1875.50

Painted by the British miniaturist George Lethbridge Saunders, this miniature is a copy of an earlier portrait, now lost.[1] Alexander Telfair (1789-1832) is pictured as an elegantly and fashionably dressed young man, with high collar and stock, muttonchop whiskers, and black double-breasted suit jacket, probably in his twenties during the second decade of the nineteenth century. If the original portrait was a full-size one, Alexander Telfair's sister Mary may have wanted a smaller version to carry with her when she traveled, thus commissioning Saunders to execute the copy.

The sixth of nine children born to Sarah Gibbons and Edward Telfair, Alexander Telfair attended the Bergen Academy in New Jersey and Princeton University before returning to Savannah, where he served in the Savannah Heavy Artillery during the War of 1812. Following the death of his two brothers in 1817 and 1818, Alexander became the head of the Telfair family and managed its business affairs for the remainder of his life, in addition to being actively involved in public service. [2]

The Telfair siblings and cousins inherited Trust Lot "N" from their uncle William Gibbons (**12**) in 1804. By February 1818, Alexander Telfair had bought the shares of all his relatives and was the sole owner of the property on which William Jay subsequently built his house, completed by the end of 1819. [3]

[1]
Also in the Telfair collection is an unsigned full-size oil portrait of Alexander Telfair, in an oval frame (Telfair Museum, 1875.51). This appears to be a later copy of the miniature, not its source.
[2]
Shellman, 1982, p. 10-12.
[3]
Ibid., p. 12.

46 a,b
William and John Frazee
(1790-1852)
American (New York)
Mantels (pair), c. 1818
White marble
55 1/4 x 75 1/2 x 13 1/2 in.
(140.3 x 191.7 x 34.2 cm.)

Inscription: on each central panel below carving, l.r. "W. & J. Frazee, Sculp."; on central panel of a., l.l. "The Shepherd Boy"; on central panel b., l.l. "And a little Child shall lead them"

Provenance: part of the original furnishings of the Telfair House, completed in 1819.
Bequest of Mary Telfair, 1875.34.1,2

The two mantels in the largest of the Telfair's rooms, the double parlor, were supplied by the New York firm of W. and J. Frazee, "marblecutters" who operated a "monument and mantelpiece business" in that city beginning in 1818. [1] Presumably ordered by Telfair himself for his new house, the mantels were apparently not the only examples of the Frazees' work in Savannah, for a shipping manifest of 1822 shows 10 boxes of marble arriving from the firm in December 1822. [2] Yet the mantels for the Telfair are the two earliest mantels known to have been made by the firm. [3]

The central panel of the mantel at the west end of the drawing room is carved with "The Shepherd Boy," a pastoral scene showing a youth playing a flute, seated beside a hollow tree. Given special treatment is the dog who looks

loyally at his master, reflecting the stonecutter's particular sympathy for animals. On vertical panels above the Ionic columns are carved sprays of flowers bound with ribbons.

At the east end the mantel features a biblical scene, taken from Isaiah 11:6, "And a little Child shall lead them," carved with lion, lamb, and child. In the background of this peaceful scene is an American landscape with log cabin, suggesting "that Isaiah's prophecy will be born out in the American wilderness." [4] The smaller panels are carved with grapes and strawberries in vases. The form and iconography of this pair of mantels is typical of the late Federal style.

[1]
Frederick S. Voss, *John Frazee 1790-1852 Sculptor* (Washington, DC and Boston: National Portrait Gallery, Smithsonian Institution and The Boston Atheneum, 1986), p. 24.
[2]
Ship *Augusta*, from New York, arriving Savannah, December 2, 1822. Consignee: Smith and Masterton, Savannah. Shipper: Wm. G. Frazee, New York (NA/ICM 36, Box 18). William Frazee was primarily involved with the commercial side of the business, while his brother John was the artist.
[3]
Voss, 1986, p. 25.
[4]
Feay Shellman Coleman, "Mantels by W. and J. Frazee, Alexander Telfair House, Savannah, Georgia" (Unpublished manuscript, Richardson-Owens-Thomas House files), p. 3. The theme of this mantel

relates to the paintings being done simultaneously by Edward Hicks, whose well-known depictions of the "Peaceable Kingdom" stemmed from his Quaker beliefs. Frazee's motivation seems less clear.

47
Unknown maker
Probably English
Mantels (pair) c. 1819
Carved marble, white and mottled gray
West wall: 55 3/4 x 72 7/8 x 11 1/2 in. (141.6 x 185.1 x 29.2 cm.)
East wall: 56 5/8 x 72 1/4 x 12 in. (143.8 x 183.5 x 30.5 cm.)

Provenance: part of the original furnishings of the Telfair House, completed in 1819.
Bequest of Mary Telfair, 1875

Marble mantels in various degrees of elaboration were imported in great number into American cities in the early nineteenth century. Italy and England were two major sources. Compared to the Frazee mantels, the carving on this pair is simpler and less sophisticated but still of high quality. A fruit-and-flower-filled basket ornaments the center plaque on each mantel, and Ionic capitals rest on plain columns. The mottled gray marble is a particularly decorative element on these otherwise restrained architectural elements. The inset cast-iron firebacks, ornamented with baskets of fruit, paterae, and reeding, appear to be original.

48
Unknown maker
English (probably Birmingham)
Oil chandelier, c. 1819
Gilt bronze; glass; cast brass
45 5/8 x 19 1/4 in. (115.9 x 48.9 cm.)

Provenance: descended in the Telfair family. Probably installed in the Octagon room at the time the house was completed.
Bequest of Mary Telfair, 1875

When this gilt-bronze oil-burning chandelier was placed in the house, it was hung from a ceiling hook and was equipped with an oil font. These features were later discarded when the chandelier was refitted, first for gas and later for electricity. It has now been restored, using photographs of the similar Bulloch-Habersham House oil fixtures as a guide. The chandelier retains its four original Argand-type burners, ring frame, and glass drippan.

The design of this chandelier as well as its construction suggests a Birmingham, England, provenance, where the finest metal light fixtures imported to America were made.[1] The ornamentation is typical of the high Regency style, consisting of such classical motifs as the Greek key, scrolls, and a central vasiform "Grecian" font from which the oil was piped.

[1]
Similar fixtures can be seen in the *Birmingham Trade Catalogue...The Argand or Air Lamps, among the following patterns are represented with glasses... lamps of every description for use and ornament*

(Winterthur Museum Library, water-marked page, 1812). For a similar lamp see The Newark Museum, *Classical America 1815-1845* (Newark, NJ: The Newark Museum, 1963), # 194.

49
Unknown maker
American
Curtain rod ends and gilt rings
c. 1820-40
White pine; gesso; gilt
arrow only, without support: 12 x 7 1/2 x 1 1/2 in. (30.5 x 17.8 x 3.8 cm.)

Provenance: part of the original furnishings of the Telfair House.
Bequest of Mary Telfair, 1875

The gods of Greek and Roman mythology were often shown with spears, symbols of power, as were Roman soldiers who represented the authority and grandeur of the ancient Roman empire.[1] But to what extent the iconography of the spear or arrow shape was significant to the Telfair family when chosen for ornamental curtain rod ends can not be known. Their simple geometric lines highlighted by gilding may have been the attraction for the dignified Telfair interior.

[1]
Among those gods shown with spears were Bacchus, Jupiter, Hercules, and Achilles. The spear figures prominently in such Roman stories as "The Oath of the Horatii."

50
Drawn by Joshua Shaw (1777-1866)
American (Philadelphia)
Engraved by W. G. Mason
(active 1822-1860)
American (Philadelphia)
Branch Bank of the United States
Savannah, 1823
Steel engraving
Published in: J. C. Kayser,
Commercial Directory, containing a Topographical Description... of Different Sections of the Union **(Philadelphia: J.C. Kayser, 1823), p. 34.**
3 7/16 x 6 3/16 in. (8.7 x 15.7 cm.)

Inscriptions: l.l. "Drawn by J. Shaw"; l.c. "William Jay Architect"; l.r. "Engraved by W. G. Mason/BRANCH BANK OF THE UNITED STATES/ SAVANNAH/Philadelphia/Published by I.C. Kayser & Co., 1823."
Loan from South Caroliniana Library, University of South Carolina
Photgraph courtesy of the North Carolina Collection, University of North Carolina Library at Chapel Hill

Headquartered in Philadelphia, the second Bank of the United States received its charter from President Madison on April 10, 1816. Within a few months, 18 branches were established "from Portsmouth, New Hampshire, to New Orleans and from Louisville to Savannah."[1] By February 6, 1817, the directors for the new bank had been selected, including Richard Richardson as president, Robert Habersham, Oliver Sturges, and Joseph Cummings.[2]

Other directors included attorneys and merchants, some with previous experience in banking.

As it was expected that each branch bank should acquire its own building, the newly appointed directors of the Savannah branch proceeded directly to plan for their structure. Serving as a precedent was the design for the Philadelphia branch by architect William Strickland (1788-1854), who had been directed to build "a chaste imitation of Grecian architecture in its simplest and least expensive form."[3] Completed in 1824, this building, on Chestnut Street between Fourth and Fifth Streets, was taken directly from the Parthenon as drawn by Stuart and Revett in *The Antiquities of Athens.*[4]

While William Jay's design for Savannah's branch bank is related to Strickland's in the use of a simple Doric portico, it was a broader, more horizontally configured building, with two wings with arched windows. It is thought that Shaw's drawing "may have been copied from the original Jay project, which suffered changes during construction."[5] For example, the arched niches in Shaw's drawing became windows in the finished building, the applied wreaths above the columns disappeared, and the balusters were eliminated.

Shaw's drawing was published in 1823 in Kayser's *Commercial Directory of the United States*, which included a separate chapter

on each state featuring an outstanding building as the chapter frontispiece. Shaw probably saw Jay's sketches for the building during a January 1820 visit to Savannah as part of a tour of the South. A native of England, Shaw settled in Philadelphia, where he became best known for his landscape paintings, his *Picturesque Views of American Scenery* being the most famous.[6]

1
Thomas Payne Govan, *Nicholas Biddle, Nationalist and Public Banker, 1786-1844* (Chicago: University of Chicago Press, 1959), p. 83; cited in Lerski, 1980, p. 149.
2
The Columbian Museum and Savannah Daily Gazette (February 6, 1817).
3
Govan, 1959, p. 82. Strickland was the architect of Savannah's monument to Major General Nathanael Greene. (16)
4
Philadelphia Museum of Art, *Philadelphia: Three Centuries of American Art* (Philadelphia: The Museum, 1976), p. 244.
5
.Lerski, 1980, p. 154. See also McDonough, 1950, p. 67.
6
Published as *Picturesque Views of American Scenery* (1819-1820), Shaw's Southern sketches were part of a series of drawings of notable sites and events along the Eastern seaboard. For this series he took subscriptions, anticipating a publication totaling six volumes with six views each. [Philadelphia Museum of Art, 1976, p. 250-251]. Among the most successful drawings from this series was Shaw's picture of the Savannah great fire of January 1820. [Illustrated in Gloria Gilda Deak, *Picturing America, 1497-1899: Prints, Maps, and Drawings Bearing on the New World Discoveries and on the*

Development of the Territory that is Now the United States (Princeton: Princeton University Press, 1988), expanded, pl. 315.11]. During his travels in the South, Shaw also gathered materials and subscriptions for his United States Directory (1822; see 54).

51
Drawn by William Goodacre (active 1829-1835)
American (New York)
Engraved by Fenner, Sears & Co.
English (London)
Branch of the United States Bank
Savannah, c. 1830-1832
Published in: John Howard Hinton, *History and Topography of the United States* v. 2 (London: I. T. Hinton, Simpkin, & Marshall, 1830-1832), pl. 71.
Tinted steel engraving
4 1/2 x 6 in. (11.4 x 15.2 cm.); o.l.: 14 3/4 x 11 3/4 in. (37.5 x 30.0 cm.)

Inscriptions: l.l. "Drawn by W. Goodacre Junr. N.Y." l.r. "Engraved and printed by Fenner, Sears & Co./BRANCH OF THE UNITED STATES BANK, SAVANNAH"
Gift of Jane Davan Forbes (Mrs. Francis Bonner), 1960.14

While the Goodacre drawing of the Branch Bank was not published until 1830-1832, it may have been executed as early as 1825 when the artist was in Savannah. He is known to have visited the city when Lafayette was there, producing an engraving of the general in his mason's apron.[1]

A landscape and still life painter, Goodacre taught drawing in New York City and executed a number of English and American views, many of which appear in Hinton's *History and Topography of the United States.*[2] Several of these were used for Staffordshire transfer printed designs, but not his drawing of the Branch Bank of Savannah.

Goodacre's view of the bank was drawn at a slight angle and incorporates several people into the picture, as well as a pair of palm trees directly in front of the two windows. The choice of Jay's bank for Hinton's book may have been a significant one. According to James Vernon McDonough, Jay's biographer, this choice may "indicate that Jay's most classic example was the only structure in Georgia acceptable to the growing Greek Revival in the North."[3]

[1]
"Among the decorations [at the Masonic Dinner] were three large allegorical paintings prepared by Mr. Rogers, and a full-length portrait of Lafayette, with a Master Mason's aporn [sic], executed by Mr. Goodacre, at present in this city." [*An Account of the Reception of Gen.* Lafayette, 1825, p. 51]
[2]
Groce, 1957, p. 264.
[3]
McDonough, 1950, p. 66.

52 a, b, c, d
a
J. and W. Ridgway Factory
England (Hanley), c. 1814-1830
Covered gravy tureen and stand
c. 1820-1830
Transfer printed creamware
Gravy tureen: on one side, *Branch Bank of the United States, Savannah*; on opposite side and on saucer, *Exchange, Charleston*
Cover: *Insane Hospital, Boston*
Stand: *Exchange Bank, Charleston*
Tureen with cover: 7 x 5 x 8 1/2 in. (17.8 x 12.7 x 21.6 cm.); stand: 6 1/4 x 8 3/8 in. (15.9 x 21.3 cm.)

Inscriptions: gravy tureen, verso "EXCHANGE CHARLESTON/BANK SAVANNAH"; cover, verso "INSANE HOSPITAL/BOSTON"; stand, verso "EXCHANGE CHARLESTON"
Source of views: both scenes from The Beauties of America *series, drawing by Joshua Shaw, engraved by W. G. Mason. Published by I. C. Kayser,* Commercial Information Relating to the State of Georgia *and* Commercial....State of South Carolina, *1823 [see 51]*
Telfair Museum of Art
Museum purchase, 1991.4

b

Relish dish with handles
Branch Bank of the United States
Savannah
c. 1820-1830
5 1/2 x 8 1/4 in. (13.9 x 20.9 cm.)

Inscription: verso "BANK SAVAN-
NAH"
Provenance: descended in the family
of (?) McClesky, president of the
Bank of Savannah (1815-1820).
Loan from Mr. Charlton Theus, Jr.

c

Small Saucer (rectangular)
Branch Bank of the United States
Savannah
c. 1820-1830
5 x 6 3/4 in. (12.7 x 17.2 cm.)

Inscription: verso "EXCHANGE
CHARLESTON"; on red bordered
label, in ink, verso "Bank of/U.S.
SAVANNAH/LAIDACKER/No 238"
Loan from H. Paul Blatner

d

Saucer (of tureen), Branch Bank of
the United States, Savannah
c. 1820-1830
6 1/8 x 8 1/4 in. (15.6 x 20.9 cm.)

Inscription: verso "BANK SAVAN-
NAH"
Loan from V & J Duncan

The well-known Shaw drawing of
the Branch Bank of the United
States in Savannah can be found
on numerous forms of earthenware, from cups, trays and tureens,
to sugar bowls and babies bath-
tubs. Shown here are only a small
assortment of the Ridgway factory's line available through retail

outlets in Savannah as well as
direct from England through
commercial shippers.[1] One slight
but notable change distinguishes
the transfer print from the Shaw
drawing: the placement of a well-
dressed couple directly in front of
the building, perhaps to make the
scene more immediate and
approachable.
The Savannah bank tureen and
saucers were part of John and
William Ridgway's series called
Beauties of America, a project
undertaken when John Ridgway
visited the United States in 1822,
"making connections with dealers,
taking orders, showing patterns,
and commissioning views."[2]
While the series primarily included views of buildings in Boston,
Philadelphia, and New York, a
small number of Southern buildings were also included, such as
the Branch Bank of Savannah and
the Exchange in Charleston. They
were often featured together in
the same service. The tureen, for
example, is decorated with the
Branch Bank on one side and the
Exchange on the other. The stand
that accompanies the tureen
shows the Exchange, while three
other small stands all feature the
Branch Bank. The cover of the
tureen includes a third print from
the *Beauties of America* series, the
Insane Hospital of Boston.[3]

[1]
A list of several known forms with this
pattern can be found in Larsen, 1939, p. 93.
Feay Coleman quotes a lengthy newspaper
advertisement of January 1, 1822, describing
the wares offered by John Thomas at his
"Staffordshire Ware-House." Among his
extensive inventory were sets of "BRITISH
VIEWS, patterns nearly all different and
the engravings executed in a very superior
style." [Coleman, 1992, p. 109]
[2]
Cooper, 1993, p. 200.
[3]
An identical tureen was sold at the
Sotheby's auction of *Important Americana:*
The Bertram K. Little and Nina Fletcher
Little Collection, Part I, (1994), # 34. A
similar, but slightly smaller example, complete with its ladle, is in the Baltimore
Museum of Art and is illustrated in
Cooper, 1993, p. 200. The majority of
Ridgway wares are unmarked, but the
attribution of this set to the partnership of
the brothers John and William is
irrefutable.

53
Cephas Grier Childs & J. W.
Carpenter (active 1822) engravers
American (Philadelphia)
Advertisement for Oran Byrd's
City Hotel
1822
Published in: Joshua Shaw,
United States Directory for the Use
of Travellers and Merchants
(Philadelphia: James Maxwell,
1822).
Paper; leather binding
3 1/2 x 6 in. (8.9 x 15.2 cm.)

Inscriptions: "SAVANNAH, GEOR-
GIA./City Hotel/ORAN
BYRD./This Elegant Establishment
which is entirely NEW with all
its/Furniture and other arrange-
ments is in the centre of BusineSs
and contiguous to the BANKS & C°
The Post Office is attached/to the

Premises__ all the Stages start from the door./Eng^d by Childs & Carpenter Phila^d/Mr Byrd likewise keeps the CITY HOTEL/76 East Bay Charleston S.C."
Photograph courtesy of The Winterthur Library: Printed Book and Periodical Collection

One of the subscribers to Joshua Shaw's *United States Directory* was Oran Byrd, proprietor of the City Hotel, Savannah. His advertisement, announcing the opening of his "Elegant Establishment," was embellished with decorative classical scrolls and flourishes, engraved by Cephas Grier Childs (1793-1871) and J. W. Carpenter of Philadelphia, whose partnership was limited to 1822. Childs, the better known of the two, was listed in the Philadelphia city directories from 1818 to 1845 as a "historical and landscape engraver."[1] Other Savannah businesses advertised in Shaw's directory: "R. Newcomb, Choice Wines &.c.; J. Shelman, Mansion House—Private Rooms Reserved for Families"; and Joseph Truchelet, Confectioner. Shaw's *U.S. Directory* has been described as "one of the most attractive publications of its kind, with fine specimens of American engraved advertising art."[2]

[1]
New York Public Library, *One Hundred Notable American Engravers 1683-1850* (New York: New York Public Library, 1928), p. 23.
[2]
Philadelphia Museum of Art, 1976, p. 250.

54
Unknown artist [possibly John Wesley Jarvis (1780-1840)]
American
***Mr. Henry McAlpin*, c. 1820-1831**
Oil on canvas
30 1/8 x 25 1/8 in. (76.51 x 63.81 cm.)

Provenance: Henry McAlpin; to his son Angus McAlpin; to his daughter Sallie McAlpin.
Gift of Sallie M. McAlpin, 1951.1

A man of vitality, ingenuity, and education, Henry McAlpin (1780-1851) is pictured here as "a man of ruddy countenance garbed in yellow waistcoat with snowy pleated frill. The straightforward blue eyes, large generous mouth, and strong chin reveal the character that gained him a place of eminence in Savannah."[1] He took possession of The Hermitage in 1815 after a friend, William I. Scott, purchased the property at public auction for $1500.[2] Shortly thereafter McAlpin begin his brickmaking concern at the plantation, followed by the establishment of an iron manufactory. In addition, his innovations included building the earliest railway in America.[3]

The portraits of Mr. and Mrs. McAlpin (**54, 55**) have been attributed to the American painter John Wesley Jarvis, who is known to have regularly visited Savannah.[4] "One of the best portrait painters active in the United States during the Neo-Classical period," Jarvis is known for his "dashing brush stroke" that endowed his portraits with a "striking immediacy."[5] His

male portraits typically feature plain backgrounds, a severity of character, and a directness of pose.[6] In fact, his portraits were rarely painted to please the sitter. Wrote Mrs. Cabell of Richmond to her step-daughter:

I have...been sitting to Jarvis for my picture. I did so contrary to my better judgment—and have therefore taken little satisfaction in it. As to the Picture I have no doubt it will be a good likeness for he hardly ever, if ever, fails—but it will not be a flattering one; neither is your Father's. His aim is not to flatter but to make the likeness as strong as possible.[7]

Jarvis, a native of England who worked all his adult life in America, is known to have painted over 400 portraits, many of famous people, including Henry Clay, James Fennimore Cooper, Washington Irving, Andrew Jackson, and John Marshall.[8] Despite his prolific output, Jarvis was considered to be an eccentric and died in poverty at the home of his sister in 1840.[9]

[1]
Granger, 1947, p. 432.
[2]
Being an unnaturalized citizen born in Scotland, McAlpin could not own land in Georgia. It was not until 1819 that he legally took ownership of the property.
[3]
Ibid., p. 435. In 1820 his railway consisted of a short length of double, flanged rails on which a four-wheeled car rolled, carrying bricks from kiln to kiln. This invention predated a similar contrivance of Solomon Willard in Quincy, outside of Boston.

4
Louis T. Cheney, "The Telfair and Its Paintings," *The Magazine Antiques*, v. 91, # 3 (March 1967), pp. 33-37.

5
Stuart P. Feld, *Neo-Classicism in America: Inspiration and Innovation 1810-1840* (New York: Hirschl and Adler Galleries, Inc., 1991), p. 29.

6
.See for example the portrait of John Frick, in Sona K. Johnston, *American Paintings 1750-1900* (Baltimore: Baltimore Museum of Art, 1983, p. 90; and the painting of Dr. John Richardson Bayard Rodgers, in The New-York Historical Society, 1974, p. 673. The portrait of Jacob Bond L'on of Charleston, attributed to Jarvis, is strikingly similar to the McAlpin portrait. It is supposed to have been painted when Jarvis visited Charleston in 1820. [Severens, 1977, p. 45]

7
Richmond Portraits in an Exhibition of Makers of Richmond 1737-1860 (Richmond: The Valentine Museum, 1949), p. 223.

8
A checklist of Jarvis's work was contained in an article by Theodore Bolton and George C. Groce, Jr. in the *Art Quarterly*, v. 1, # 4 (Autumn, 1938).

9
Harry B. Wehle, *American Miniatures 1730-1850* (New York: Garden City Publishing Company, Inc., 1937), p. 90.

55
Unknown artist [possibly by John Wesley Jarvis (1780-1840)]
American
Mrs. Henry McAlpin (Ellen McInnis McAlpin), c. 1820-1831
Oil on canvas
30 1/8 x 25 1/8 in. (76.5 x 63.81 cm.)

Provenance: Mrs. McAlpin; to her son Angus McAlpin (1825-1888); to his daughter Sallie McAlpin. Gift of Sallie Mary McAlpin, 1951.2

Ellen McInnis McAlpin (c. 1799-1831), daughter of Dorothy Mary and Joseph McInnis of Charleston, was Henry McAlpin's second wife and mother of his seven children.[1] She died after the birth of her last child, Donald, at the age of 32. Following her death the children were cared for by the mother of Henry McAlpin's first wife, Mary Melrose.

Like the pendant portrait of her husband, the painting of Ellen McAlpin has also been attributed to John Wesley Jarvis. In contrast to the plain backgrounds of his male portraits, Jarvis's paintings of females frequently contain windswept curtains and landscapes. The column and scroll-arm couch are two additional elements which place this painting strongly in the neoclassical tradition. The artist's focus on detail, as seen in the cluster pearl earrings, the carefully articulated amber brooch, and the delicately painted lace, are marks of Jarvis's concern for precision and realism.[2]

1
The seven children were James, Angus, Henry, Wallace, Donald, Ellen (Mrs. John Schley), and Isabel (Mrs. William Schley).

2
Jarvis's portrait of Mrs. John Richardson Bayard Rodgers (1768-1818), painted c. 1810-1815, includes similar earrings and brooch. [The New-York Historical Society, 1974, p. 674].

56
Edgerton Chester Garvin (1881-1950)
American (Georgia)
The Hermitage, Savannah, Georgia (June 1915)
Platinum print
3 x 4 15/16 in. (7.6 x 12.6 cm.)

Provenance: Edgerton G. Garvin; to his wife Frances McCoy Garvin; to two nieces; Francis McNairy; High Museum of Art. Photograph courtesy of the High Museum of Art

This rare, early photograph of The Hermitage, built for Henry McAlpin, was taken by Edgerton Chester Garvin, a civil engineering graduate of George Washington University and amateur photographer who lived in Augusta, Georgia, from 1909 and 1947. During those years he recorded hundreds of landscapes, people, and buildings in the Southeast while he worked as an engineer in Georgia and Florida.[1]

The house and its numerous outbuildings were made of bricks produced on the plantation and laid by McAlpin's own slaves.

With the exception of marble for the stairs and mantels, and slate for the roof, all the building materials were produced on the premises.[2] The McAlpin family lost possession of The Hermitage during the Civil War, but the plantation was purchased by Aaron Champion, father-in-law of Henry McAlpin's son James.[3]

During the postwar period the house was largely unoccupied until Henry McAlpin, son of James and Maria Champion McAlpin, moved into it with his wife Isabel E. Wilbur and his daughter Claudia. He invested $25,000 in refurbishing the house.[4] By 1915 when this photograph was taken, however, the family had long since moved back to the city to their house on Orleans Square. The plantation house was demolished in the 1930s.

[1]
Garvin's work and its later discovery is chronicled in Beth Bassett, "Edgerton Chester Garvin: Photographer," *Brown's Guide to Georgia* (June 1980). The photograph of The Hermitage was one of many pictures purchased by Francis D. McNairy from two of Garvin's nieces in 1978. Accompanying the photographs was a logbook in which the circumstances under which the pictures were taken – lighting, location, time of day – were recorded. This notebook remains in a private collection in Savannah.

[2]
Henry McAlpin, *Souvenir of the Hermitage* (Savannah: privately printed, 1916).

[3]
Albert Sidney Britt, Jr. *The Champion-Harper-Foulkes House: Headquarters of the Cincinnati in the State of Georgia* (Savannah: Society of the Cincinnati, 1988), p. 8.

[4]
Granger, 1947, p. 446-447.

57
Rembrandt Peale (1778-1860)
American (Philadelphia)
Dr. George Jones, c. 1838
Oil on canvas
30 1/16 x 25 1/8 in. (76.36 x 63.81 cm.)

*Provenance: Dr. George Jones; to his son George Wymberley Jones DeRenne [George Frederick Tilghman Jones]; to his son Wymberley Jones DeRenne; to his son Wymberley Wormsloe DeRenne; M. Knoedler & Co. Inc., 1937; to Mrs. Joseph Bickerton, 1937; to Elfrida DeRenne Barrow (sister of W.W. DeRenne), 1937; to her son Craig Barrow Jr., 1970; to The Wormsloe Foundation, Inc., 1973; to the Telfair Museum of Art.
Gift of the Wormsloe Foundation, 1981.14.3*

Descended from a line of prominent Georgians, Dr. George Jones (1766-1838) continued the family legacy of political, philanthropic, cultural, and business leadership. His father, Dr. Noble Wimberly Jones (1722-1805), was a physician and political activist; his grandfather Noble Jones was a physician, soldier, surveyor, and aide to General Oglethorpe.[1] George Jones, the first of his family to have been born in America, was mayor of Savannah from 1812

to 1814, a member of the Georgia House of Representatives, state treasurer, judge of the superior court and Eastern Judicial Court, United States Senator, a practicing physician, first president of the Georgia Medical Society, and official host to Lafayette when he visited Savannah in 1825.

This portrait, attributed to Rembrandt Peale, formerly hung over the figural marble mantelpiece in the south living room at Wormsloe. Rembrandt was a son of Charles Willson Peale and one of his many children named after old master artists. Like his father, he was a portrait painter. He was also president of the American Academy of Fine Arts in New York and founder of the National Academy of Design.

During his long, active life as an artist, Rembrandt Peale painted some of America's best known patriots, including George Washington, Governor DeWitt Clinton of New York, Senator Charles Carroll of Maryland, and Representative Thomas Sumter and Senator John C. Calhoun, both of South Carolina. The portrait of Dr. Jones is painted much as that of Calhoun, "as an eager and alert figure" whose "dynamism" is captured in the image.[2] It has been suggested that the portrait was painted posthumously, after Rembrandt Peale settled in Philadelphia and Senator Jones's widow, Eliza Smith Jones (1782-1857), returned to her native city after his death.[3]

Typical of Peale's later work, a golden light surrounds the figure of George Jones, and the portrait combines a strong sense of both the real and the ideal.[4]

1
Lee Giffen, "Living with Antiques: Wormsloe, The Home of Mrs. Craig Barrow," *The Magazine Antiques*, v. 91, # 3 (March 1967), p. 50-51.
2
Severens, 1977, p. 63.
3
Letter from Feay Shellman to Ms. Lynn Miller, Athens, Georgia, March 7, 1986 (Telfair Museum archives). A portrait of Eliza Smith Jones's mother, Letitia Van Deren Smith (1759-1811), now in the collection of the Telfair Museum, was painted by Charles Willson Peale. Rembrandt Peale is known to have visited Savannah much earlier in his career, advertising in the *Georgia Republican and State Intelligencer* and the *Columbian Museum and Savannah Advertiser* in 1804 that he was planning to paint several portraits. This plan necessitated his closing of the exhibition of the Mammoth which had brought him to the city initially. (February 10, 1804; February 8, 1804).
4
Carol E. Hevner, "Rembrandt Peale, Art and Ambition," *The Magazine Antiques*, v. 127, # 2 (February 1985), p. 467.

58
Attributed to Raphaelle Peale
(1774-1825)
American
Senator George Jones, **1822**
Watercolor on ivory
3 3/8 x 2 1/2 in. (8.6 x 6.35 cm.)
Signed: u.l. "R. P./ 1822"

Provenance: Senator George Jones; to Noble Wimberly Jones (1787-1818); George Noble Jones (1811-1876); George Fenwick Jones (1841-1876); to George Noble Jones (1874-1955) and his wife Frances Casey Meldrim (1883-1965); to her daughter Caroline Wallace Jones Wright.
Loan from Caroline Jones Wright

This miniature of Senator George Jones has long been attributed by the family to Raphaelle Peale, miniaturist and still life painter. Son of Charles Willson and younger brother of Rembrandt, Raphaelle Peale worked throughout the South, including in Savannah (1804 and 1805), Charleston, Norfolk, and Baltimore.

This attribution is based on a number of stylistic similarities to Peale's work, including the fact that the initials "R.P." next to Jones's shoulder are Raphaelle Peale's typical signature. Most of Peale's sitters were men, with hair described as either "a wooly wig" or "wiry," and sloped shoulders.

Furthermore the faces "are painted in very pale skin tones and modeled with blue hatches. The backgrounds are light, often blue and white striated to suggest sky, and occasionally incorporating an unusual combination of lavender, pale yellow, and pink."[1]

The 1822 date painted on this miniature is problematic, however. Around 1805, Peale began to drink heavily, his health declined, and he developed severe gout, prompting his hands to swell. He largely stopped painting miniatures in favor of full-scale still lifes, which were easier for him to paint. From 1818 until September 1821, however, Peale traveled again in the South, although ill with gout and "drowning his pain with alcohol." He was in Charleston in the winter of 1824, where he would have had the opportunity to paint this miniature of Senator Jones.[2]

1
Johnson, 1990, p. 175.
2
Philadelphia Museum of Art, 1976, p. 265.

112

Savannah, Georgia

1800 – 1840 / 1840

When Tyrone Power (1794-1841) visited Savannah in 1834, he observed a city somewhat faded from its 1820 splendor, the result of economic depression. He recorded his impressions of the city and published them upon his return to London:

Here are, however, several very ambitious looking dwellings, built by a European architect for wealthy merchants during the balmy days of trade; these are of stone or some composition, showily designed, and very large, but ill-adapted, I should imagine, for summer residences in this climate. They are mostly deserted, or let for boarding-houses, and have that decayed look which is so melancholy, and which nowhere arrives sooner than in this climate. Here is a well designed and well-built theatre, but, like the houses I speak of, a good deal the worse in consequence of neglect: the materials and design were, I understood, all imported from England, at a prodigious cost when the smallness of the population is considered; but it is now, I fancy, rarely occupied.

Despite the gloomy nature of these words, however, Power offered a reason for optimism:

The trade of this port was at one period great; it offered at this time a cheerful prospect of well-lined quays, and I was glad to learn that the prospects of the community were again brightening; indeed, the high prices of produce this year are infusing additional life and spirit into the whole Southern community: the speculators in cotton are ardent, and the prices continually on the rise.[1]

Although another depression struck the city in 1837 with significant detriment to its growth and prosperity, it rebounded quickly.

By 1839, the Savannah visited by world traveler James Silk Buckingham (1786-1855) seemed to be bustling:

The population of Savannah is estimated to be at present 10,000, of whom about 5,000 are whites, and the remainder mostly slaves, though there are some free coloured people residing here. ... Like the society of Charleston, this of Savannah is characterized by great elegance in all their deportment; the men are perfect gentlemen in their manners, and the women are accomplished ladies **(59)**.[2]

The Impact of the Railroad on Savannah

Savannah's prosperity in the 1830s and 1840s was largely due to the introduction of the railroad that linked the port city with Georgia's interior as well as with other states. Chartered in 1833, the Central of Georgia Railroad line from Savannah to Macon was completed in 1843, with a later spur to Augusta.[3] While Savannah had previously been eclipsed by her northern neighbor Charleston, the Georgia city began to gain ground in the 1840s. As one observer of the effects of the railroad wrote: "Thus year by year, as road after road was completed, opening up in the State and pouring its products in the lap of Savannah, her merchants reaped the reward due them for their foresight, zeal, and enterprise,..."[4]

Furthermore, improved water navigation brought increasing wealth to the city, particularly as the steamship began to monopolize trade between Savannah and Augusta. The Georgia Steamboat Company ran the greatest number of vessels, but a second firm, The Iron Steamboat Company, was also noteworthy. Its organizer, Gazaway B. Lamar (1798-1874), made Savannah the site of another first in maritime history in 1834 when he assembled the first iron vessel in America, the SS *John Randolph* **(60)**.[5] Passenger steamships continued to ply the coastal waters between Savannah and the northern ports, but it was not until 1848 that the next transatlantic voyage was undertaken, almost 30 years after the tragic demise of the SS *Savannah*.[6]

59
George Washington Conarroe
*(*1802-1882*)*
American (Philadelphia)
Joseph Habersham, 1837
Oil on canvas

60
William Gale, Jacob Wood,
Jasper W. Hughes
(active 1836-1845)
possibly retailed in Savannah
by Moses Eastman (1794-1850)
American (New York)
Tea service (5 pieces)
c. 1836-1838
Sterling silver

The Waning of Classicism

By the 1830s the Greek Revival style of architecture had eclipsed all others in the South, bequeathing a "heritage of monumental beauty which has never been surpassed."[7] Furnishing these houses were goods representing a variety of styles, the most modern being in the French Restauration taste.[8] Furniture in this style incorporated broad veneered surfaces with scroll supports or veneered pillars, the ornament being derived more from form, color, and contrast than carving, inlay, and subtle details.

One advocate of this style was the firm of Joseph Meeks & Sons, Manufactory of Cabinet and Upholstery Articles. A New York family of cabinetmakers, the Meekses had exported furniture to Savannah beginning in the late eighteenth century, and continued to provide goods to the Southern market through the mid-nineteenth century (**61**).[9] New technology, such as veneering machines and steam-driven band saws, made furniture in this "pillar and scroll" style financially accessible to a wider market. The transportation revolution led to widespread distribution of these goods, to places as far away as the West Indies and South America.

116

61
Unknown maker
American (New York)
Pier table
c. 1830-1840
Mahogany; white pine

62
Peter Laurens
American
(in Savannah 1836-1853)
Gilbert Butler
c. 1840
Oil on canvas

By 1840, people of modest means were also able to afford to have their likenesses painted, while earlier, only people of wealth were the subject of portraits. Included in these pictures are "all of the appropriate symbols of refinement, taste and fashion": the requisite column and drapery, a handsome scrolled chair or sofa, a marbletop table, a vase of flowers, or the tools of the sitter's trade — all representing material success.[10] The pair of portraits painted by Peter Laurens, for example, show Gilbert Butler (1797-1875), a Savannah builder of average means, and his wife Jane Stillwell (1800-1895), in their prime in 1840 (**62, 63**).

118

63
Peter Laurens
American
(in Savannah 1836-1853)
Jane Stillwell (Mrs. Gilbert) Butler
c. 1840
Oil on canvas

New Products, New Life Styles

It was not long until a profusion of new styles
began to compete with the Classical Revival for
the public's favor. A host of other revival styles,
the French Rococo, the English Elizabethan,
the Egyptian, the Italian Renaissance, and the
Louis XVI, among others, offered the American
consumer a wide variety of choices. Of these,
the Rococo was the most popular, particularly
in furniture and silver design (**64 a,b**). While the
supremacy of the Classical Revival was eclipsed,
it never completely lost favor. In fact, throughout
the nineteenth century, decorative objects in the
classical taste continued to be made along with
other more exotic creations.

64
b
Attributed to Samuel Child Kirk
(1792-1872; active 1815-1872)
American (Baltimore)
Silver ewer
c. 1840
Sterling silver
a
Attributed to Samuel Child Kirk
(1792-1872; active 1815-1872)
American (Baltimore)
Silver ewer
c. 1840
Sterling silver

NOTES

1

Tyrone Power, *Impressions of America* (London, 1836), excerpted in *The Rambler in Georgia* (Savannah: The Beehive Press, 1973), pp. 109-110.

2

Buckingham, 1842, excerpted in Lane, 1973, p. 139.

3

Hardee, 1928, p. 79.

4

Lee and Agnew, 1867, p. 136.

5

Federal Writer's Project, 1937, p. 40.

6

Hardee, 1928, p. 82.

7

Nichols, 1976, p. 54.

8

The Restauration of the French Monarchy (1814-1830) coincided with a decorative style that has been described by some as "plain and ponderous" and reflecting "obese decadence". However, many examples of this style are monumentally graceful, such as the 1837 commission for the parlor of Samuel A. Foot executed in the shop of Duncan Phyfe (now in the Metropolitan Museum). See Ruth Ralston, "The Style Antique in Furniture: II. Its American Manifestations and their Prototypes," *The Magazine Antiques*, v. 48, #4 (October, 1945), pp. 206-209, 220-223. The Phyfe suite is illustrated in Metropolitan Museum, 1970, # 79.

9

Joseph Meeks "on Morel's Wharf" advertised in the *Columbian Museum and Savannah Advertiser* (Savannah) on March 20, 1798: "Cabinet-Maker from New York, Informs the Public that he has lately arrived and has for sale a handsome assortment of elegant Mahogany Furniture and will dispose of it at very reasonable prices." Quoted in Mrs. Charlton Theus, *Savannah Furniture 1735-1825* (Savannah: Privately printed, 1967), p. 81. The names of members of the Meeks family—Robert, Edward, and Thomas—appear in Savannah-related documents in the nineteenth century.

10

Cooper, 1993, p. 219.

CATALOGUE ENTRIES

59
George Washington Conarroe
(1802-1882)
American (Philadelphia)
Joseph Habersham, **1837**
Oil on canvas
29 x 25 ½ in. (73.6 x 64.7 cm.)

Inscription: signed, l. quadrant at height of "v" of coat "G.W. Conarroe/1837"

Provenance: Marie Delores Boisfeuillet Colquitt-Floyd (1887-1965); to her son Adrian B. Colquitt (b. 1908).
Loan from Adrian B. Colquitt

While little is known about this particular Joseph Habersham (b. 1810), he came from a illustrious Savannah family. Joseph Habersham's father, Robert (b. 1783), was an eminent merchant and a distinguished man of the church; his grandfather, Colonel Joseph Habersham (1751-1815), had been Postmaster General of the United States. These ancestors were two in a line of wealthy and notable citizens of Savannah, many of whose images were preserved in full-size portraits and in miniatures (**9,41**).

Joseph Habersham's portrait was painted by George Washington Conarroe, a portraitist and genre painter who made his home primarily in Philadelphia.[1] He paid a brief visit to Savannah from November 1836 to March 1837, during which time he solicited business. As references he listed Robert Habersham, Joseph W. Jackson, I. K. Teffts, and Charles Henry.[2] Perhaps he had already

painted their likenesses. Earlier, Conarroe had painted a portrait of Colonel Joseph Habersham which was included in Herring and Longacre's 1834-1840 publication, *The National Portrait Gallery*.[3] Conarroe's final advertisement in a Savannah newspaper appeared on February 18, 1837, announcing that he intended to leave the city the following month, but meanwhile he was happy to "execute further orders."[4]

1
Groce, 1957, p. 143.

2
In the *Savannah Georgian* (November 28, 1836), Conarroe advertised that "being on a professional leave to this city," he had taken a room on Broughton Street.

3
Ibid. See also correspondence from Robert G. Stewart, Curator, National Portrait Gallery, Smithsonian Institution, to Louis T. Cheney, Director, Telfair Academy of Arts and Sciences, April 30, 1968. According to Stewart, the Conarroe painting was a copy after Douglas, and the *Daily Georgian* advertisement states that Conarroe's portrait was a copy of the original "de(s)igned expressly for the National Historic Portrait Gallery." In a letter of March 20, 1969 to Adrian B. Colquitt, John C. Milley, Museum Curator, Independence National Historic Park, hypothesized that Conarroe was commissioned by Herring and Longacre to copy Douglas' portrait.

4
The Daily Georgian (February 18, 1837).

60

William Gale, Jacob Wood, Jasper W. Hughes (active 1836-1845); possibly retailed in Savannah by Moses Eastman (1794-1850)
American (New York)
Tea service (5 pieces), c. 1836-1838
Sterling silver
Teapot: 12 ½ x 12 ⅛ x 6 ¾ in. (31.8 x 30.8 x 16.7 cm.); hot water pot: 12 ⅛ x 12 x 6 ½ in. (30.8 x 30.5 x 16.5 cm.); cream pitcher: 7 ⅛ x 7 ¾ x 4 ⅜ in. (18.1 x 19.7 x 11.1 cm.); waste bowl: 6 ¾ x 7 ½ x 5 ⅛ in. (17.2 x 19.1 x 13 cm.); sugar bowl: 11 x 9 x 4 ¾ in. (27.9 x 22.9 x 12.1 cm.)

Mark: verso of each piece in Roman capitals, in rectangle "G W & H", spread eagle in circle, sovereign's head in oval

Provenance: Gazaway Bugg Lamar; to Armand John deRosset II, M.D. (1767-1859); to his son Armand John deRosset III, M.D. (1807-1897); to his son Armand Lamar deRosset (1842-1910); to his son Armand Lamar deRosset, Jr. (1871-1957); to his sister Tallulah Low deRosset Peschau (Mrs. John Bauman) (1878-1964); to her daughter Tallulah Lamar Peschau Morton (Mrs. James White) (b. 1914). Loan from Mrs. James White Morton, Jr.

William Gale, founder and principal partner with several other silversmiths in New York City beginning in 1821, was associated with Jacob Wood and Jasper W. Hughes between 1835 and 1845.[1] A late 1830s date for the manufacture of this tea set is implied by its shape and decoration. The forms combine the spherical, lobed bodies and wide, rounded shoulders which became popular in the 1840s with the earlier simple lines seen in the ornament and handles.

The year of 1838 was one of great personal tragedy for Gazaway Bugg Lamar (1798-1874) and many other Savannahians. In the summer of that year, the steam packet Pulaski, bound from Savannah to New York, exploded and sank off the coast near Wilmington, N.C. Lamar, his wife, sister, and six of his children were among the 131 passengers. Lamar was one of the 54 survivors along with his sister and one son who were rescued after three days at sea.[2] According to one account, "in this pitiable condition, [the Lamar family members] were taken by Dr. [Armand John] deRosset to his home, where for many weeks they were tenderly nursed by his daughters."[3] In appreciation for restoring the health of his sister, Rebecca Lamar, and his only surviving son, Charles Augustus Lafayette Lamar, Gazaway Lamar sent this tea service to Dr. deRosset. The great, great granddaughter of Dr. deRosset is the current owner.

1
Naeve and Roberts, 1986, p. 90. The dates for the firm of Gale, Wood & Hughes are based on information provided by Robert Alan Green, who states that the firm was listed in Longworth's and Trow's New York City directory in 1835 to 1837 and 1841 to 1845, first at 116 Fulton and later at 46 Charles. ["William Gale and Son, New York," *The Magazine Silver*, v. II, no. 2 (March-April, 1978), p. 11]. Traditionally the dates for the firm have been recorded as 1833 or 1836-1845, based on the entry in Dorothy Rainwater. *Encyclopedia of American Silver Manufacturers* (Hanover, PA: Everybodys Press, Inc., 2nd ed., 1975), p. 55 and p. 191.
2
Mrs. Hugh McLeod (Rebecca Lamar), "The Loss of the Steamer Pulaski," *Georgia Historical Quarterly*, v. 3, # 2 (June, 1919), p. 95.
3
Catherine deRosset Meares, *Annals of the deRosset Family* (Columbia, SC: R. L. Bryan, Co., 1906), p. 69.

61

Unknown maker
American (New York)
Pier table, c. 1830-1840
Mahogany; white pine
34 ¾ x 40 ½ x 18 in. (88.3 x 102.9 x 45.7 cm.)

Provenance: descended in the Dunn family; to Mary Ann Daily Dunn Farrell; to her son William Farrell; to his daughter Margaret Farrell Braziel; Francis D. McNairy. Loan from Francis D. McNairy

The style of this pier table is commonly termed "pillar and scroll," referring to its principal elements: plain, round or angular pillar supports, and broad, veneered scroll shapes. By the mid-1830s, regional preferences and variations blended into one homogenous Late Classical or "Grecian" style.

While perhaps the product of any one of a number of urban centers, this pier table was most likely made in New York, based on its affinity to other New York tables of this type. A pier table with canted legs has been attributed to Duncan Phyfe's workshop based on two other documented examples.[1] Another pier table, labeled J. & J.W. Meeks of New York City, closely resembles this table, particularly in the shape of the legs and the distinctive lotus feet. The Meeks table was owned in Natchez, Mississippi, in the 1830s.[2] Furthermore, the motif on the apron of the Savannah-owned table can be found on the crest rail of a set of Late Classical balloon-back chairs thought to have been made in New York, reinforcing the attribution to a maker of that city.[3]

[1]
Metropolitan Museum, 1970, # 80.
[2]
Cooper, 1993, p. 217.
[3]
See Robert Bishop, *Centuries and Styles of the American Chair, 1640-1840* (New York: E. P. Dutton & Co., Inc., 1972), pp. 312-313. A set of four of these chairs was sold recently at auction as probably New York, 1825-1840. [Christie's sale, Prior-8066 (June 2, 1990), Lot 250].

62
Peter Laurens
American
(in Savannah 1836-1853)
Gilbert Butler, **c. 1840**
Oil on canvas
45 ⁵/₁₆ x 38 ⁵/₁₆ in. (115.1 x 97.3 cm.)

Inscriptions: recto, in script, signed on architectural drawing l.r. "P. Laurens/Pinxt."; verso on canvas "1840/Age ᵈ 41 Years."; verso, covered by lining, stamped "PREPARED BY/EDWARD DECILIUX/NEW YORK"

Provenance: descended in the Butler family; Mrs. Ouida H. White, 1946; Mrs. L. Roy Riddick; to her son Daniel D. Riddick; Marion Cooper; Ben Adams, 1987; Francis D. McNairy, 1987.
Loan from Francis D. McNairy

The handsome pair of portraits of Mr. and Mrs. Gilbert Butler by Peter Laurens were painted in the same tradition as the more opulent pendant portraits of Mr. and Mrs. Henry McAlpin (**55,56**). The Butlers, however, were of Savannah's upwardly mobile middle class, of modest wealth and background, rather than members of society's elite. Butler (1797-1875) was born in Hudson, New York, and arrived in Savannah by 1825 when he married Jane R. Stillwell, daughter of a local carpenter.[1] The young couple moved briefly to Liberty County, Georgia, but by 1829 returned to Savannah where they remained together until his death in 1875.

During his years in Savannah, Butler was active in the community, as a member of the Odd Fellows and the Savannah Fire Company, as director of the Mechanics Saving Bank and, in 1866, as an elected member of the Board of Health.[2] Deeds record his ownership of several lots in the city, including the site of his lumber and carpentry business, established with J. B. Richmond in 1832.[3] For the following three years Butler and Richmond did carpentry work for the city, erecting a cupola on the guardhouse and making repairs in the City

Exchange. After their partnership dissolved in 1835, Butler worked alone as carpenter, master builder, and contractor on such projects as Christ Church, a synagogue on Whitaker Street, the Masonic Hall at Bull and Broughton Streets, the Hall and Engine House for the Metropolitan Steam Fire Engine Company, and numerous residences.[4]

While the exact building represented by the elevation drawing held in Butler's hand is not known, it resembles a number of Savannah's brick houses built early in the nineteenth century, such as the 1820 residence of carpenter-builder Isaiah Davenport (1784-1827).

[1]
Savannah Republican (June 17, 1825).
[2]
Butler also ran, unsuccessfully, for Tax Collector of Chatham County, Coroner and Alderman.
[3]
Savannah Georgian (March 5, 1832).
[4]
The genealogical information about Gilbert Butler was compiled by Elisabeth Evans, October, 1988.

122

63
Peter Laurens
American
(in Savannah 1836-1853)
Jane Stillwell (Mrs. Gilbert)
Butler, **c. 1840**
Oil on canvas
36 ¼ x 29 ¼ in. (92.0 x 74.2 cm.)

Inscriptions: verso on canvas
"1840/Age 39 Years."; verso, covered
by lining, stamped "PREPARED
BY/EDWARD DECILIUX/NEW
YORK"

Provenance: descended in the Butler
family; Mrs. Ouida H. White, 1946;
Mrs. L. Roy Riddick; to her son,
Daniel D. Riddick; Marion Cooper;
Ben Adams, 1987; Francis D.
McNairy, 1987; Telfair Museum of
Art.
Gift of Francis D. McNairy, 1993.4

Jane Stillwell Butler (1800-1895)
lived most of her 95 years in
Savannah, where her family had
moved in 1810. Her father, John
Stillwell, was a carpenter, shop
and ship joiner, who advertised
"sashes, panel work and chimney
pieces of the latest fancy work" to
be made at his shop on Bryan
Street.[1] Fifteen years later she
married a young carpenter from
New York and had six children,
four of whom survived into adult-
hood. Sometime after her husband
died, Jane Butler moved to
Augusta, perhaps to live near her
daughter Lydia Elizabeth Butler
Tarver. She is buried, however, in
Laurel Grove Cemetery in
Savannah.

Little is known about the painter
Peter Laurens. Local newspaper

notices suggest that his first career
was that of the proprietor of the
Lafayette Coffee House, where he
served "Oysters and Venison
Steaks" in addition to "Superior
Soda Water" and coffee in an
atmosphere arranged "to afford
every comfort to visitors, and its
decorations elegant."[2] This business closed and was sold in 1828.[3]
Six years later a letter to the editor appeared in the Savannah
Georgian calling attention to the
merits of Peter Laurens, portrait
painter. Perhaps written by the
artist himself, the letter extols the
artistry of Laurens, whose

likenesses are excellent, his coloring
fine, rich and mellow, his execution
bold. The correctness, delineation and
striking expression he so happily
throws in representations of his sub-
jects, entitle them to be truly called
'tableaux parlans.' – Whilst the eye is
delighted to dwell on the painting,
so true to nature, the imagination is
witchingly, for a moment led away,
and expectation on 'tip-toe,' sees the
lips move and hears the canvass
[sic] speak.[4]

According to this letter, Laurens
was "well known" to Savannah,
but previously his "talents as an
artist were not known." One
assumes that he was self-taught
and that his subjects were probably drawn from the local community. Two other signed portraits
by him are known, one of a Mr.
Leigh, c. 1830, and a second of
Captain Steigin, dated 1853, commissioned by the German
Volunteer Company for their
commanding officer.[5]

1
The Republican and Savannah Evening
Ledger (December 27, 1810).
2
Savannah Georgian (November 26, 1827);
Ibid. (May 25, 1825); *Ibid.* (November 29,
1827).

3
Ibid. (March 3, 1828).
4
Ibid. (June 14, 1834).
5
Letter from Mrs. Henry W. Howell, Jr.,
Frick Art Reference Library, November 21,
1966, to Louis B. Cheney, Director, Telfair
Academy of Arts and Sciences [Telfair
Museum files]

64 a, b
a
Attributed to Samuel Child Kirk
(1792-1872; active 1815-1872)
American (Baltimore)
Silver ewer, **c. 1840**
Sterling silver
16 ¾ x 8 in. (19.3 x 15.9 cm.)
Unmarked

Inscription: engraved in script sur-
mounted by lion passant on cartouche
on body under spout "G.W.O."

Provenance: George Welshman
Owens (1796-1856); to his son
George Savage Owens (1825-1897);
to his son George Welshman Owens
Jr. (1852-1924); to his daughter Mai
Owens Coxe (1895-1972); Telfair
Museum of Art.
Gift of Eckley Coxe, in memory of
Mrs. Mai Owens Coxe, 1975.4

b
Attributed to Samuel Child Kirk
(1792-1872; active 1815-1872)
American (Baltimore)
Silver ewer, **c. 1840**
Sterling silver
16 ¾ x 8 in. (19.3 x 15.9 cm.)
Unmarked

*Inscription: engraved in script sur-
mounted by lion passant on cartouche
on body, under spout "G.W.O.";
engraved in script on foot ring on
pitcher "Given to the Georgia Society
of Colonial Dames by Margaret
Gray Thomas, November 8, 1951."*

*Provenance: George Welshman
Owens (1796-1856); to his daughter
Margaret Wallace Owens Thomas
(1829-1915); to her daughter
Margaret Gray Thomas (1871-1951);
The National Society of The
Colonial Dames of America in
the State of Georgia.
Loan from the Andrew Low House,
The National Society of The
Colonial Dames of America in
the State of Georgia*

The tall, narrow "gourd" shape of
these ewers, with their angular
handle with cast ram's head, was
used by the Kirk firm from the
middle of the 1820s through the
mid-twentieth century.[1] Overall,
the pitchers are adapted from
eighteenth-century neoclassical
forms and the ram's head masks
recall French Neoclassical precedents. This type of pitcher was
one of Samuel Kirk's "most popular and influential designs," in
which neoclassical forms are
incorporated into an eclectic blend
of Rococo and English Baroque
elements typical of mid-century

Baltimore silver.[2] Beginning
around 1840, tiny buildings set in
a dense landscape of flowers and
scrolls became a favorite
Baltimore motif. These miniature
buildings were at first in the
Gothic or "Tuscan" style, but
sometimes they were substituted
with "Chinoiserie-style" scenes,
or with representations of actual
buildings.[3] Today, antique dealers
sometimes refer to this type of
silver as "landscape pattern," but
Samuel Kirk, himself, called it
"Etruscan."[4]

The ornate Rococo répoussé decoration for which Kirk is known
was both technically and artisti-
cally innovative. Baltimore
Répoussé-style silver became
tremendously popular during the
1840s and 1850s, particularly in
the South where it was extensively
imported.[5]

One such Southern purchaser was
George Welshman Owens, a
prominent attorney, and the original owner of these ewers.
Beginning in 1830, Owens resided
in the house formerly owned by
Richard Richardson. According to
one early account, he

*was prompted not alone by the desire
to have one of the most comfortable
and beautiful of dwellings in making this purchase, but likewise by the
impulse to own and protect in days
to come the house which had grown
to be regarded as one of the pillars of
the early structure of Savannah,
which stood for historic value as well
as intrinsic worth. The commendable
spirit prompted him to take posses-*

*sion of the place and preserve it in
much the same form as it had been
left by the architect, and it is to his
credit that this old place remains today [1897] a monument to the early
period of Savannah's history.[6]*

His civic spirit was unflagging,
serving as mayor of Savannah,
(1832-1833) and member of
Congress (1835-1839). The
Richardson-Owens-Thomas
House remained in his family
until it was given to the Telfair
Academy of Arts and Sciences in
1951.

1
Jennifer Faulds Goldsborough, *Eighteenth
and Nineteenth Century Maryland Silver in
the Collection of the Baltimore Museum of
Art* (Baltimore: The Baltimore Museum of
Art, 1975), p. 163. A cream pitcher in the
Winterthur Museum is dated c. 1828, based
on the makers mark impressed on the base
(DAPC ACC. No. 74.1679), as is a second
cream pitcher at Winterthur, bearing an
1828 assay mark. (DAPC Acc. No. 69.251).
For a succinct description of Samuel Kirk
and his company see *Treasures of State*,
1991, p. 365.
2
Treasures of State, p. 365.
3
Jennifer Faulds Goldsborough, *Silver in
Maryland* (Baltimore: Museum and
Library of Maryland History, Maryland
Historical Society, 1983), p. 13.
4
Gregory R. Weidman and Jennifer F.
Goldsborough, et. al., *Classical Maryland
1815-1845: Fine and Decorative Arts from
the Golden Age* (Baltimore: Maryland
Historical Society, 1993), p. 161.
5
Goldsborough, 1983, p.13.
6
Savannah Morning News (May 16, 1897).

Classical Furniture
in
Savannah

NEW YORK FURNITURE

Many examples of furniture in the classical taste with a history of ownership in early nineteenth-century Savannah survive today. Some of these are of superior quality, apparently the result of a custom order direct from the cabinetmaker, while others are of a more moderate grade, probably purchased at a furniture store in Savannah from a warehouseman who imported quantities of goods on speculation. What survives is typical of what one would expect to find in any major city of that period, with one important distinction: upper class consumers in Savannah preferred furniture in the English taste, ignoring a number of forms in the French style that were popular in Boston, New York, and Philadelphia, such as the pillared fall-front secretary and veneered column pier table. Of all the imported furniture, products of New York manufacture were the most readily available, followed by those from Philadelphia. Other cities represented in the coastal furniture trade to Savannah included Boston, Providence, Newburyport, and Portsmouth, among others.

Every form of high-style New York furniture appears to have been available in early nineteenth-century Savannah. An 1819 announcement of goods to be sold by William Barnes, cabinetmaker from New York, at his store on "Barnard Street, near the bay," suggests the variety of forms one could purchase:

Cabinet Furniture, Looking-Glasses; Fancy and Windsor Chairs, &c; Elegant Sideboards of various patterns; Secretaries and Bookcases and Secretary; Sets of dining tables and dining do; Pillar and claw card and breakfast do; Handsome mahogany high post Bedsteads; Field Bedsteads and crib Cradles; Elegant ladies' toilet Glasses, with and without drawers; Gilt chimney and pier Glasses; Rose wood cane bottom, rose wood rush bottom, fancy and Windsor Chairs.[1]

Numerous examples of Classical-style sideboards, secretaries, tables, chairs, and bedsteads, made in New York and owned in Savannah during the first four decades of the nineteenth century, can be found in Savannah today.

Several known examples of New York- and Philadelphia-made furniture ordered by members of one Savannah family, the Telfairs, offer rich documentation for the prevailing taste and sources for goods imported into Savannah between 1800 and 1840. This group of furniture represents a portion of the contents of the house of Alexander Telfair and his maiden sisters Mary and Margaret, designed by William Jay and completed in 1819.[2] In addition to the actual objects, written accounts of many of these purchases remain, indicating that these furnishings were generally ordered directly from the cabinetmakers, not purchased through a retailer in Savannah.[3]

New York Case Furniture

Best known of the cabinetmakers patronized by the Telfairs was Duncan Phyfe (1768-1854). Phyfe's first shipment to Savannah is recorded in October 1817, when he shipped six boxes and one bundle to George Anderson and Son (active 1817-1839).[4] He continued to send furniture to Savannah for the next several years, the largest shipment of 44 boxes arriving on January 31, 1821, on board the ship *Comet*.[5] From 1821 until 1823, Isaac W. Morrell (working 1811-1865), cabinetmaker and warehouseman, served as Phyfe's agent, offering

Side boards with/without Liquor cases, sets of dining tables, single do., sofas and couches, Rosewood and Mahogany, Pier Tables with marble tops, card tables, Tea tables . . . Mahogany Book Cases and chairs, Curled maple do., and Rosewood do., High post Rose-wood Bedsteads and field do....[6]

A June 1822, advertisement suggests that Morrell annually left Savannah in the early summer for New York where he procured stock for his store. He took with him orders "for furniture of the newest fashions made by D. Phife of New York" which could either

65

Attributed to Duncan Phyfe (1768-1854)
American (New York)
Secretary bookcase
c. 1816-1817
Mahogany; poplar, white pine, mahogany
81 ¾ x 36 x 22 ¼ in.
(207.6 x 91.4 x 56.5 cm.)

*Provenance: Mary Telfair (1791-1875); Telfair
Museum of Art; Edward V. Jones; to his
daughter Mrs. Jeanette Jones Balling.
Loan from Mrs. Jeanette Jones Balling, 1.1981*

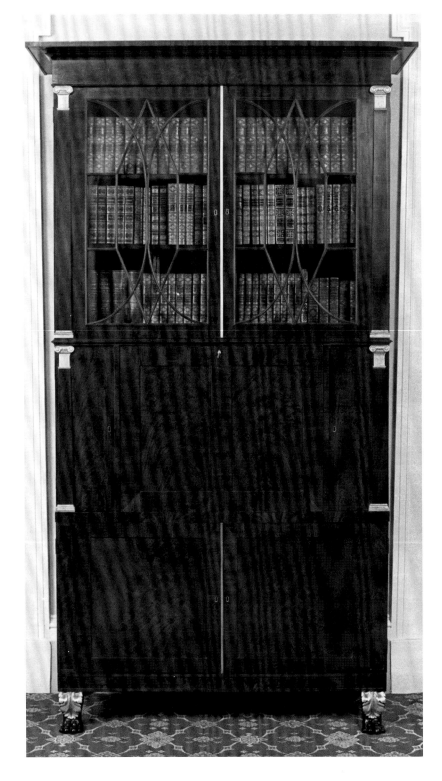

66

Attributed to Duncan Phyfe (1768-1854)
American (New York)
Secretary bookcase
c. 1815-20
Mahogany, satinwood, rosewood;
mahogany, pine, poplar
98 ½ x 57 x 19 ½ in.
(250.2 x 144.8 x 49.5 cm.)

Provenance: Colonel Charles H. Olmstead
(1837-1926); to his daughters Susan and
Florence Olmstead; A.J. Lomel; Mrs. Walter
Strong; Francis D. McNairy.
Loan from Francis D. McNairy

be delivered over the summer or "brought out on my return in October."[7]

Through Mary Few, her friend in New York, Mary Telfair (1791-1875) ordered a secretary and a worktable from Phyfe. In a letter dated October 28, 1816, Mary Telfair inquired, "Have you paid Phyfe a visit & what does he say about the Secretary?-... PS Keep the change of the hundred after you settle with Phyfe [ ] and pay for the blank book as I may trouble you soon if you have no objection to being my Banker."[8] The overall form of this secretary (65) is related to a labeled example made in 1820 for Thomas Lattimer Bowie (1808-1838) of Philadelphia, and it features rosettes similar to ones under the soffit on the wardrobe sold by Phyfe in 1816 to James Lefferts Brinckerhoff (1791-1846) of New York.[9] Inspired by the designs of Thomas Sheraton, the secretary relates to a number of case pieces associated with Phyfe with projecting cornices, Gothic tracery, and highly figured veneers.[10]

One of these related examples is a three-part secretary-bookcase, formerly owned by the Savannah military officer and businessman Colonel Charles Hart Olmstead (1837-1926), and perhaps originally owned by his parents, Jonathan and Eliza Hart Olmstead (66).[11] The bookcase features the marked overhanging cornice and other Phyfe trademarks such as interior satinwood drawer fronts, crisp moldings, and exceptionally fine veneers.[12]

Other New York case

furniture owned in the period by Savannah families documents the variety of forms available at the time. A chest of drawers (67) with cupboard doors below was owned by the family of George Welshman Owens (see 64).[13] With two small drawers at the top, a larger drawer below, each with lion's head brasses, and sliding shelves behind the doors, the chest would have been used for storage of clothing or linen. The acanthus carving and paw feet, the banded and crotched veneering, and the canted corners all speak to a New York provenance.

A New York sideboard also descended in the Owens-Thomas family (68). This side-

67

Unknown maker
American (probably New York)
Chest with cupboard
c. 1820-1830
Mahogany, white pine; mahogany, white pine, poplar, cherry
48 ¼ x 47 ⅜ x 21 ¼ in.
(122.6 x 120.3 x 54 cm.)

Provenance: George Welshman Owens (1786-1856); to his daughter Margaret Wallace Owens Thomas (1829-1915); to her daughter Margaret Gray Thomas (1871-1951); Telfair Museum of Art. Bequest of Margaret Thomas, OT 1951.9

129

68

Unknown Maker
American (New York)
Sideboard
c. 1815-1820
Mahogany; mahogany, pine, poplar
56 ⅝ x 65 ½ x 25 in.
(143.8 x 166.4 x 63.5 cm.)

Provenance: descended in the Owens-Thomas families; bought from the Owens-Thomas House by Mr. and Mrs. A. J. Lomel after 1951; to Ruth Lomel Mullininx.
Loan from Ruth Lomel Mullininx

board is similar to one illustrated in Nancy McClelland's book on the furniture of Duncan Phyfe. It also relates closely to a labeled sideboard by Michael Allison (d. 1855).[14] Originally owned by Allan Bradley, the sideboard in McClelland's book features long drawers, cupboards, and two deep drawers for bottles. Bands of veneer outline the doors, and the splashboard consists of columns with pineapple finials, a rectangular panel, and a broken pediment.[15] Within the break is a

small reeded plinth, on which sits a third finial, also a pineapple. (The Owens sideboard is missing its third finial.)[16]

While neither the Bradley sideboard nor the Owens's can be definitively attributed to a specific cabinetmaker's workshop, they both can reasonably be given a New York provenance.[17] Classical motifs found on the Owens sideboard include leaf and paw carving on the front feet, acanthus capitals, and a broken pedimented splashboard.

Suggesting the coming popularity of the Gothic Revival style are the arched, pointed panels flanking the corners of the large drawers. Although smaller in overall length than some others of the period, George Owens's sideboard would have comfortably served the function of holding and displaying the necessary accoutrements for elegant dining of the period. It includes drawers to accommodate silver flatware, cupboards to store serving dishes, pullout slides at each end to expand the serving area, and a top for displaying the finest china and silver.

One of the most archaeologically correct classical elements incorporated into furniture of the early nineteenth century was the curule or Grecian cross, used on seating and case furniture, most prevalently in New York. The Garlington family dressing bureau with curule base, rectangular mirror, and S-shaped scroll supports is a particularly high-style example of New York furniture (**69**). The overall design is related to a plate in George Smith's *Cabinet-maker and Upholsterer's Guide* (London, 1826).[18]

In addition to being stylish, this dressing bureau was an extremely functional piece of furniture. The looking glass could swing back and forth on carved and shaped supports, attached

69

Unknown maker
American (New York)
Dressing bureau
c. 1820–1830
Mahogany; pine, poplar, mahogany
60 x 36 ¾ x 18 ¾ in.
(152.4 x 91.4 x 47.6 cm.)

Inscription: verso, red edged label on middle of drawer support "Antique/French Dresser/Mahogany inlaid/with brass./Stobo D. Garlington's Mother's"

Provenance: Susan Washington James Garlington; to her son Stobo Dickie Garlington (b. 1838); descended in the Garlington family of Savannah; Francis D. McNairy; Telfair Museum of Art. Museum Purchase from Francis D. McNairy, OT 1978.5

with brass knobs; drawers stored necessary items of hygiene, and the high stance of the case permitted a stool or chair to slip underneath.

New York Tables

A group of card tables owned in Savannah during the first four decades of the nineteenth century illustrate the variety of styles available to the well-to-do consumer. A Telfair card table is also related to Phyfe's furniture for Brinckerhoff.[19] With canted corners, four turned and carved supports, painted paw feet, gilded acanthus leaves, and brass trim, the Telfair card table may have been made by Phyfe, or another of New York's finest craftsmen (**70**). The table is distinguished by a pivot

mechanism introduced by French émigré craftsman Charles Honoré Lannuier that allows the tabletop to swivel and eliminates the need for a gate leg and hinged rails.

A second card table, formerly in the Phillips family, has standard New York legs with ring-turned capitals and tapered reeding, and vasiform feet ending in brass casters, but its overall design and quality suggest a first rate maker (**71**).[20] The elliptical shaped top and the fifth leg, which swings to the rear, relate to a New York table labeled by John T. Dolan, a contemporary of Duncan Phyfe.[21] A nearly identical example with a swag carved central panel is illustrated by Charles O. Cornelius in his book on Duncan Phyfe, and similar elements can be found on the work of such

70

Unknown maker
American (New York)
Card table
c. 1810-1820
Mahogany; cherry, poplar, white pine, mahogany; brass
30 ¾ x 36 ½ x 18 ¾ in.
(78.1 x 92.7 x 47.6 cm.)

Provenance: part of the original furnishings of the Telfair House; Telfair Museum of Art. Bequest of Mary Telfair, 1875, 00.425

71

Unknown maker
American (New York)
Card table
c. 1810-1820
Mahogany; white pine, cherry
29 x 36 x 35 ½ in.
(74.9 x 91.4 x 90.2 cm.)

Provenance: descended in the Cohen and
Phillips families of Savannah; Telfair
Museum of Art.
Gift of Miss Fanny Phillips, OT 1974.4

133

72

Unknown maker
American (New York)
Card table
c. 1810-1820
Mahogany; poplar, cherry, mahogany
30 ⅛ x 35 ⅝ x 18 in.
(76.5 x 90.5 x 45.7 cm.)

Provenance: descended in the Charlton or
Hartridge families of Savannah.
Loan from Mrs. Walter C. Hartridge

notable cabinetmakers as George Woodruff, Michael Allison, and Charles Honoré Lannuier.[22]

The table that descended in the Charlton or Hartridge families of Savannah was of the type commonly referred to in newspaper advertisements as a "Pillar and Claw" card table (**72**). For example, in 1817 New York cabinetmaker John H. Oldershaw advertised in a Savannah newspaper: "Piller, Claw, Card and Pembroke Tables … just received from New-York by brig *Actress*…."[23] The canted corners of the top, the shape of the base, and the style of carving are all typical of furniture made in New York. As on the Phillips

table, centered in the apron on this card table is a plaque with carved drapery and tassels, a New York hallmark. A mahogany table with a similar base bears the label of "M[ichael] Allison's Cabinet and Upho… Furniture Warehouse-1817."[24]

While many of George Owens's furnishings came from New York, he did not exclusively patronize cabinetmakers of that city. A richly carved card table from England, for example, with heavy paw feet, exaggerated scrollwork, and a multitude of classical motifs was part of his household inventory in the mid-nineteenth century (**73**). Like the

134

73

Unknown maker
English
Card table with four carved supports
c. 1830-1840
Mahogany; pine, mahogany, spruce; green felt
30 ½ x 36 x 17 ¾ in.
(77.5 x 91.4 x 45.1 cm.)

Provenance: George Welshman Owens (1796-1856); to his son George Savage Owens (1825-1897); to his son George Welshman Owens Jr. (1852 1924); to his daughter Mai Owens Coxe (1895-1972); Telfair Museum of Art.
Gift of Mrs. Eckley Coxe (née Mai Owens), OT 1956.6

Garlington dressing bureau, Owens's English table is related to an 1826 George Smith design: a library table in the *Cabinet-Maker's and Upholsterer's Guide* features scroll shaped trestle supports resting on a rectangular horizontal plinth with paw feet.[25] Tables of this type continued in popularity for many years and were published in English design books of the late 1840s and 1850s.[26]

A pier table owned by the Stuart family of Savannah was also imported from England (**74**). Painted to simulate rosewood veneer and metal inlay, and decorated with gold, red, and white paint, the table relates to designs in Sheraton's *Cabinet-Maker and Upholsterer's Drawing Book*.[27] The "most salient reference" to Sheraton's design is the incurvate platform connecting the legs.[28] Of these tables, Sheraton wrote:

As pier tables are merely for ornament under a glass, they are generally made very light, and the style of finishing them is rich and elegant. Sometimes the tops are solid marble, but most commonly veneered in rich satin, or other valuable wood, with a cross-band on the outside, a border about two inches richly japanned, and a narrow cross-band beyond it, to go all round.[29]

74

Unknown maker
English
Pier table
c. 1810–1815
Pine; rosewood grained, stenciled and hand-painted highlights
35 ¾ x 30 ¾ x 15 ½ in.
(90.8 x 76.7 x 39.3 cm.)

Inscription: in script in chalk under top "Betton" or "Belton"

Provenance: descended in the Stuart family of Savannah; Telfair Museum of Art. Bequest of Mrs. Charles J.B. Stuart, OT 1967.1

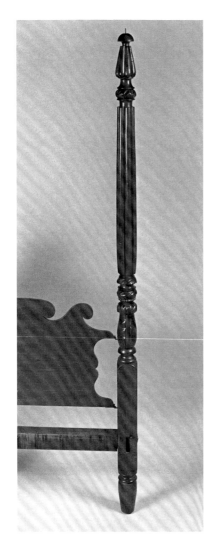

75

Unknown maker
American (New York)
Four-posted bed with canopy
c.1820–1840
Mahogany; maple
78 ¾ x 65 ½ x 104 ½ in.
(2 x 1.66 x 2.7 m.)

*Provenance: George Welshman Owens
(1786–1856); to his daughter Margaret
Wallace Owens Thomas (1829–1915);
to her daughter Margaret Gray Thomas
(1871–1951); Telfair Museum of Art.
Bequest of Margaret Thomas, OT 1951.8.1–4*

The Stuart table follows the form of Sheraton's designs and is painted to imitate the "rich and elegant" materials described in the *Drawing Book*. While handsome in its own right, the final product is a far less expensive one than the designer described.

New York bedroom furniture

According to John Bivins:

The production of elaborate, tall mahogany beds was best suited to large urban shops equipped with long-bed lathes and efficient carvers, and of late Neoclassical bedsteads surviving in much of the South, including the backcountry and the Mississippi Valley, the vast majority are of New York origin.[30]

The bed owned by George Owens, is typical of those made in New York, with common features including the shape of the reeding and the type of leaf carving on the turnings (**75**). Bedsteads in this style were probably similar to those imported and sold by Havens and Bilbo, who advertised "bedsteads with carved and fluted posts," and Joyner and Fenno, auctioneers, who sold "10 elegant carved post mahogany bedsteads."[31] Owens's bed was probably one of the hundreds of beds that arrived regularly in Savannah from New York cabinetmakers and were listed separately from other furniture arriving in cases and boxes. For example, John Hewitt shipped one case of furniture and "30 pieces bedsteads" to Benjamin Ansley in

May 1803 and six bedsteads in February 1811 to Paul Chase, J. G. Bullock, and Gorham and Miller.[32] In March 1825, Isaac W. Morrell received "14 bundle posts, marked S L B" from J. L. Brower.[33]

By the early nineteenth century, the dressing or "swing" glass was a common article for the well-appointed bedroom. Generally used on a bureau or a dressing table, the glass could swivel for increased visibility. The dressing mirror which descended in the Phillips and Cohen families was another product of New York

76

Unknown maker
American (New York)
Dressing mirror
c. 1815
Mahogany; poplar
29 ⅝ x 26 x 10 ¼ in.
(75.2 x 66 x 26 cm.)

*Provenance: descended in the Cohen and
Phillips families of Savannah; Telfair
Museum of Art.
Gift of Miss Fanny Phillips, OT 1974.5*

craftsmanship that made its way to Savannah in the early nineteenth century (**76**). Called "toilet glasses" in one advertisement and dressing glasses" in another, stands "of this sort usually consisted of a rectangular or oval mirror between two posts, resting on a case with one to three drawers.[34] Lion head brasses and reeded posts make this dressing glass a particularly elegant example.

Another form of looking glass that became popular during the early decades of the nineteenth century was the "screen dressing glass," "horse dressing glass," or "cheval glass," a tall dressing glass between columns resting on pairs of legs. This screen dressing glass, decorated in the classical manner with stenciled anthemia and pineapple finials, was owned by the Woodbridge family of Savannah (**77**). First illustrated by Sheraton in 1793, looking glasses of this type were made in abundance in New York, where they frequently followed the French Empire style.[35] Mirrors of this design were of many specialized furnishings that became popular in this period. The existence of the cheval glass depended on improvements in plate-glass manufacturing that "made it possible to use sheets large enough to show the whole figure."[36] According to *The Repository of Arts*, published by Rudolph Ackermann (1764-1834), "These moving glasses are now generally introduced in the sleeping-apartments and dressing-rooms of our nobility and persons of distinction."[37]

137

77

Unknown
American (probably New York)
Screen dressing glass
c. 1825-1840
Mahogany; oak, white pine
Stencilling redone by Mr. and Mrs. N.K. Clark, Spring, 1954
85 ¾ x 41 x 24 ½ in.
(217.8 x 104.1 x 62.2 cm.)

Provenance: descended in the Woodbridge family of Savannah; Telfair Museum of Art. Gift of Miss Caroline Lamar Woodbridge, OT 1954.4

78

Unknown maker
American (probably New York)
Dining chair
c. 1805-1815
Mahogany; ash, poplar
32 x 18 ½ x 18 ⅛ in.
(81.3 x 47 x 46.0 cm.)

Provenance: purchased by William Huger at 1916 Habersham house sale; to his cousin Eliza Mackey Huger Harrison (1875-1952) as a wedding gift; to her daughter Isabel Ritchie Harrison (1902-1978); to her daughter Elizabeth Harrison Austin (b. 1933). Loan from Mrs. Lawrence Austin

Formal Seating Furniture

By the end of the eighteenth century, the most fashionable houses normally included dining rooms. Inventories of this period suggest that certain features of this room were predictable: a sideboard, dining table, one or more looking glasses, polished fireplace equipment, and a sizeable set of chairs. These ubiquitous elements of the dining room were described by Thomas Sheraton in his style-setting *Cabinet Dictionary*: "The large sideboard… the handsome and extensive dining table; the respectable and substantial looking chairs; the large face glass; the family portraits; the marble fireplaces; and the Wilton carpet; are the furniture that should supply

the dining room."[38]

Chairs used in Savannah dining rooms in the first decades of the nineteenth century were generally of two varieties, those referred to as "mahogany" and those that were painted. In sets of eight to eighteen, the typical mahogany dining chairs of the period were in the "Grecian" style, with front leg, rail and stile forming a continuous curve, ending in a shaped back splat. The chairs from the Habersham House are a model made in Boston, Baltimore, and New York (78).[39] Featuring a pierced splat with a classical rosette flanked above and below by channeled carving within horizontal attenuated scrolls, the chairs relate to a "chaise curule" illustrated by Pierre La Mésangère

79

Unknown maker
American (New York)
Dining chair, one of eighteen
c. 1825-1835
Mahogany, rosewood; cherry
31 ½ x 18 ¼ x 17 ¾ in.
(80.0 x 46.4 x 45.1 cm.)

Marks: stamped on slip seat frame "VIII"; later in pencil "IV"; stamped on chair rail "VI"; later in pencil "V"
Inscription: ink stamp on back seat rail, in script "Stewben spring 1934"; in black marker "7-6-9 Historic Savannah Foundation"

Provenance: William Scarbrough (1776-1838) or Godfrey Barnsley (1805-1873); descended in the family of Godfrey Barnsley; purchased from Barnsley family by Mrs. Bulow Campbell in the 1930s; to her daughter Mrs. Richard Winn Courts; Historic Savannah Foundation; Telfair Museum of Art. Transfer from Historic Savannah Foundation, 1991.5.7-8

80

Unknown maker
England
Side chair
c. 1825-1835
Mahogany, various dyed wood inlays;
birch
33 ¾ x 19 ½ x 20 in.
(85.7 x 49.5 x 50.8 cm.)

*Provenance: descended in the family of
Emma Preston Roberts of Savannah.
Loan from Emma Walthour Morel Adler*

(1761-1831) in 1819.[40] A nearly
identical set of chairs with a
strong New York history is
said to have been made by
Duncan Phyfe for the house of
Charles March at 16 Warren
Street, New York City.[41]

Another set of chairs
made in New York were owned
by Savannah merchant William
Scarbrough or his son-in-law
Godfrey Barnsley (**79**). Originally
one of eighteen, this chair is also
in the antique klismos form as
adapted by English and American
craftsmen of the early nineteenth
century. The adaptation includes a
broad paneled back splat between
channeled stiles. The carved back
rail features scrolls, anthemia, and
a pineapple, all common classical
motifs.[42]

Other mahogany dining
room and parlor chairs owned in
Savannah were imported from
England. An example of the late
Regency design is the chair with

81

Unknown maker
English
Side chair (one of four)
c. 1825-1840
Mahogany; beech; cane seat
35 ½ x 18 ½ x 19 ½ in.
(90.2 x 47 x 50 cm.)

*Provenance: thought to have come from James
Troup House, Darien, Georgia, 1824, home of
James Troup and his wife Camilla Braisford
Troup; descended in the Braisford/Dent fam-
ily to Ophelia Dent, great-granddaughter of
James Troup; Telfair Museum of Art.
Gift of Ophelia Dent, OT 1954.3*

an inlaid crest rail, featuring a
classical urn and arabesques (**80**).[43]
The turned legs and broad over
hanging crest rail suggest a date
around 1830 when furniture in this
style was referred to as "Grecian"
or "modern" and was characterized
by "sober solidity and good
taste."[44]

An elaborate set of fifteen English chairs is thought to have been owned by Dr. James McGillivray Troup (1784-1849) of Darien, Georgia (**81**).[45] Originally fitted with cane seats, these chairs reflect the "growing fondness for rounded forms" beginning at the start of the second quarter of the nineteenth century.[46] The classical vocabulary of earlier in the century — reeding, scrolls, and anthemia — continued to be popular, as did the overall klismos form, but the extravagance of the carving suggests the Victorian era in design.

New York Fancy Chairs

A generation before Alexander Telfair was furnishing his Savannah house, his uncle William Gibbons (1754-1804) traveled to New York to secure clothing, dishes, silver, and furniture. Gibbons's inventory of 1804 and account book of 1802-1804 give a remarkable record of the buying habits of one wealthy Savannahian, including purchases from New York furniture craftsmen George Shipley (active 1791-1803), Samuel and William Burling (working together c. 1804-1808), and Duncan Phyfe (from whom he bought a pair of card tables and a tea table).[47] During an 1802 buying trip to New York he also bought "a dozen bamboo gilt chairs at $3.50 each and $4.50 for 2 armed" from chairmaker William Palmer (active 1796-1831) and a dozen black and gilt rush seat chairs from Joseph Riley for $19.50.[48] A single armchair from the Palmer set (**82**) and four side chairs from the Riley purchase (**83**) are all that remain in the Telfair collection from a total of four dozen painted "fancy chairs" in Gibbons's possession at the time of his death in 1804.[49]

82

Attributed to Joseph Riley
American (New York)
Side chair, one of four
1802
Painted wood, rush bottom, birch, maple, ash, oak
37 ⅞ x 18 ⅛ x 16 in.
(83.6 x 46.1 x 40.7 cm.)

Provenance: William Gibbons (1754-1804); to Mary Telfair (1791-1875); Telfair Museum of Art.
Bequest of Mary Telfair, 1875.29.1-4

83

Attributed to William Palmer
American (New York)
Fancy armchair
c. 1802
Mixed woods including oak, rush seat
33 ¼ x 18 ¹/16 x 16 ⅛ in.
(84.5 x 45.9 x 41 cm.)

Provenance: William Gibbons (1754-1804); to Mary Telfair (1791-1875); Telfair Museum of Art.
Bequest of Mary Telfair, 1875

84

Unknown maker
American (probably New York)
Painted fancy chair
c. 1820-1840
Painted wood, rush seat
15 ¾ x 33 x 17 ½ in. (40 x 83.8 x 44.5 cm.)

Provenance: descended in a Savannah
family.
Loan from Will Theus

By the mid-nineteenth century so-called "fancy chairs" were considered to be middle-class furniture, but earlier they were a fashionable alternative to mahogany chairs and were owned by the wealthiest homeowners who displayed them side-by-side with more formal furniture in parlors and dining rooms.[50] The Palmer chairs were turned in imitation of bamboo, a fashionable decorative style described in Sheraton's Cabinet Dictionary.[51] In poor condition now, and earmarked for conservation, the surviving chair was originally painted white with gilt highlights. The narrow members, broad seat, and curve of the arms and back suggest its early date. The Riley chairs were originally painted black, perhaps with rosewood graining and gold highlights.[52]

Two other New York fancy chairs with Savannah

85

Unknown maker
American (probably New York)
Painted fancy chair
c. 1825-1840
Painted wood, rope seat
17 x 32 ¾ x 16 ⅛ in. (45.1 x 83.2 x 40.9 cm.)

Provenance: descended in a Savannah
family.
Loan from Will Theus

histories, dating from the first two decades of the nineteenth century, have survived in unrestored condition (**84**; **85**). They are both similar in form to the Riley chairs with only slight differences in decoration.[53] New York City chairmaker Thomas Ash (active

86

Unknown maker
American (probably New York)
Child's chair
c. 1830-1840
Maple; ash, cane
21 ⅞ x 12 ⅜ x 11 ¹¹⁄₁₆ in.
(53.3 x 31.4 x 29.6 cm.)

*Provenance: Martha Jane Gallaudet Hardee
(1832-1900); to her daughter Harriet
Brailsford Hardee (b. 1866); Telfair
Museum of Art.
Gift of Harriet Brailsford Hardee, OT 1957.4*

1815-1824) illustrated chairs of this variety in his 1815 advertisement in *Longworth's Directory*, and Charles Fredericks (active 1812-1837), another New York chairmaker, advertised chairs with balls between the slats in the same directory, suggesting the wide availability and popularity of this particular style, called "ballback" in the period.[54] Both Ash and Fredericks are known to have exported chairs to Savannah.[55]

After 1825, the continuous stiles containing the back splat on fancy chairs gave way to an overhanging crest rail, and the rounded seat became square. An example is a child's chair, painted and stenciled, with a square caned seat (**86**). It belonged to Martha Jane Gallaudet Hardee (b. 1832), daughter of James Gallaudet (1795-1878), founder of Gallaudet College for the Deaf, and wife of noted Savannah historian Charles Seton Hardee (1830-1927). Chairs of this type were available to a

growing market of middle class consumers. They were made in abundance, shipped "knocked down" in bundles, and assembled in Savannah.[56] The advantage of this method of producing chairs was described by Savannah chairpainter Silas Cooper in an advertisement for his stock of "rush and cane seat fancy and Windsor CHAIRS and SETTEES," principally from New York: these "chairs possess the advantages of being finished on the spot, and consequently are not injured by transportation."[57] Chairs in this style continued to be popular throughout the 1840s.

As was the case with mahogany chairs, not all fancy chairs found in Savannah were imported from Northern American cities. In the early decades of the nineteenth century, England was a source for painted chairs as well. For example, merchants John and Robert Bolton received in 1803 from Liverpool

87

Unknown maker
English
Painted side chair
c. 1810-1820
Varied woods, caned seat
32 x 15 x 15 ½ in. (81.2 x 38.1 x 39.4 cm.)

*Provenance: George Welshman Owens (1786-
1856); to his daughter Margaret Wallace
Owens Thomas (1829-1915); to her daughter
Margaret Gray Thomas (1871-1951); Telfair
Museum of Art.
Bequest of Margaret Thomas, 1875, X-130*

"elegant black & gold chairs with organ backs."[58] The following year Robert Mackay wrote from Liverpool to his wife, Eliza Anne Mackay (1778-1862), "I hope the Chairs will be ready to go by the same Ship, I have not yet chose Curtains."[59] In fact, throughout the United States, "among the most popular English items imported in the early 1800s were painted chairs, described variously in newspaper advertisements and inventories as "gilt" or "japanned."[60] Particularly fashionable were English chairs painted black and gold with reeded crest rails and caned seats, such as those owned by the Telfair family of Savannah (**87**).

Other Painted Furniture

Three other outstanding examples of New York-made painted furniture descended in the family of George Welshman Owens: a pair of window seats and a marbletop center table. The window seats are grained to simulate rosewood and ornamented with a multitude of handsome and varied stencils (**88**). The quality of decoration is representative of the early years of stenciling following 1820, when work "could be quite inventive and exciting in its variety."[61] Stencils on the more elaborate painted furniture of this period were often derived from French and English sources, particularly from the designs of Percier and Fontaine, Thomas Hope, and Thomas Sheraton.[62]

A center table would have been a necessary piece of furniture in any well kept parlor of the 1830s, placed in the center of the room as the focus of family activities. With either a center pedestal or three or four legs, the center table was considered by Andrew Jackson Downing as "the emblem of the family circle."[63] Owens's rosewood and mahogany table is a particularly outstanding example of the central pedestal form (**89**). It has unusually elongated paw feet, finely applied powdered gilt stenciling, and a carefully carved anthemion collar at the base of the pedestal. The majority of painted and stenciled center tables of the early nineteenth century are thought to have been made in New York.

88

Unknown maker
American, New York
Window seat (one of a pair)
c. 1820-1825
Maple or birch; rosewood grained, stenciled and hand-painted highlights
33 ½ x 15 x 52 in.
(85.1 x 38.1 x 132.1 cm.)

Provenance: George Welshman Owens (1786-1856); to his daughter Margaret Wallace Owens Thomas (1829-1915); to her daughter Margaret Gray Thomas (1871-1951); Telfair Museum of Art.
Bequest of Margaret Thomas, OT 1951.10

PHILADELPHIA FURNITURE

While vast quantities of New York-made furniture were advertised in early nineteenth-century Savannah newspapers, furniture made in Philadelphia was rarely mentioned. Yet shipping manifests document significant amounts of furniture made in Philadelphia arriving in Savannah during this period.[64] In fact, between 1789 and 1815, Philadelphia led all foreign and American cities, except New York, in furniture exports to Savannah.[65] Some of these goods were sold at auction. Philadelphia cabinetmaker Otto James, for example, shipped almost 30 boxes of furniture to auctioneer Moses Herbert in 1817 and 1819.[66] Other shipments were sent from Philadelphia craftsmen to general merchants such as Sturges and Burroughs, R. and J. Habersham, and A. B. Fanning Co., who brokered the furniture through retail outlets.[67] Perhaps the largest quantity of Philadelphia furniture in Savannah was purchased directly from the maker and shipped to the purchaser.[68]

For example, members of the Telfair family also turned to Philadelphia cabinetmakers for their furniture needs. A circular dining table was ordered by Margaret Telfair in 1836 from Thomas Cook (**90**). Probably commissioned during the Telfairs' annual trip North, the table was ready before the Misses Telfair returned to Savannah. According to a letter from Mary Telfair in Philadelphia to her sister Margaret in New York,

89

Unknown maker
American (probably New York)
Center table
c. 1825-1830
Rosewood, ebonized mahogany; ash, mahogany; marble; bronze powdered stencilling
29 x 36 in.(73.7 x 91.4 cm.)

Provenance: George Welshman Owens (1786-1856); to his daughter Margaret Wallace Owens Thomas (1829-1915); to her daughter Margaret Gray Thomas (1871-1951); Telfair Museum of Art.
Bequest of Margaret Thomas, OT 1951.7

Just as I had dispatched my last epis-tle my dear Margaret—the above named Franklin bowed himself into our presence with Bill of Lading...in one hand, and a receipt in the other —I seated his Honor, gave him this sheet of paper, and dispatch[ed] his autograph, paid him your money, talked of Armoures to him and wished him good morning.[69]

Based on an English design, the table accommodates demi-lune leaves that fit around the central circular tabletop.[70] The top rests on S-scroll carved upright legs resting on a shaped platform base.
    Thomas Cook (working 1819-1837) and his partner Richard Parkins (working 1819-1840) sup-plied furniture to other Savannah customers, including members of the Kollock and Jones families.[71]

In an August 1831 letter to his brother George Jones Kollock (1810-1894), who was acting as agent for the family while in Philadelphia, Dr. Phineas Miller Kollock (1804-1872) requested a number of pieces of furniture: chairs, a sideboard, a sofa, a maple dressing table, and a maple wash-stand. Of the sofa he wrote,

I am very much surprised at the information you give me concerning the sofa—Aunt Harriet did not give more than $50.00 for both of hers exclusive of the cushions, & I cannot imagine how these last can cost more than $15.00 or $20.00—If you can-not however, procure a Sofa of the description I mention (which I do not think Cook could have under-stood) I will thank you to endeavour to procure one of any cheaper pattern

90

Thomas Cook (active 1800-1837)
American (Philadelphia)
Circular dining table (with leaves)
c. 1836
Mahogany; oak, pine
28 5/16 x 52 ½ in.
(71.5 x 133.3 cm.); dia. (with small leaves)
72 ½ in. (184.2 cm.); dia. (with large
leaves) 85 ½ in. (216.2 cm.)

Provenance: Margaret Telfair (1797-1874); to Mary Telfair (1791-1875); Telfair Museum of Art.
Bequest of Mary Telfair, 1875.57

145

146

91

Unknown maker
American (Philadelphia)
Center table
c. 1825-1830
Bird's-eye maple, mahogany; pine,
poplar, oak
29 x 48 ⅛ in. (73.7 x 122.2 cm.)

*Provenance: part of the original furnishings
of the Telfair House; Telfair Museum of Art.
Bequest of Mary Telfair, 1875.16*

*they may think not much experienced
in such matters. In regard to the
Sofa, if you cannot do better, I should
like a Lounge like those which Aunt
used to have in her rooms, which I
should suppose were not quite as
expensive—Whatever you get, desire
the man to keep a particular description of it, as I may at some future
period desire to get a match for it—
If possible I do not wish the Sofa &
cushions to cost more than $50.00—*[72]

A year later, George Kollock
received an additional request
from his brother who wished him
to order

*at Cooke's a small sized center table,
of a size suitable for such a room as
Aunt's front parlor (for mine is
about the size) of the best bird's eye
maple, perfectly plain, without black
moulding, the pedestal exactly after
the pattern of that of my dining
tables. Mr. Wm. W. Gordon of this
City has one exactly of the description which I wish- I think he*

*which Aunt Jones may like—If it
will not be giving Aunt too much
trouble, I wish you would consult her
in regard to every thing which you
purchase, inasmuch as the people
with whom you have to deal will be
very apt to impose upon one whom*

92

Unknown maker
American (Philadelphia)
*Side Chair (one of fifteen; originally
one of eighteen)*
c. 1825-1830
Curly maple, tiger's eye maple; maple;
caned seat
33 x 19 x 22 in.(83.9 x 48.3 x 55.9 cm.)

*Provenance: part of the original furnishings
of the Telfair House; Telfair Museum of Art.
Bequest of Mary Telfair, 1875.1-15*

purchased it in Philadelphia, proba-
bly at Cooke's, & I think I have
understood that it cost about $30.00.
I wish you would charge Cooke to be
very sure, that the wood of which he
makes the furniture is well seasoned;
for the maple furniture which he has
sent me has warped in some places,
& opened at the joints.[73]

Perhaps the table Kollock had in
mind resembled the one owned by
the Telfairs (**91**), a bird's eye maple
center table with lion paw feet
and hexagonal pedestal.[74] Maple
as a primary wood was particularly
popular in Philadelphia,
where it was used extensively in
the early nineteenth century by
such preeminent cabinetmakers as
Anthony Gabriel Quervelle (1789-
1856), Michel Bouvier (1792-1874),
and Joseph Beale (active 1801-

1820).[75] The Telfair's table incorporates many elements of the
Classical Revival, including lion's
paw feet, scrolls, and anthemia.
The Gothic panels around
the base of the table suggest
the revival of that style which
came into fashion beginning in
the 1830s.[76]

A set of eighteen maple
chairs (**92**) and mirror-image sofas
(**93**) were also part of the original
Telfair furnishings, presumably
purchased at the same time as the
center table.[77] The design of the
Telfair chairs relates closely to
that of a "dining and drawing
room chair" illustrated in an 1815
issue of Rudolph Ackermann's
Repository of Arts.[78] Described as a
"design of a very splendid character, and suited to the most embellished drawing room," the English

93

Unknown maker
American (Philadelphia)
Pair of mirror image recamier sofas
c. 1820-1830
Curly maple, tiger's eye maple; maple;
caned seat
33 x 66 x 20 in.(83.8 x 167.6 x 50.8 cm.)

Provenance: part of the original furnishings
of the Telfair House; Telfair Museum of Art.
Bequest of Mary Telfair, 1875.17.1-2

94

Joseph Barry (c. 1757-1838)
American (Philadelphia)
Armchair
c. 1829-1833
Mahogany; secondary woods unknown
45 ½ x 23 ¾ x 25 in. (15.6 x 60.3 x 63.5 cm.)

*Mark: verso, front seat rail, branded
"J. BARRY & CO."*
*Provenance: Isaac Minis (1780-1856);
descended in the Minis family; Margaret
Caldwell and Carlo Florentino.*
*Loan from Margaret Caldwell and Carlo
Florentino*

148

chair features legs in the form of
Greek crosses, chair rails that end
in scrolls at the front, a cane seat,
and a concave crest rail.

Another Philadelphia
cabinetmaker associated with
Savannah was Joseph B. Barry
(c. 1757-1839), who announced in
the *Columbian Museum and
Savannah Advertiser* for October
5, 1798, that he had "Lately landed
from Philadelphia" and had for
sale at Messrs. Mein and
MacKay's store "A most compleat
Assortment of Elegant and warranted well finished MAHOGANY
FURNITURE..."[79] He returned to
Philadelphia less than two months
later, but continued his relationship with that city for many decades, providing furniture for some
of Savannah's most prosperous
citizens. A set of armchairs made
by Barry 30 years after his brief
sojourn in Savannah (**94**) was
originally owned by Isaac Minis
(1780-1856). Active in financial

95

Unknown maker
American (possibly Savannah)
Armchair with inlay
c. 1815-1840
Mahogany, unknown light wood inlay,
burned tips; secondary woods
undetermined
39 x 24 x 28 in. (99 x 60.9 x 71.1 cm.)

*Inscription: engraved on silver plaque on
crest rail "A W A"*
*Provenance: may have belonged to Ann Wylly
Adams Habersham (1795 1876) (**9**), wife of
Dr. Joseph Clay Habersham; descended in the
Habersham family to Josephine Habersham
Connerat; John D. Duncan.*
Loan from V & J Duncan

and civic activities in Savannah, Minis regularly summered in Philadelphia and wintered in Savannah.[80] The imposing size and design of these chairs make them unusual examples of late classical American furniture, related more to French than English examples.[81]

In addition to the Barry armchairs, Isaac Minis owned another high-backed armchair, this one made locally. A group of chairs with similar turnings, form, and light inlay (**95**), all of which were owned by Savannah families in the early nineteenth century, offer an interesting comparison with the chair made in Philadelphia by Barry.[82] Each of these turned and inlaid chairs has the same rosette inlay on the crest rail, but other details vary. The unsophisticated nature of the detailing and construction indicate that these chairs were made in the Savannah area by an untrained craftsman, but the overall form suggests an awareness of high-style furniture.

Other Philadelphia-made furniture by unknown cabinet makers was owned by Savannahians in the early nineteenth century. Although typically attributed to the shop of Henry Connelly (active 1801-1823), the extension dining table owned by James Proctor Screven (1799-1887) (**96**) could have been made by any one of several first-class craftsmen whose goods were exported to Savannah.[83] Extension tables came into use around 1800, meeting the need of accommodating large parties yet collapsing when not in

96

Unknown maker
American (Philadelphia)
Extension dining table
c. 1815-1820
Mahogany; pine, maple
Folded: 28 ⅞ x 51 ½ x 50 in. (73.3 x 130.8 x 127 cm.); leaves 23 ¼ x 23 x 24 ³⁄₁₆ in. (59.1 x 58.4 x 61.4 cm.); open with four leaves 146 x 52 x 29 in. (370.8 x 132.1 x 73.7 cm.)

Provenance: descended in the Screven family to Miss Maude Bryan Foote, great-granddaughter of Dr. James Proctor Screven (1799-1859); Telfair Museum of Art.
Museum purchase for the Richardson-Owens-Thomas House with funds from Mrs. George Lorimer (Mrs. Lee Mingledorff), OT 1958.30.1-16

149

97

150

Unknown artist
American
Possibly James Proctor Screven
(1799-1859)
c. 1810
Watercolor on ivory; leather case with brass
hooks; inside fibrous filler covered with what
remains of green silk
2 ¼ x 2 ½ x ½ in.(5.7 x 6.4 x 1.3 cm.)

Provenance: descended in the Screven family;
Telfair Museum of Art.
Gift of the Estate of Maude Bryan Foote,
1994.4.3

use.[84] One plan for an "extensible dining table" was illustrated in the 1821 version of the *London cabinet-makers book of prices*, incorporating a similar diamond-shaped telescoping mechanism as the Screven table.[85] An expensive purchase when it was acquired by Screven (**97**), a physician who later abandoned his medical practice to devote himself full-time to his Savannah River plantation, the table expands to hold five leaves, seating 20 people.[86] Tables of this description were imported into Savannah as early as 1817 when cabinetmakers Faries and Miller advertised "patent extensible Dining Tables" among their stock of furniture from New York and Philadelphia.[87]

A set of mahogany dining chairs was also owned by James

and his wife Hannah Georgia Bryan Screven (1807-1887) (**98**). Related to a group of Classical style-chairs made in Philadelphia, these klismos chairs incorporate the saber legs, curved stiles, pierced splats, and shaped back so popular in the first three decades of the nineteenth century. The overhang on the crest rail and the shape of the front leg suggest that these chairs were made in the 1820s.[88]

George W. Owens owned a dressing table made in Philadelphia (**99**). This dressing table consists of a case with drawers on legs and a rectangular mirror between supports. In this instance, there are two small drawers on either side of a recessed top, probably originally fitted with marble. The mirror is

98

Unknown maker
American (Philadelphia)
Dining chairs (one of twelve)
c. 1815-1825
Mahogany, ebonized stringing; maple
33 ¼ x 19 ½ x 21 ¼ in.
(84.4 x 48.2 x 45.7 cm.)

Provenance: descended in the Screven family
to Miss Maude Bryan Foote (d.1974), great-
granddaughter of Dr. James Proctor Screven
(1799-1859); Telfair Museum of Art.
Gift of Miss Maude Bryan Foote, OT
1959.14.1-4, OT 1971.2.1-2; Purchased from
Miss Maude Bryan Foote with funds from
Mrs. Everette E. Ellis, OT 1961.25.1-2; Gift
in memory of Miss Maude Bryan Foote by
Miss Letitia Sproul, OT 1974.9.1-4

suspended between veneered columns with modified Corinthian capitals, the whole set below a triangular pediment surmounted by turned and carved urn finials. The legs of the table are turned and carved in a manner suggesting a Philadelphia origin. Likewise the diagonal gadrooning on the apron is a feature often seen on furniture from that city.[89]

The large arched looking glass from the Bulloch-Habersham House (**100**) may have been made in Philadelphia by one of the manufacturers who specialized in mirrors and frames, such as Caleb P. Wayne (1776-1849) and James E. Earle (1807-1879), who shipped their goods to Savannah.[90] A New York provenance is also possible, as looking glasses of New York origin are known to have been imported into Savannah as well.[91] In 1818, for example, J. H. Oldershaw's New York-made stock included: "Heavy pillard, double twisted pillard, single twist pillar, moulding-framed, mantle & pier glasses . . ."[92] Originally gilded, the simple molded looking glass was undoubtedly an expensive acquisition, considering the large expanse of plate glass that would have required special handling in shipping.

151

99

Unknown maker
American (probably Philadelphia)
Dresser with mirror
c. 1830
Mahogany; poplar, mahogany, white pine
71 x 38 ½ x 19 in. (180.3 x 97.7 x 48.2 cm.)

Provenance: George Welshman Owens (1786-1856); to his daughter Margaret Wallace Owens Thomas (1829-1915); to her daughter Margaret Gray Thomas (1871-1951); Telfair Museum of Art.
Bequest of Margaret Thomas, OT 1951.20

100

Unknown maker
American (Philadelphia or
New York)
Gold and green mirror
c. 1820-1830
Gilt wood (pine); later sea-green paint
59 ½ x 80 ½ in. (1.5 x 2.0 m.)

Provenance: from the Bulloch-Habersham
house sale, 1916; Margaret Vernon Stiles; to
Laura Knapp Palmer Bell (1885-1972); to her
son Malcolm Bell Jr. (b. 1913); Mr. and Mrs.
John Cay III.
Loan from Mr. and Mrs. John Cay III

Two examples of Massachusetts-made furniture indicate the presence in Savannah of goods from that state as well. A survey of ten years of coastal shipping manifests yields numerous references to furniture shipments from Boston from a variety of makers, including such well known craftsmen as John Doggett (1780-1857), Emmons and Archibald (active 1813-1825), William Hancock (b. 1794), and Isaac Vose and Son (1819-1824).[93] As was the case with Philadelphia manufactures, Boston goods were rarely mentioned in newspaper advertisements, with the exception of Boston-made fancy chairs. For example, in 1840 F. W. Heinemann advertised a shipment of chairs just arrived on the *Susan Drew* from Boston:

1 doz harp back cane seat chairs; 4 do. flat top do.do. do.; 2 do. imitation mahogany wood seats do.; 3 and 1/2 do. double back chairs; 7 doz mortice top do.; 2 do. Baltimore pattern; 4 cane rocking chairs; 4 scroll do. do. do., 4 flat do.; 4 toilet tables, 4 stands; 6 children's chairs, assortments; 15 doz painted parts.[94]

The rosewood couch from the Scarbrough/Barnsley family is a handsome Boston adaptation of an English Regency form (**101**).[95] The broken-scroll arms relate to a design in Thomas King's *Modern Style of Cabinet Work Exemplified*, published in London in 1835, and the exuberantly carved C scrolls, leafage, and paw feet relate to designs in George Smith's published plates.[96] The quality of construction, woods, and carving of

101

Unknown maker
American (probably Boston)
Grecian couch
c. 1825-1835
Brazilian rosewood; birch, pine
83 ⅛ x 37 ½ x 29 in. (211.2 x 95.1 x 73.7 cm.)

Provenance: William Scarbrough (1776-1838) and/or Godfrey Barnsley (1805-1873); descended in the family of Godfrey Barnsley; purchased from Barnsley family by Mrs. Bulow Campbell in the 1930s; to her daughter Mrs. Richard Winn Courts; The National Society of The Colonial Dames of America in the State of Georgia.
Loan from Andrew Low House, The National Society of The Colonial Dames of America in the State of Georgia

153

this couch indicate that this was an expensive purchase; the legs, for example, are made of 4 1/2" solid rosewood, and the feet are elaborately detailed.

According to Charles Montgomery, "a rectangular top with circular projections at each end was... common to much furniture made in Massachusetts in the early 1800's."[97] Legs of Massachusetts worktables of this period typically descend directly below the corners of the top. The four colonettes clustered under the center of the Lynah family work-table (**102**) are unusual.[98] The reeded upswept legs meeting at a rectangular base are a feature found on other tables from eastern Massachusetts, and the sophisticated combination of turnings, carving, reeding, and brass paw feet found on this worktable suggests an urban provenance. The top drawer is fitted for writing implements, while the lower, larger drawer is undivided.

102

Unknown maker
American (Massachusetts)
Worktable
c. 1815-20
Mahogany; mahogany, white pine
30 ¾ x 22 x 19 in.
(78.1 x 55.9 x 48.3 cm.)

Provenance: descended in the Lynah family of Savannah; Marie Glover Lynah Jenkins (b. 1854); to her daughter Marie Jenkins; to her great niece Elizabeth Harrison Austin. Loan from Mrs. Lawrence Austin

Music was an important part of nineteenth-century life among the middle and upper classes. From the President of the United States down to the average American, music was found to be an "elevating and delightful recreation."[99] Without question the most important music-making instrument in the house was the piano, called by one historian "the Romantic-era instrument par excellence."[100] As Elizabeth Donaghy Garrett has written:

The proliferation of the [piano] in the early nineteenth century was an indication of the diffusion and diversity of consumer demand and of the growing emphasis on the polite accomplishments deemed necessary to a polished young lady. When a

daughter sat down to perform for a parlorful of guests, such tunes pronounced the genteel education her parents had procured her, and not without considerable expense. Even if not used, "the diminutive, thin-legged, wheezy piano, purchased during some paroxysm of thoughtless extravagance," stood triumphant as a symbol of the family's recognition of polite refinements.[101]

By the 1830s pianos could be found in many well-to-do American homes, mostly in the form of the pianoforte, either square or cabinet. In 1829, it was "estimated that twenty-five hundred Piano Fortes, of the aggregate value of $750,000, were made this year in the United States, of which nine hundred were made in

103

Thomas & John Loud (1817-25)
American (Philadelphia)
Piano Forte
c. 1817-1825
Mahogany, purple heart (?) light wood stringing; white pine, poplar; brass stringing, stamped brass mounts
33 ¾ x 67 ⅛ x 25 in.
(85.7 x 170.5 x 63.5 cm.)

Inscription: on soundboard "Thomas & Joh…oud/ Grand and Square Piano Forte Manufacturers/ Philadelphia"

Provenance: William Washington and Sarah Stites Gordon; to their daughter Eliza Gordon Stiles; to Margaret Vernon Stiles; Susan and Walter Hartridge. [Accompanying letter by Margaret Vernon Stiles reads: "Came from Gen. [William] Gordon's (1796-1842) old home over a hundred years ago [written in 1949]. Length about five feet. 24" D. Made by Thomas about 1813."]
Loan from Mrs. Walter C. Hartridge

155

Philadelphia, eight hundred in New York, seven hundred and seventeen in Boston, and a considerable number in Baltimore."[102]

In Savannah, music was clearly a priority to the upper-class citizens, given the number of pianos imported during the early nineteenth century, primarily by

Lowell Mason, who with his partner Stebbins, advertised "Elegant Piano Fortes" for sale.[103] While Mason and Stebbins's principal supplier was the firm of John and George D. MacKay of Boston, other furniture dealers in Savannah sold pianos made by manufacturers in New York,

104

P. Schultz
British
Harp
c. 1820
Rosewood, mahogany (?); pear, apple, fir, maple; brass
67 ⅜ x 26½ x 36 ½ in.
(171.1 x 67.3 x 92.7 cm.)

Inscription: engraved in script on proper right of necking "P[?] Schultz/Harp Maker from London/St. Petersburg"; engraved on rectangular brass plaque applied to proper left of sounding board "Harp 1830/owned by Miss Isabella Habersham/Gift of Mr. Arthur Beverly Elliott"; in ink on gilded tape applied proper right of sounding board "Gift of Arthur Beverly Elliott/(harp of Miss Isabella Habersham)/presented 1936"

Provenance: Isabella Charlotte Habersham (b. 1815); by descent to her great-great nephew, Arthur Beverly Elliott; Telfair Museum of Art.
Gift of Arthur Beverly Elliott, OT 21.1954

156

Baltimore, and Philadelphia. For example, in 1820 John Oldershaw, whose stock was from New York, offered "two very elegant PIANO FORTES, of the best quality" in addition to "a general assortment of *Musical Instruments*, Such as Violins, Flutes, Clarionets, Fifes, etc."[104] First class piano factories whose goods were imported into Savannah included John Abbott and Co. (New York); Alpheus Babcock (Boston and Philadelphia); Jonas Chickering (Boston); Henry Erben (New York: organs); John A. Geib (New York); Thomas Gibson (New York); Eben Goodrich (Boston: organs); William Knabe (Baltimore); and Thomas and John Loud (Philadelphia).[105] A piano from the firm of Thomas and John Loud was owned by the Gordon family of Savannah (**103**).

The Loud piano company, in business for about 45 years, was one of the "largest and most

105

J. Delveau & Co.
British (London)
Harp
c. 1840
Maple, pear, apple; fir, pine and other woods
70 ⅜ x 20 ¼ x 37 ½ in.
(179.3 x 51.4 x 95.2 cm.)

Inscription: "J. Delveau & Co/18, Berners St./Oxford St. London: Patent # 2265"; on a brass plaque on slanting upright support "Dieu à Mon Droit" and crest with horse

Provenance: Hannah Levy Florance (d. 1866); to her granddaughter Maria Minis (1853-1941); Telfair Museum of Art. Bequest of Maria Minis, in memory of her mother Lavinia Florance Minis, 1941.7

prominent businesses of its kind in America."[106] At their factory on Chestnut Street they made both works and cases, which were sold throughout the country and overseas.[107] The Loud factory was the largest piano factory in Philadelphia where the approximately 80 piano-makers produced more than one-third of all U.S.-made pianos in 1829.[108]

Based on a stenciled inscription on the soundboard, the Gordon piano was made c. 1817 to 1825 when brothers John and Thomas Loud were in partnership alone. The case is quite simple, featuring large, plain veneered surfaces decorated by inlaid brass

106

Unknown maker
American (probably New York)
Music Stand
c. 1820-1830
Mahogany, rosewood; white pine; brass inlay; bronze stencilling
46 ⅞ x 18 ⅞ x 13 ¾ in.
(119.1 x 48 x 35 cm.)

Provenance: George Welshman Owens (1786-1856); to his daughter Margaret Wallace Owens Thomas (1829-1915); to her daughter Margaret Gray Thomas (1871-1951); Telfair Museum of Art.
Bequest of Margaret Thomas, OT 1951.114

stringing and applied chased brass moldings. On either side of the label are a pair of elaborate classical brass mounts, and the turned and diagonally reeded legs end in elegant fire gilded brass capitals.[109]

While not as common as the piano in early nineteenth-century Savannah homes, the harp was a similarly important symbol of culture and refinement. In fact, the harp, a classical and ancient musical instrument, was seen by some as the ultimate symbol of taste and accomplishment. As one writer put it, "there could be nothing more picturesque than a gilded harp standing near the piano," or as stated by another commentator, "in the window embrasure stands the most Regency of instruments, with Ossianic associations, the harp."[110]

Harps owned in Savannah by members of the Habersham and Minis families feature a wealth of classical motifs popular during the period. Mythological characters were commonly pictured on musical instruments, particularly gods and goddesses endowed with musical powers, such as Apollo, Orpheus, and the nine muses of Mount Parnassus (2).[111] The forepillar of Isabella Habersham's harp (**104**), for example, consists of a molded circular cornice with a classical frieze of Neptune figures flanking lyres; a second deeper frieze features winged caryatids joined by rose garlands and acanthus forms, surmounting a classical fluted column.[112] The flared base is ornamented with winged sea horses. This model of harp was apparently a popular one: similar harps were owned by Eliza Ridgely of Hampton (outside Baltimore) and by Sophronia Pickerell, a student at Georgetown Academy in 1839-1845.[113] The Ridgely, Pickerell, Habersham, and Minis harps were all made in London.

Allegorical figures of the Muses holding musical instruments decorate the Minis family harp (**105**).[114] While the hexagonal forepillar is ornamented with gothic decoration, the Classical style can be found in winged lions and hairy paw feet on the base and the scroll foliate motif on the soundboard. Made by J. Delveau & Co., the Minis harp resembles a double action harp made in the London branch of Pierre Erard and patented in 1836.[115]

A music stand would have been a necessary accessory for a harp in the well-equipped parlor. Rosewood graining, hand-painted gilding, bronze stenciling, and brass inlay, using classical anthemia and scrolls, are decorative features on George W. Owens's music stand (**106**). Another music stand (**107**), tiered to store sheet music not in use, has a long history of ownership in Savannah and may have been made locally, based on the use of yellow pine as a secondary wood.[116] An extremely functional design, the square base opens to reveal a small flat compartment for further storage, and the lift-up music rest is ratcheted for flexibility.[117] The small urn finials, vase turned stiles, and tapering reeded legs all reflect the influence of neoclassicism.

107

Unknown maker
American (Savannah)
Music Stand
c. 1810-1820
Mahogany, yellow pine
50 x 18 x 16 ½ in.
(127 x 45. 7 x 42 cm.)

Provenance: descended in a Savannah family; Collection of the Museum of Early Southern Decorative Arts.
Photograph courtesy of the Museum of Early Southern Decorative Arts

159

LOCALLY MADE FURNITURE

For all the furniture that was imported from Northern cities into Savannah, there was also a market for locally made manufactures. The firm of Faries and Miller appealed to the Savannah consumer in their 1819 notice:

The subscribers return their thanks to their friends and fellow citizens, for the liberal encouragement afforded them in their business, and respectfully inform them, that they have turned their attention principally to manufacturing, for which purpose they have procured some of the first rate workmen and materials, and will be able to execute orders for any description of Furniture in a style equal to any Northern City, and at as low a rate. They hope, by punctual attendance to business, to give satisfaction to those who may feel disposed to encourage Savannah manufactories.[118]

Some of this locally produced furniture may have been stylistically similar to the goods imported from the North, but what can be identified today as Savannah-made is generally more provincial in nature. While related in overall form to Northern manufactures and sometimes incorporating simplified classical elements, these pieces are generally quite plain and somewhat old-fashioned in execution, making it difficult to date a piece by style alone.[119]

Objects of coastal manufacture are best identified on the basis of local ownership and the presence of native woods. For example, a side table which has descended in the Barrow family of Savannah is made entirely of yellow pine, one of the favorite softwoods in Georgia (**108**).[120] It retains vestiges of brown paint. The ring turnings on the legs,

108

Unknown maker
American (Savannah)
Side table
c. 1810-30
Yellow pine (replaced drawer pulls)
34 ⅛ x 41 ¼ x 23 ½ in.
(86.7 x 104.8 x 59.7 cm.)

Provenance: descended in the Barrow family of Savannah; to Muriel Barrow Bell; to Mr. and Mrs. Lamaund E. Wells.
Loan from Mr. and Mrs. Lamaund E. Wells

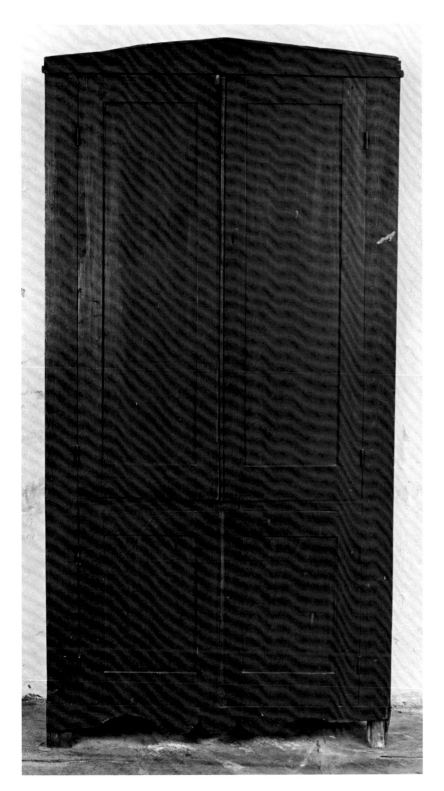

109

Unknown maker
American (Georgia)
Kitchen cupboard
c. 1820–1840
Yellow pine, poplar; poplar
83 x 42 ¾ x 17 in.
(210.8 x 91.4 x 56.5 cm.)

Provenance: part of the original furnishings
of the Telfair House; Telfair Museum of Art.
Bequest of Mary Telfair, 1875.6

161

110

Unknown maker
American (possibly Savannah)
Turned candlestand
c. 1830
Mahogany
24 x 19 ⁹⁄16 x 27 ¼ in.
(60.9 x 49.6 x 69.2 cm.)

*Provenance: possibly owned by William
Washington Gordon I (1796-1842) and his
wife Sarah Anderson Stites Gordon (1816-
1882); associated with the Gordon family of
Savannah.*
Loan from Juliette Gordon Low Birthplace

162

the flattened ball feet, and small gouged lines at the top and bottom of the drawer all point to a maker concerned with appearance and style, but the end result is a much plainer table than those imported from England or the North.

A kitchen cupboard owned by the Telfair family is made of yellow pine and poplar (**109**). The skirt is reminiscent of eighteenth-century furniture, but the slightly triangulated pediment suggests the later Classical style, such as on the dresser with mirror owned by George Welshman Owens (**99**). A small rectangular tilt-top table owned by William W. and Sarah Gordon is made entirely of mahogany (**110**).[121] While candlestands were made in the eighteenth century and into the nineteenth in every region of the United States, a very similar table has a history of having been made by Savannah cabinetmaker Isaac Fell (1758-1818).[122] The form is generic, but the proportions of the pedestal, the massing of the bulbous turned rings, and the use of double incised lines to highlight the legs may point to a local provenance.[123]

Assembled by M. and W. Dyer, Savannah
Parts probably made in Connecticut (perhaps by
Eli Terry)
Shelf Clock
c. 1830
Mahogany; poplar, white pine; glass;
metal with wooden works
34 ½ x 17 ½ x 4 ½ in.
(87.6 x 44.5 x 11.4 cm.)

*Paper label: "Patent/CLOCKS,/Invented
by/Eli Terry/made by/M.&
W.Dyer,/Savannah, Georgia./Warrented
if well used."*
Loan from H. Paul Blatner

163

Another essential item for the parlor of the 1830s was a shelf clock, first introduced by Eli Terry (1772-1853) about 1816.[124] Several examples with Savannah histories and labels of local assemblage have survived, but to what extent shelf clocks were actually made in Savannah is undetermined; quantities were imported into Savannah from New York, many manufactured by Seth Thomas (1785-1850) and other Connecticut clock-makers.[125] In fact, several Connecticut clock manufacturers moved in the 1830s to Georgia, "where they would assemble Northern clockworks in Northern-made cases, gluing thereon their own `Manufactured in Georgia' labels... They were peddled all over [the] state. Sometimes peddlers themselves affixed their own Georgia-made labels to Northern made clocks."[126]

Assembled by A. Sage and Company,
Savannah
Parts probably made in Connecticut
Shelf Clock
c. 1837
Mahogany; poplar and white pine; glass
and metal; with
brass works
38 ¾ x 18 x 5 ½ in.
(98.4 x 45.7 x 14 cm.)

*Paper label: "PATENT/EIGHT-DAY/BRASS
CLOCKS/MADE AND SOLD BY A. SAGE
& CO./WHOLE-SALE AND
RETAIL,/SAVANNAH, GEO./WARRANT-
ED IF WELL USED."*

*Provenance: Jerry's Antiques; Alex Raskin;
H. Paul Blatner.*
Loan from H. Paul Blatner

113

Assembled by John Stevens
& Company, Savannah
Parts probably made in Connecticut
Shelf Clock
c. 1840
Mahogany; poplar, white pine; glass;
metal, with brass works
35 ½ x 17 x 5 in.
(90.1 x 43.2 x 12.7 cm.)

Paper label: "EIGHT DAY/BRASS
CLOCKS/MADE AND SOLD BY/JOHN
STEVENS & CO./SAVANNAH GEO."
*Provenance: purchased by a Savannah fami-
ly; H. Paul Blatner.*
Loan from H. Paul Blatner

Ranging in quantity and
type of decoration and quality of
construction, many of these clocks
feature that most American of
ornaments, the eagle. Three clocks
decorated with eagles bearing the
labels of Savannah companies are
illustrated here. The earliest is
that of M. & W. Dyer, based on
the presence of 30-hour wooden
works and a plain scrolled pediment with stenciled eagle (**111**).[127]
The label reads "Patent CLOCKS,
INVENTED BY ELI TERRY, MADE
BY M. & W. DYER, SAVANNAH,
GEORGIA."[128] The word "made" in
this instance probably refers to the
assembly of the clock, not to the
actual making of the individual
parts of the case.

The use of attenuated
freestanding columns terminating
at corner blocks ornamented with
bull's eyes suggests a relatively
early date for the eight day clock
labeled by A. Sage and Company
(**112**).[129] The eight-day mechanism
required a weight fall of 24 to 30
inches, necessitating an elongated
vertical case, which in this example is relatively ornate.
Fashionable features include
handsome painted glass panels,
pillars marbleized with ivory and
brown paint, gilded capitals and
bases, and a carved and gilded
eagle. The Sage clock resembles
one in the Baltimore Museum
with the label of Philip Barnes
& Co., Bristol, Connecticut. Even
the painted scene on the center
panel is the same, probably the
ubiquitous War of 1812 battle of
the Constitution and Gurriere.[130]

A similar but less ornate
clock with carved eagle contains
the label of John Stevens & Co.,
maker and seller of "eight day
brass clocks" (**113**).[131] The eagle is
not gilded, nor are the columns
painted. The lower section of the
case is supported by cyma consoles, suggesting the popular pillar
and scroll motifs on late Classical
furniture.[132]

NOTES

1

The Savannah Republican (January 28, 1819).

2

After Alexander's premature death in 1832, the house became the property of Alexander's two maiden sisters, Mary and Margaret. The 1875 bequest of Mary Telfair gave the house to the Georgia Historical Society as an Academy of Arts and Sciences, now called the Telfair Museum of Art.

3

According to Forsyth Alexander, "between 1798 and 1820, more than thirty cabinet warehousing concerns advertised in Savannah newspapers. Most of them were established by relocated artisans, many from New York." ["Cabinet Warehousing for the Southern Atlantic Ports 1783-1820," *Journal of Early Southern Decorative Arts*, v. 15, # 2 (November, 1989), p.29.] Among the New York City area cabinet and chair makers who exported furniture to Savannah in the early nineteenth century were David Alling (Newark), P. J. Arcularius, Thomas Ash, Benjamin J. Barnes and William Barnes and William Osborne, John L. Brower, Matthias Bruen (Newark), Joel Clarkson, Job K. Cowperthwaite, Abraham Cross (Newark), Fredericks and Farrington, William Hall, John Hewitt, Charles Honoré Lannuier, William Macrae, William Mandeville, Edward and Joseph Meeks, John H. Oldershaw and Nathaniel Phillips, William Osborne, William Palmer, Duncan Phyfe, George Shipley, John Voorhis, and Wheaton and Davies. While many of these craftsmen never traveled to Savannah, several established warehouses in Savannah on a temporary basis. They included Barnes, Clarkson, Hewitt, Macrae, Joseph Meeks, and Oldershaw. Furniture makers who shipped goods from Philadelphia to Savannah included Joseph Aikens, Richard Alexander, Joseph Barry, Joseph Burden, Joseph Burr, Cook and Parkins, William Cox, John R. Davey, William Fling, William Haydon, John Huniker, Otto James, Isaac H. Laycock, David Lyndall, John Patterson (or Peterson), William Mitchell, James Pentland, Benjamin Snowden, Anthony Steel, William H. Stewart, Stewart and James, Robert West, and James Whitaker. Many of these names were found in the Outbound Foreign Manifests, Port of Philadelphia, Record Group 36, as analyzed by Deborah Ducoff-Barone for her two-part article on the Philadelphia furniture industry. ["Philadelphia Furniture Makers, 1800-1815," *The Magazine Antiques*, v. 139, # 5 (May, 1991), pp. 982-995; "Philadelphia Furniture Makers, 1816-1835," *The Magazine Antiques*, v. 145, # 5 (May, 1994), pp. 742-755] Ducoff-Barone notes that during the 1820s, furniture shipments from Philadelphia expanded from their earlier principal markets of Charleston and Cuba to include Savannah and New Orleans, along with other cities on the Atlantic coast and in the Caribbean and South America p. 742.

4

Marilyn A. Johnson, "John Hewitt, Cabinetmaker," *Winterthur Portfolio*, v. 4 (1968), p. 192.

5

National Archives, Inward Coastal Manifests, Port of Savannah, Record Group 36 (NA/ICM 36), Box 15.

6

Savannah Museum (January 4, 1822).

7

Savannah Museum (June 12, 1822).

8

Mary Telfair letter to Mary Few, October 28, 1816, William Few Papers, Georgia Department of Archives and History, quoted in Coleman, 1992, p. 70.

9

Nancy McClelland, *Duncan Phyfe and the English Regency, 1795-1830* (New York: William R. Scott, 1939; reprinted New York: Dover Publications, Inc., 1980), Pl. 251; Jeanne Vibert Sloane, "A Duncan Phyfe bill and the furniture it documents," *The Magazine Antiques*, v. 131, # 5 (May, 1987), p. 1109. The rosettes on the Brinckerhoff wardrobe relate to those on a desk-and-bookcase illustrated in Metropolitan Museum, 1970, # 20. This feature may derive from a plate from Peter Nicholson's *Principles of Architecture* (London, 1798), showing the underside of a soffit. Our thanks to William Rutledge for calling this plate to our attention. An 1818 newspaper notice of booksellers S.C. and J. Schenck includes a book of Peter Nicholson, *The Carpenter's New Guide*, with 84 plates, suggesting the availability and interest in these sources. [*Savannah Republican* (October 15, 1818)] Sloane points out that applied rosettes were also used on furniture made by Lannuier, citing a pier table in the Metropolitan Museum of Art and a pier table illustrated in *The Magazine Antiques* (October, 1945), p. 207, Fig. 6 (p. 1113).

10

See, for example, the desk-and-bookcase in Celia Jackson Otto, *American Furniture of the Nineteenth Century* (New York: The Viking Press, 1965), # 139.

11

Coleman and Gurr, 1983, p. 763.

12

Unusual in its height, this bookcase relates to an English example from the collection of the Earl of Lucan, illustrated in the *Antique Dealer and Collector's Guide* (March, 1989), and to a German neoclassical secretary in three sections, sold at Sotheby's, September 26, 1992.

13

The chest was at some point converted to a Butler's desk, so the larger drawer front now opens to reveal compartments and small drawers.

14

McClelland, 1980, p. 172. The Allison sideboard was sold at Neal Auction Co., February 18, 1995, Lot 364. It is dated February 1819.

15

The veneers on the cupboards of the Thomas sideboard are slip matched, while those on the Bradley sideboard are book-matched.

16

No evidence of a finial remains today, but the top of the plinth may have been replaced, covering the trace of a hole for the finial.

17

A similar sideboard with ball finials was sold at Christie's, June 22, 1994, Lot 255.

18

This plate is one of more than twenty copied by Joseph Meeks & Sons's lithographed advertisement, published in 1833. [see Bishop, 1972, # 512]

19
Sloane, "A Duncan Phyfe bill," p. 1111.

20
According to Mrs. Charlton Theus, the table was "bought from one of the New York shipments early in the nineteenth century…" [Theus, 1967, p. 77]

21
Helen Comstock, *American Furniture: A Complete Guide to Seventeenth, Eighteenth, and Early Nineteenth Century Styles* (New York: The Viking Press, 1962), # 557. Comstock relates this table to one by Phyfe from Mrs. J. Insley Blair's collection.

22
Charles Over Cornelius, *Furniture Masterpieces of Duncan Phyfe* (Garden City, NY: Doubleday, Page & Company, 1922; reprinted New York: Dover Publications, Inc., 1970), Pl. XIX; Montgomery, 1966, # 331, 198, 306

23
Columbian Museum & Savannah Daily Gazette (April 10, 1817).

24
Otto, 1965, # 173. According to John Bivins, tables of this type are often "assigned dates later than their actual manufacture." [Bivins, 1989, p. 78]

25
Illustrated in *Pictorial Dictionary of British 19th Century Furniture Design* (Suffolk, GB: Antique Collectors' Club, 1977), p. 505. See also John N. Pearce, Lorraine W. Pearce, and Robert C. Smith, "The Meeks family of cabinetmakers," *The Magazine Antiques*, v. 85, # 4 (April, 1964), for a sofa table with scroll and pedestal ends, Pl. CXVIII, from Smith (1826). This table was reproduced in Joseph Meeks & Sons' 1833 advertisement as Item 26 (p. 415)

26
See, for example, the designs of Henry Wood (1848) and William Smee & Sons (1850), illustrated in *Pictorial Dictionary*, 1977, pp. 509, 510.

27
Thomas Sheraton, *Cabinet-Maker and Upholsterer's Drawing-Book* (London, 1793-1802; reprinted New York: Dover Publications, Inc., 1972), Appendix, Pl. 4: "Pier Tables."

28
William Voss Elder, *American Furniture 1680-1880 from the Collection of the*

Baltimore Museum of Art (Baltimore: Baltimore Museum of Art, 1987), p. 159. The modified D-shape of the top, in particular, was a popular one in Regency England.

29
Sheraton, 1793-1802, p. 152.

30
Bivins, 1989, p. 79.

31
Columbian Museum and Savannah Advertiser (June 23, 1808); *Savannah Republican* (January 8, 1821). Their shipments arrived from New York.

32
May 12, 1803; February 2, 1811 (NA/ICM 36, Box 1).

33
March 7, 1825 (NA/ICM 36, Box 21).

34
Faries & Miller who had lately received a shipment "from the best manufactories in New York" advertised "toilet glasses" in *The Savannah Republican* (November 6, 1818). I. W. Morrell, "agent for the well-known factor of D. Phyfe, the city of N.Y." offered "Dressing glasses of every description." [*Savannah Museum* (January 4, 1822)]

35
The earliest version of this form was mentioned in the 1788 London price book; the illustration was in the 1793 Appendix of Sheraton's *Drawing Book* (published in 1802). Barquist lists a number of French and English designers who featured standing dressing glasses in their publications: Charles Percier, Thomas Hope, George Smith, Richard Brown, and Peter and Michael Angelo Nicholson. [Barquist, 1992, p. 362] According to Gregory Weidman, the derivation for this style of mirror is the grand miroir or psyché. She illustrates a cheval glass attributed to Charles Honoré Lannuier, based on both provenance and design. Lannuier's paper label was in the shape of a cheval glass. [Gregory Weidman, *Furniture in Maryland 1740-1940* (Baltimore: Maryland Historical Society, 1984), p. 146]

36
Marshall B. Davidson and Elizabeth Stillinger, *The American Wing: The Metropolitan Museum of Art* (New York:

Alfred A. Knopf, 1985), p. 148.

37
The Repository of Arts (1827), quoted in Barquist, 1992, p. 362.

38
Thomas Sheraton, *Cabinet Dictionary* (London, 1803; reprinted New York: Dover Publications, Inc., 1970), v. 2, p. 218.

39
The family history of ownership by the Habershams is corroborated by an 1890s inventory of the Habersham House on Orleans Square. In pencil next to the entry of a mahogany dining table and eight horsehair-covered dining table chairs is the note, "Bot by Wm. Huger for Eliza H. Harrison." [Private Collection, Savannah]

40
Pierre La Mésangère, *Collection des Meubles et Objets de Goût*, v. 2 (1819), # 483.

41
McClelland, 1980, pp. 283-6.

42
A chair with a similar back rail is illustrated in Newark Museum, 1963, # 40. It is attributed to New York.

43
The herringbone inlay may be a later addition.

44
Edward T. Joy, *English Furniture 1800-1851* (London: Sotheby Parke Bernet Publications, 1977), p. 76.

45
Troup was a planter and physician who served in the Georgia state senate, was justice of the county, and a bank president. Some have suggested that Troup's house was designed by William Jay in 1824, but Jay had long since left Savannah by that date, so this attribution seems unlikely. [Lerski, 1983, p. 173]

46
Ibid., p. 80.

47
William Gibbons's Household Memo, 1802 (Telfair Family Papers, 1751-1875. Manuscript Collection 793, Georgia Historical Society). These accounts have been transcribed by Feay Shellman Coleman

48
A single shipment of "48 fancy chairs" from William Palmer, New York, to Joseph

Clare, Savannah, is noted in a Savannah port manifest of December 16, 1818 (NA/ICM 36, Box 11).

49
At his death Gibbons owned a dozen black and yellow, a dozen white and gilt, and two dozen red and green painted chairs. [Inventory of William Gibbons, 1804, Chatham County Probate records, I & A Book F, 1805-1806]

50
According to Ulysses Dietz, the term "fancy" referred "not to the degree of elaboration of the ornament on a piece, but to the fanciful nature of the decoration." [Century of Revivals: Nineteenth-Century American Furniture from the Collection of the Newark Museum (Newark: The Newark Museum, 1983), p. 8] Charles Montgomery refers to painted furniture as "the dernier cri in English taste," a fashion which "American fancy-furniture makers quickly followed." [American Furniture: The Federal Period 1768-1825 (New York: The Viking Press, 1966), p. 446] For more on the derivation of "fancy" as a style, see Sumpter Priddy, "Fancy, Acceptance of an Attitude, Emergence of a Style" (Unpublished M.A. Thesis, University of Delaware, Winterthur Program in Early American Culture, 1981).

51
Otto, 1965, # 19.

52
The current paint scheme is probably the fourth. The balls at the back of the chair may have originally been gilt.

53
The use of balls between horizontal back rails is a feature on New York fancy chairs of the first quarter of the nineteenth century, as is the rounded seat of painted rush, and front legs that splay outwards.

54
Esther S. Fraser, "Painted Furniture in America: Part I. The Sheraton Fancy Chair 1790-1817," The Magazine Antiques, v. 5, # 6 (June, 1924), p.303.

55
Ash (active 1815-1824), son of chairmaker William Ash, sent 60 fancy chairs to Savannah in 1816. [February 3, 1816 (NA/ICM 36, Box 5)] Charles Fredericks and his partner Benjamin Farrington

(active 1818-1826) shipped dozens of fancy chairs to Savannah in 1822 and 1823, primarily to cabinetmaker and warehouser Isaac W. Morrell. [November 25, 1822; December 2, 1823 (NA/ICM 36, Box 18, 20)]. Fredericks began working as a chairmaker by 1812, and after his partnership with Farrington, continued to ply his trade until 1837. Other New York chairmakers who shipped their wares to Savannah included David Alling (whose business was located in Newark, N.J.), Philip J. Arcularius, Jr., Benjamin Barnes and William Osborne, William Brown, Samuel Campbell, Augustus Cornwe[a]ll, Job Cowperthwaite, Fu[o]rno[a]te and Clark, William Hall, and Wheaton and (William A.) Davis. In addition, Thomas Howard of Providence shipped hundreds of chairs to Amassa Humphrey in Savannah between 1818 and 1821. Howard, a cabinetmaker and furniture retailer, was the sole agent for Tunis and Nutman, fancy chairmakers of Newark, New Jersey. [Providence Gazette (April 3, 1813)] In 1822 he advertised the availability of "4,000 Fancy and Windsor Chairs," at his store in Providence. [Christopher P. Monkhouse and Thomas S. Michie, American Furniture in Pendleton House (Providence, RI: Museum of Art, Rhode Island School of Design, 1986), p. 186] The chairs that he shipped to Savannah were probably made in Newark or New York, not in Rhode Island.

56
The inventory of Nathaniel Brown, Savannah chairmaker and importer originally from Philadelphia, included "a lot of chairs bottoms, sticks, bows, etc. say for 125 chairs" @ 37 1/2 ¢ each, as well as "a lot of paints, oil, jugs, brushes pt. stones," presumably for finishing and decorating the imported parts. [Chatham County Probate records, I & A, Book E, 1794-1805, p. 379 (December 6, 1804)]

57
Cooper announced that his shipment of chairs had arrived "by the schooner Edmund," which had arrived from New York in late February 1810. [Republican and Savannah Evening Ledger (March 3, 1810; March 1, 1810)]. He had "just returned from the north, & has now an opportunity of offering for sale an elegant assortment

of the most fashionable CHAIRS." In addition to selling new chairs, he also repainted and regilded old chairs. [Columbian Museum and Savannah Advertiser (November 11, 1811)]

58
Georgia Republican and Savannah Intelligencer (December 27, 1803).

59
Robert Mackay to Eliza Anne Mackay, Liverpool 7th Septr. 1804 (Walter Hartridge, ed., The Letters of Robert MacKay to His Wife, Written from Ports in America and England, 1795-1816 (Athens, GA: The University of Georgia Press, under the auspices of The Georgia Society of The Colonial Dames of America, 1949), p. 141. Mackay was a prominent and successful Savannah merchant who was a partner of Alexander and William Mein, trading in foreign commodities including slaves and wine. [Bell, 1987, p. 535]

60
Cooper, 1993, p. 53. French chairs in this style were illustrated in La Mésangère, v. 2 (1819) and described as a "chaise curule," (# 483).

61
Dean A. Fales, Jr., American Painted Furniture 1660-1880 (New York: E.P. Dutton and Company, Inc., 1972), p.186. Fales describes the process for decorating these window seats: "black-over-red rosewood paint was first applied. Then a coat of binder such as varnish and turpentine was put on; and when this had nearly dried, a stencil was laid flat on the surface to be decorated, and the metallic powders were brushed on with small velvet or leather pads. Several stencils were used to achieve a single design, each adding its bit to the fineness of detail. Bronze powder, which could be of several colors, was normally used due to its low cost, but any powdered metal, such as brass, zinc, aluminum, silver, or gold, could be used as well. Stripings were then added and the piece varnished."

62
For a discussion of these sources see Weidman and Goldsborough, 1993, pp. 95-106. For more on the development of stenciling in America, see Esther S. Fraser, "Painted Furniture in America: II.

The Period of Stencilling," *The Magazine Antiques*, v. 6, # 3 (September, 1923), pp. 141-146

63

Andrew Jackson Downing, *The Architecture of Country Houses* (New York: D. Appleton & Company, 1850; reprinted New York: Dover Publications, Inc., 1969), p. 429.

64

Kathleen Catalano recorded a total of 955 individual pieces, 142 boxes, 485 bundles, and 3 shipments of furniture from Philadelphia to Savannah between 1820 and 1840. ["Cabinetmaking in Philadelphia 1820-1840, Transition from Craft to Industry," *Winterthur Portfolio*, v. 13 (1979), p. 83]

65

Katherine Wood Gross, "The Sources of Furniture Sold in Savannah, 1789-1815" (Unpublished M.A. Thesis, University of Delaware, Winterthur Program in Early American Culture, 1967), pp. 9, 62, 93.

66

April 17, 1817; November 10, 1817; April 24, 1819 (NA/ICM 36, Box 7, 8, 12).

67

George Mitchell to Sturges and Burrows (Burroughs), 35 boxes clocks, November 13, 1818 (NA/ICM 36, Box 11); Isaac Laycock to R. and J. Habersham, 6 bundles chairs, January 4, 1825 (NA/ICM 36, Box 21); Robert West to A.B. Fanning Co., two packing boxes and one doz chairs, April 15, 1823 (NA/ICM 36, Box 19).

68

Kathleen Catalano proposed that "craftsmen preferred this type of marketing because they retained the greatest control over the prices of their wares." [Catalano, 1979, p. 84]

69

Mary Telfair's letter to Margaret Telfair, October 25, 1836 (Manuscript Collection 793, Georgia Historical Society, quoted in Shellman, 1992, p. 67). "Franklin" was acting as Cook's messenger, by delivering the bill and accepting payment for the table.

70

A "new design for a dining table," from Thomas Sheraton, *Designs for Household Furniture* (London, 1812) and a "dining table" from Richard Brown, *The Rudiments of Drawing Cabinet and Upholstery*

Furniture (London, 1822) are illustrated in Coleman, 1992, p. 66. The connection between the Cook table and English design sources is described in *Ibid.*, pp. 65-67.

71

The partnership of Cook and Parkins lasted from 1819 to 1833. Thomas Cook worked on his own from 1833 until 1837, Parkins until 1840. Ducoff Barone lists shipments from Cook and Parkins to Savannah in 1823, 1824, 1828, and 1830, and, in addition, the Savannah port manifests include references to Cook and Parkins in 1825. [Ducoff-Barone, 1994, p. 746; NA/ICM 36, Box 21] A sideboard by the firm is illustrated in Cooper, 1993, p. 57. Cook and Parkins chose another English design as the source for the sideboard, a plate in Thomas Hope's *Household Furniture and Interior Decoration* (London, 1807)

72

Dr. P.M. Kollock, Savannah, to George J. Kollock, Wrentham, Mass., August 17th, 1831, in "The Kollock Papers," *Georgia Historical Quarterly*, v. 31, no. 1 (March, 1947), pp. 64-65.

73

P.M. Kollock, Savannah, to George J. Kollock, 297 Spruce St., Philadelphia, Pa., Sept. 18th, 1832. "Kollock Papers," *Georgia Historical Quarterly*, v. 31, # 2 (June, 1947), pp. 128-9. The "Mr. Wm W Gordon" of whom Kollock speaks is William Washington Gordon, probable owner of the Loud piano (103) and a locally made table (110). Gordon was the grandfather of Juliette Magill Kinzie Gordon Low (1860-1927), the founder of the Girl Scouts of America. Perhaps he acquired his table in 1831 when he purchased the house of his uncle James Moore Wayne (1790-1867) on the corner of Oglethorpe and Bull Streets in Savannah (now known as the Juliette Gordon Low Birthplace).

74

The Telfairs and Kollocks were friends, and members of both families were in Philadelphia in 1831 and 1832 when Cook and Parkins were executing orders for maple furniture for Savannah clients. When Alexander Telfair died in 1832, he was on his way to Philadelphia to visit his sisters, Mary and Margaret.

75

A center table by Quervelle (1789-1856) in the Baltimore Museum of Art has many features in common with the Telfair table: a triangular platform base with concave sides supported by carved paw feet and a pedestal with hexagonal lower half. [Illustrated in Elder and Stokes, 1987, pp. 174-5] The sophisticated card table by French émigré cabinetmaker Bouvier (1792-1874) in a private collection is veneered in curly maple. [Illustrated in Donald L. Fennimore, "A Labeled Card Table by Michel Bouvier," *The Magazine Antiques*, v. 103, # 4 (April, 1973), p. 760] A worktable made by Joseph Beale for Nicholas Biddle is illustrated in Ducoff-Barone, 1994, p.750.

76

A similar center table with a Richmond history is in a private collection. It too has carved paw feet and Gothic panels. A maple armchair at Nicholas Biddle's home on the Delaware River, Andalusia, also features Gothic details. Although the maker is unknown, a pair of maple center tables owned by Biddle bear the label of Quervelle.

77

Alexander Telfair's inventory included "18 large maple chairs, 12 small do. do." as well as "one center table." [Chatham County Probate Records, Book H, 1823-1836, p. 222-32] An identical pair of chairs in the collection of the Minneapolis Museum of Art was purchased from a Philadelphia dealer. The dining chairs in the Georgia Governor's Mansion are copies of the Telfair chairs. Sofas in the collection of the Philadelphia Museum of Art and ones in the William Mason Smith House (now in a private collection) are nearly identical to the Telfair pair. The Charleston sofas were part of a seventeen-piece set of curly maple furniture that belonged to Thomas Bennett (1781-1863), Governor of South Carolina from 1820 to 1822, and illustrated in Samuel and Narcissa Chamberlain, *Southern Interiors of Charleston, South Carolina* (New York: Hastings House, 1956), p. 35.

78

Rudolph Ackermann, *The Repository of Arts*, Pl. 21, p. 239 (London: October, 1815)

79
For more on Barry's stay in Savannah, see Robert T. Trump, "Joseph B. Barry, Philadelphia cabinetmaker," *The Magazine Antiques*, v. 106, # 1 (January, 1975), pp. 94-5. A breakfront secretary with the label of Joseph B. Barry & Son was originally owned by Robert Mackay of the firm of Meins & Mackay, importers (see note 59; illustrated in Theus, 1967, p. 84). A number of examples of documented furniture by Barry are illustrated in Donald L. Fennimore and Robert T. Trump, "Joseph B. Barry, Philadelphia cabinetmaker," *The Magazine Antiques*, v. 135, # 5 (May, 1989), pp. 1212-1225.

80
Isaac Minis served on the Chatham County grand jury, was fire chief for the city for two terms, was alderman, and served as county representative to the state legislature. He was a private with the Savannah Heavy Artillery and commissioner of the Central Railroad and Banking Company of Georgia. He also owned considerable real estate. For more on Minis, see Kaye Kole, *The Minis Family of Georgia 1733-1992* (Savannah: Georgia Historical Society, 1992), p. 50. Two more chairs from this set were illustrated in Ducoff-Barone, 1994, p. 749.

81
A carved mahogany armchair, stamped by Georges Jacob (1739-1814), was part of the furnishings of the Tuileries when it was occupied by Napoleon Bonaparte as First Consul. The tapering carved and turned front legs, raked rear legs, flat straight arms, broad seat, and elongated back relate to the proportions and form of the Barry chair. [Illustrated in Leon de Groër, *Decorative Arts in Europe 1790-1850* (New York: Rizzoli, 1985), p. 22]

82
According to family tradition, this chair was a wedding present to Ann Wylly Adams Habersham in 1817, but stylistically the chair appears to have been made later.

83
The Connelly attribution was first made in 1953 by Marian S. Carson, in her article "Sheraton's influence in Philadelphia," *The Magazine Antiques*, v. 63, # 4 (April, 1953), p. 86. Tables of this form have recently been predominantly attributed to New

York, and a Baltimore example was published in a Sotheby's catalogue, Sale # 6589 (June 23-4, 1994), # 469. Coleman attributed the table to Philadelphia based on the overall quality of the workmanship, the low relief carving and the use of reeding and rosettes. [Coleman, 1992, p. 63]

84
Richard Gillow (1734-1811) of London and Lancaster, England, took out a patent in 1800 for a "telescopic principle for extending dining room tables, the detached leaves being carried on a hinged diamond shape underframing which extends and collapses the table top." [Geoffrey Beard and Christopher Gilbert, eds., *Dictionary of English Furniture Makers 1660-1840* (Leeds, GB: Furniture History Society, 1986), p. 341]

85
Plate 5, from *The London Cabinet-makers Book of Prices*, ...(London, 1821), is illustrated in Coleman, 1992, p. 64.

86
For more on the use of the extension table in the dining room see Coleman, 1992, p. 63. A handsome, mahogany, custom-made table-leaf rack accompanies the Screven dining table. Made to hold five leaves, the rack consists of four carved and turned vertical supports, a rectangular top and bottom, each with five grooves into which slide the leaves, and two medial turned braces [62 1/2 x 24 1/8 x 15 7/8 in. (158.8 x 61.3 x 40.3 cm.)] For more on Screven see Rowland, 1985, p. 60-61. The table may have been acquired in 1826 at the marriage of Hannah Georgia Bryan and James Proctor Screven, although stylistically the table appears to have been made earlier.

87
Columbian Museum and Savannah Daily Gazette (October 25, 1817).

88
Montgomery illustrated a side chair with a similar profile. He used the period term "tablet top" to describe the scrolled contour of the overhanging splat. [Montgomery, 1966, p. 131]

89
For other examples of Philadelphia furniture with gadrooning see the series of articles by Robert C. Smith, "The furniture of Anthony G. Quervelle, Part I: The Pier

Tables," *The Magazine Antiques*, v. 103, # 5 (May, 1973), pp 984-994; "Part II: The Pedestal Tables," *The Magazine Antiques*, v. 104, # 1 (July, 1973), pp. 90-99; "Part III: The Worktables," *The Magazine Antiques*, v. 104, # 4 (October, 1973), pp. 260-268. For a related dressing table, see Part I, Fig. 5 (p. 986).

90
C.P. Wayne to Jos. Kopman and Co., nine cases Looking Glasses marked JK and Co., April 4, 1825 (NA/ICM 36, Box 21); Earle and Brothers to T. Butler, 12 boxes looking glass, September 16, 1820 (NA/ICM, Box 14). For information about Earle's factory see Robert C. Smith, "Architecture and sculpture in nineteenth-century mirror frames," *The Magazine Antiques*, v. 109, # 2 (February, 1976), pp. 354-355. David Barquist has written that approximately two-thirds of American looking-glass makers working in America before 1860 worked in Boston, New York City, or Philadelphia, and these makers carried on a brisk business in trade to other American cities. Many looking glasses were imported from England as well, and even the presence of American pine does not guarantee a United States provenance, since pine was exported to England. [Barquist, 1992, p. 296]

91
D. Williford of Savannah advertised in 1819 "an invoice of well made N.Y. Furniture, consisting of . . . Looking Glasses of Various descriptions." [Theus, 1967, pp. 90-91]

92
Columbian Museum and Savannah Daily Gazette (January 6, 1818).

93
John Doggett to Moses Herbert, five boxes looking glass, November 11, 1818 (NA/ICM 36, Box 11); Emmons and Archibald to Stephen Lynch, 7 cases furniture, January 12, 1818 (NA/ICM 36, Box 9); Hancock and Otis to A.G. Symmes, three boxes cabinet furniture, four bundles field post beds, May 12, 1817 (NA/ICM 36, Box 7); Isaac Vose and Son to M.H. McAllister, one case furniture marked M H McA, April 26, 1823 (NA/ICM 36, Box 19). In the period 1789-1815, numerous shipments as well as numerous individual pieces of

furniture from Boston were included in shipping manifests, newspapers, and other sources. [Gross, 1967, plate 12]

94
Daily Georgian (November 5, 1840).

95
This is one of two matching sofas now in the Andrew Low House. According to furniture conservator Gregory W. Guenther, however, the second is a later copy, based on a comparison of the frame structure and quantity and quality of carving. [Furniture Conservation Report, April 20, 1993]

96
For a discussion of a sofa with a similar arm, see Page Talbott, "Seating furniture in Boston, 1810-1835," *The Magazine Antiques*, v. 139, # 5 (May, 1991), pp. 960, 963.

97
Montgomery, 1966, p. 411.

98
Weidman illustrates a worktable attributed to John Needles of Baltimore with four slender tapered columns with acanthus carved bases. She refers to the four-column support seen on early Empire card, dining, and pembroke tables of New York and Philadelphia origin, but states that this form of support is "seldom, if ever, found on worktables from other locales." [Weidman, 1984, p. 190]

99
Catherine Beecher and Harriet Beecher Stowe, *American Woman's Home* (New York: J.B. Ford and Co., 1869), p. 296.

100
Hugh Wiley Hitchcock, *Music in the United States: A Historical Introduction* (Englewood, NJ: Prentice, Hall, 1974), p. 73.

101
Elizabeth Donaghy Garrett, *At Home: The American Family, 1750-1870* (New York: Harry N. Abrams, Inc., Publishers, 1990), p. 52. In this citation, Garrett quotes from Abram C. Dayton, *Last Days of Knickerbocker Life in New York* (New York: George W. Harlan, 1882), p. 28.

102
J. Leander Bishop, *A History of American Manufactures from 1608-1860*, v. 2. (Philadelphia: Edward Young and Company, 1866), p. 339, quoted in Cooper, 1993, p. 263.

103
See, for example, *Savannah Republican* (March 26, 1817; April 1, 1817; June 10, 1817). In the latter advertisement, they featured "1 grand upright piano, additional keys; 2 grand pianos, with claw ft & pillar; 2 grand square corners."

104
Savannah Daily Republican (November 25, 1820).

105
This information is based on inward coastal ship manifests and Savannah newspaper advertisements 1800 to 1840. For more on each of these factories, see Edna Deu Pree Nelson, "When is a Piano?," *The Magazine Antiques*, v. 29, # 6 (June, 1936), pp. 247-249.

106
Kathleen M. Catalano, "The Empire Style: Philadelphia," in Mary Jane Madigan, ed., *Nineteenth Century Furniture: Innovation, Revival and Reform* (New York: Art and Antiques, 1982), p. 13.

107
The Louds are known to have sent pianos to South America and the West Indies as early as 1821 and were among Philadelphia's most prominent exporters. [Laurence Libin, *American Musical Instruments in the Metropolitan Museum of Art* (New York: W. W. Norton & Company, 1985), p. 177]

108
Ibid., p. 176.

109
Although more elaborate, this piano relates to another early Loud example in the Smithsonian Institution (Hugo Worch Collection). The Gordon piano is missing its damper pedal assembly.

110
Maria Richards Dewing (Mrs. C.W.), *Beauty in the Household* (New York: Harper and Brothers, 1882), p. 127; Morley, 1993, p. 406.

111
For more on mythological motifs on musical instruments, see Christopher Rueger, *Musical Instruments and their Decoration: Historical Gems of European Culture* (Cincinnati: Seven Hills Books, 1986), pp. 61-64.

112
Isabella Charlotte Habersham was the daughter of Elizabeth Neyle and Robert Habersham, son of Lt. Col. Joseph Habersham and Isabella Rae. She never married, but her brother William Neyle Habersham (b. 1817) had twelve children.

113
Eliza Ridgely's harp was purchased in 1817 from Sebastian Erard (1752-1831) of Paris and London. Erard's first double action harp, patented in June, 1810, was decorated with "a half circle of Grecian maidens, and the base of the harp had a traditional motif of winged Grecians holding lyres." For more on this harp, see Page Talbott, *Furnishing the Music Room (1850-1890)* (Baltimore: Hampton National Historic Site, 1994), pp. 98-100. According to Beth Miller, the Erard harp was probably the "earliest of its type to be imported to the U.S." ["The Ridgely's of Hampton: New Perspectives on Musical Life in Nineteenth Century Baltimore" (Paper delivered at the 1988 annual conference, The American Museological Society), p. 3] Pickerell's harp is illustrated in Cooper, 1993, p. 265, and discussed on p. 266.

114
The Minis harp may have originally been owned in New Orleans, the home of Hannah and Jacob Florance until the 1840s when they moved to Philadelphia. [Kole, 1992, p. 87]

115
Pierre Erard was the nephew of Sebastian. His "Erard Gothic Harp" is illustrated in Roslyn Rensch, *The Harp, Its History, Technique and Repertoire* (New York and Washington: Praeger Publications, c. 1969), Pl. 34b. "A larger and more durable instrument, with greater distance between the strings…(the Gothic harp) featured angelic figures in pointed archways. In this design gilded plaster effectively trimmed black lacquered or highly polished wood." (Rensch, 1969, p. 70) Another Erard Gothic Harp is illustrated in Professor Roger Bragard and Dr. Ferdinand J. De Hen, *Musical Instruments in Art and History* (London: Barrie and Rockliff, 1967), Pl. VI-2. What appears to be an Erard Gothic harp was illustrated in Hunter, 1958, p. 8. Miss Angela Altick of Savannah is pictured with the harp which belonged to her grandmother, Josephine Clements O'Byrne, "an accomplished

singer as well as harpist [who] took part in popular musicals of the era." The O'Byrne family is said to have "occupied the Scarbrough house until the fire of Sherman's approach was heard." [*Ibid.*, p. 6]

116
According to staff at the Museum of Early Southern Decorative Arts, "the decoration of horizontal lines at the front leg tops is unusual and may prove to be a trademark by which we identify pieces more strongly with Savannah." A related "dumb waiter" was formerly on loan to the Telfair Museum by Mr. Anderson Bouchelle.

117
Gregory Weidman refers to a similar Baltimore "music shelf" as "an enlarged and somewhat later version of the canterbury." [Weidman, 1984, p. 153]

118
Savannah Daily Republican (December 7, 1819). This partnership must have been a failure, as the firm dissolved by mutual consent only nine months later. [Ibid. (August 12, 1820)]

119
For more on the old-fashioned nature of Georgia-made furniture, see William W. Griffin, et al., *Neat Pieces: The Plain-Style of Furniture and Nineteenth Century Georgia* (Atlanta: Atlanta Historical Society, 1983), pp. 5-11. [Mrs.] Charlton Theus has written that "the majority of Savannah made furniture that has been identified is in the Classic style," but the pieces illustrated in her article on Savannah furniture are not in the high style classical mode. Most examples made in the first half of the nineteenth century are in the Sheraton style or in a subdued French Empire style using broad expanses of veneer and little carved decoration. [(Mrs.) Charlton M. Theus, "A concise guide to Savannah furniture and cabinetmakers," *Connoisseur*, v. 169, # 680 (October, 1968), p. 128]

120
Griffin, 1983, p. 6. The drawer pulls have been replaced. Originally the drawer was divided into three sections; the dividers are missing. The top of the table has been turned. The original paint color can be seen on the reverse side of the current top.

121
Although not indigenous to Georgia, mahogany was imported from the West Indies and Northeastern states well before the advent of railroads. [Griffin, 1983, p. 6]

122
Barquist, 1992, p. 232-233. The Fell table is illustrated in Theus, 1968, p. 124. Theus describes the table as "mahogany throughout, in the Sheraton style with a ringed pedestal on a tripod base." The table top and legs are nearly identical and the rings on the pedestal, while not exactly the same, are equally broad and varied.

123
The latch has been replaced, and two legs have been repaired; otherwise, the table is entirely original.

124
Snowden Taylor, *The Development Era of Eli Terry and Seth Thomas Shelf Clocks* (Fitzwilliam, NH: Ken Roberts Publishing Co., 1985). Terry is best known for being the first man to produce cheap clocks in large quantities, making them accessible to middle-class consumers throughout the United States.

125
For example, a total of 48 Seth Thomas clocks were recorded in Savannah ship manifests for 1822: February 2, March 23, April 8, December 24 (NA/ICM 36, Box 17). The Connecticut clockmaking-industry in the early nineteenth century is described by Kenneth D. Roberts in "Some Observations Concerning Connecticut Clockmaking, 1790-1850", Supplement to the *Bulletin of the National Association of Watch and Clock Collectors*, # 6 (1970). According to Roberts, so large was the quantity of clocks produced by these factories annually that they were "almost all sent abroad for a market, and principally to the southern and western states" (p. 20).

126
Griffin, 1983, p. 6.

127
Wooden works were used exclusively from around 1817 until the end of the 1820s when brass works became popular. The introduction of brass movements necessitated a somewhat larger case to provide the increased distance for the weight drop. [Lee H. Davis, "The Greek Revival Influence on American Clock Case Design

and Empire Clock Case Development," Supplement to the *Bulletin of the National Association of Watch and Clock Collectors, Inc.*, # 18 (Spring, 1991), p. 10]. Davis illustrates in Fig. 9 a Seth Thomas wood movement clock of about the same date. It too is decorated with a stenciled eagle. According to Davis, "Stencilled designs in bronzing powder on 30-hr wood movement clock cases were extremely popular and found on almost all Connecticut short pendulum, half column cases" (p. 17).

128
Two related clocks are illustrated in Edgar G. Miller, *American Antique Furniture*, v. 2 (Baltimore: The Lord Baltimore Press, 1937; reprinted New York: Dover Publications, Inc., 1966), # 1936 and 1937. Both have painted glass panels below the clock face, a feature that presumably was present in the Dyer clock originally. Clock # 1937 is labeled "Patent clocks. Invented by Eli Terry. Made and sold at Terryville, Connecticut, by Eli Terry, Jr." (1824-1841) Terry received eight patents for brass- and wooden-wheeled clocks between 1815 and 1845, but many other makers "took advantage of his inventiveness by copying these various improvements along with those of their own devising." [Cooper, 1993, p. 223]

129
Davis, 1991, pp. 9-23. Other clocks with the Sage label are known in Savannah, including a similar example with gilded eagle in the Telfair Museum collection which was the bequest of Mary Telfair, 1875, X-66.

130
Miller, 1966, # 1939.

131
A related clock, with the label of Dyer, Wadsworth & Co., was sold in Augusta, Georgia between 1836 and 1840. It is illustrated in Smith, 1985, # 92. Clocks such as this one, called a "triple decker column case" were generally priced at $ 18 - $ 22. [*Ibid.*, p. 158]

132
This clock, too, is missing the painted glass panels.

Checklist of Other Objects

Select Bibliography & Index

114

Unknown maker
Probably English
Mantel
c. 1819
Black polished marble
43 ⅛ x 68 ¾ x 12 in.
(109.5 x 174.6 x 30.5 cm.)

*Provenance: part of the original furnishings
of the Telfair House, completed in 1819;
Telfair Museum of Art.
Bequest of Mary Telfair, 1875*

115

Raphaelle Peale (1774-1825)
American
Physiognotrace of Sarah Ann Hollis
1804
Paper; original burnished gilt frame
6 ½ x 5 ½ in. (16.5 x 14 cm.)

*Provenance: Sarah Ann Hollis (Mrs. Silas)
(1788-1838); to her daughter Maria Louise
Hollis Low (Mrs. James Hugh) (1818-1886);
to her daughter Tallulah Ellen Low deRosset
(Mrs. Armand Lamar) (1845-1901); to her
daughter Tallulah Low deRosset Peschau
(Mrs. John Bauman) (1878-1964); to her
daughter Tallulah Lamar Peschau Morton
(Mrs. James White) (b.1914); to her son
James White Morton III.
Loan from James White Morton III*

116

Unknown artist
American
Mourning pendant
1800-1825
Watercolor on ivory; hair; brass; blue glass
2 ¹/16 x 2 ¹/16 in. (5.2 x 5.2 cm.)

*Inscriptions: recto, on tomb "PEACE"; verso,
on hair, cut out of copper, in script
"souvenir/SM"*

*Provenance: descended in the Dent family;
Telfair Museum of Art.
Gift of Miriam and Ophelia Dent, 1945.2*

117

Unknown artist
American
Miniature pendant
1810-1830
Watercolor on ivory, surrounded by
golden colored hair decoration; copper
frame; blue glass
3 ¼ x 2 ⅜ in. (8.3 x 6.1 cm.) (includes ring)

*Inscription: verso, etched on center of an
ivory oval on a hair background
"Ann Caroline Wylly"*

*Provenance: Ann Caroline Wylly; to her niece
Margaret Wylly Couper (1839-1897) and
Robert Mackay Stiles (1836-1874); to their
daughter Caroline Couper Stiles Lowell
(1862-1947); to her sister Mrs. Margaret
Screven Duke; Telfair Museum of Art.
Gift of Harriet L. Houston, from the estate of
Mrs. Margaret Screven Duke, OT 1964.29*

118

Angelica Kauffman (1741-1897), painter
Swiss
Jean Marie Delattre (1746-1848), engraver
French
*Beauty Directed by Prudence Rejects with
Scorn the Solicitations of Folly*
1783
Stipple engraving
Framed: 17 ¾ x 15 ⅝ in. (45.0 x 38.73 cm.);
image: 10 ½ x 11 in. (26.6 x 27.9 cm.)

*Inscriptions: l.l. "Angelica Kauffmann pinxt";
l.r. "J M Delattre Sculpsit"*

*Provenance: George Welshman Owens
(1786-1856); to his daughter Margaret
Wallace Owens Thomas (1829-1915); to her
daughter Margaret Gray Thomas (1871-1951);
Telfair Museum of Art.
Bequest of Margaret Thomas, OT 341*

119

Angelica Kauffman (1741-1807), painter
Swiss
Francesco Bartolozzi (1725/7-1813),
engraver
Italian
Cupid Binding Aglaia to a Laurel
c. 1784

Stipple engraving; original gilt frame
with painted glass
Framed: 15 ¼ x 13 ¼ in. (38.7 x 33.6 cm.);
Image: 11 ¼ x 9 ¼ in. (28.6 x 23.5 cm.)

*Inscriptions: l.l. "Angelica KauffmannP^t";
l.r. "Bartolozzi S^t"*

*Provenance: George Welshman Owens
(1786-1856); to his daughter Margaret
Wallace Owens Thomas (1829-1915); to her
daughter Margaret Gray Thomas (1871-1951);
Telfair Museum of Art.
Bequest of Margaret Thomas, OT 1951.82*

120

Angelica Kauffman (1741-1807), painter
Swiss
Francesco Bartolozzi (1725/7-1813),
engraver
Italian
Cupid Disarm'd by Euphrosine
c. 1784
Stipple engraving; original gilt frame
with painted glass
Frame: 15 ½ x 13 ½ in. (38.7 x 34.3 cm.);
image: 10 ⅜ x 8 ½ in. (26.4 x 21.6 cm.)

*Inscriptions: l.l. "Angelica KauffmannP^t"; l.r.
"Bartolozzi S^t"*

*Provenance: George Welshman Owens
(1786-1856); to his daughter Margaret
Wallace Owens Thomas (1829-1915); to her
daughter Margaret Gray Thomas (1871-1951);
Telfair Museum of Art.
Bequest of Margaret Thomas, OT 1951.81*

121

Giovanni Battista Cipriani (1725-1813),
painter
Italian
Francesco Bartolozzi (1725/7-1813),
engraver
Italian
*Perseus Cautiously Relating to Andromeda
the Transforming Power of Medusa's Head*
1789
Stipple engraving
14 x 17 in. (35.6 x 43.2 cm.)

Inscriptions: *l.l. "Drawn by I.B.Cipriani.";
l.c. "Pub. by R Ackermann. 101 Strand.";
l.r. "Engraved by F.Bartolozzi, R.A.
Historical Engraver to His Majesty."; l.c.
"Perseus cautiously relating to Andromeda/the
transforming power of Medusa's Head."*

*Provenance: George Welshman Owens
(1786-1856); to his daughter Margaret
Wallace Owens Thomas (1829-1915); to her
daughter Margaret Gray Thomas (1871-1951);
Telfair Museum of Art.
Bequest of Margaret Thomas, OT 1951.113*

122 a,b,c

Lavinia, Countess of Spencer (d. 1831),
painter
English
Giovanni Mariano Bovi (b. 1753), engraver
Italian
Bacchantes (three)
1791-1792
Mezzotints
12 ⅞ x 10 ½ in. (32.7 x 26.67 cm.)

Inscriptions: *on all three l.l. "Drawn by
Lavinia CounteSs of Spencer"; l.c. "BAC-
CHANTE"
a (OT 9.1.54): l.r."Engraved by M. Bovi late
Pupil of F. Bartolozzi R.A."; l.c. "PubliSh'd
Sept. 1791. by M^no Bovi N° 207 Piccadilly,
London"
b (OT 9.2.54): l.r. "Engraved by M. Bovi late
Pupil of F.Bartolozzi"; l.c. "c. PubliSh'd Jan.
1st 1792. by M^no Bovi N° 207 Piccadilly
London"
c (OT 9.3.54): l.r. "Engrav'd by M.Bovi late
Pupil of F.Bartolozzi R.A."; l.c. "c. PubliSh'd
Jan. 1st 1792. by M^no Bovi N° 207 Piccadilly
London"*

*Provenance: descended in the Nightingale
family; Telfair Museum of Art.
Bequest of Miss Francis N. Nightingale,
OT 9.1-3.1954*

Henry Singleton (1766-1839), painter
English
Haveill Gillbank (active late 18th c.-early
19th c.), engraver
English
Coriolanus and Hersilia
c. 1802
Aquatint on paper; in original frame with
painted glass
Framed: 40 ¾ x 32 ½ in. (103.5 x 82.5 cm.);
image: 31 ½ x 23 ½ in. (80 x 59.7 cm.)

Inscriptions: *l.l. "H. Singleton pinx";
c. "HERSILIA"; l.c. "London, Published
March 25. 1802,by James Daniell,& Co.,
480 Strand. The Battle of the Romans &
Sabines"; l.r. "H Gillbank Sculp."*

*Provenance: George Welshman Owens
(1786-1856); to his daughter Margaret
Wallace Owens Thomas (1829-1915); to her
daughter Margaret Gray Thomas (1871-1951);
Telfair Museum of Art.
Bequest of Margaret Thomas, OT 1951.90*

124

M. Dubourg (active 1786-1838), engraver
English
*Vues des Restes des Constructions Antiques
de Rome et de Ses Environs (three plates)*
1820
Aquatints
Ponte Lucarno: 16 ¹⁵/₁₆ x 13 ¹¹/₁₆ in. (43 x
34.8 cm.); *Arch of Titus:* 16 ⁹/₁₆ x
13 ¹²/₁₆ in. (42.1 x 34.9 cm.); *Ponte Salaro:*
18 ¹/₁₆ x 14 ⅞ in. (45.9 x 37.8 cm.)

Inscriptions: *recto on all three, l.l. "Engraved
by M. Duborg"; Ponte Lucarno: l.c. "Plate
11./PONTE LUCARNO./London. Publish'd
as the Act Directs, 1820."; Arch of Titus: l.c.
"Plate 15./ARCH of TITUS."London,
Publish'd as the Act Directs_ . 1820."; Ponte
Salaro: l.c. "Plate 24./PONTE
SALARO./London, Publish'd as the Act
Directs_ . 1820."*

*Provenance: descended in the Huger/Barrow
family.
Loan from Caroline Gordon Armstrong*

William Jay (1792-1837)
English
*South Elevation, Robert Habersham House,
probably drawn in Savannah*
c. 1818/1819
Photographic reproduction
Sheet: 17 ½ x 20 ⅜ in. (44.5 x 51.8 cm.);
Image: 15 ½ x 18 ½ in. (39.4 x 47 cm.)

Inscriptions: *recto, in script u.l. "No 5"; c.l.
"Windows or Doors Down to the floor"; l.l.
"Robt Habersham Esq/Savannah"; l.c. "South
Elevation"; l.r. "William Jay/Architect"*

*Provenance: the original was discovered (with
two other drawings) in a drawer of a nineteenth-century washstand found in Savannah
in the 1940s, and is now in a private collection in Savannah.
Telfair Museum of Art Study Collection*

126

Unknown artist
American (Savannah)
Small girl and African American nurse
c. 1820
Pastel on paper, ink; graphite
Image: 10 ½ x 12 ¾ in. (26.7 x 32.4 cm.)

*Provenance: descended in the Morrell family
to Ernestine Cutts Morrell (1890-1973) and
William Goodrich Morrell (1890-1976);
to their daughter Jeanne Morrell Garlington
(b. 1926).
Loan from Jeanne Morrell Garlington*

127

W. J. (or T.) Williams
American
United States Barracks (Savannah)
c. 1835
Watercolor on paper
Overall: 11 x 9 ⅛ in. (27.9 x 23.2 cm.);
image with border: 6 x 8 ¼ in.
(15.2 x 20.9 cm.)

Inscriptions: *ink in script, l.c. "United States.
Cantonment. in_Savannah. Georgia."; ink
in script, l.r. "Executed by. MJ Williams."
Loan from Georgia Historical Society*

128

Unknown artist
American
Mrs. Ruth Ehlrich Welman
c. 1815
Pastel on paper; original frame of gilt
and gesso on poplar
Frame: 31 ¼ x 27 in. (79.4 x 68.6 cm.)
Image: 24 ⅞ x 20 ⅝ in. (63.2 x 52.4 cm.)

Inscription: *verso, c. "Mrs. Ruth Welman/
formerly Miss Ehlrich of Savannah"*

Provenance: *Ruth Ehlrich Welman (1785-
1822); to her husband Francis Harvey
Welman; Sumpter Priddy III, Inc.
Loan from Sumpter Priddy III, Inc.*

129 a,b

Attributed to Jean-Baptiste Boyer (b. 1793)
French
Narcissus and Echo (pair)
n.d.
Bronze
10 ½ x 6 ⅛ in. (26.6 x 15.5 cm.)

Signed: *base of both, recto, in script "Boyer"*
Inscriptions: *base of Echo (1951.29.1), rough
etched "BxJ"*

Provenance: *George Welshman Owens
(1786-1856); to his daughter Margaret
Wallace Owens Thomas (1829-1915); to her
daughter Margaret Gray Thomas (1871-1951);
Telfair Museum of Art.
Bequest of Margaret Thomas, OT 1951.29.1-2*

130

Unknown maker
French
Napoleonic Column, Place Vendôme, Paris
c. 1830-1848
Bronze
18 ⅛ x 5 ½ x 5 ½ in. (45.7 x 13.9 x 13.9 cm.)

Provenance: *George Welshman Owens
(1786-1856); to his daughter Margaret
Wallace Owens Thomas (1829-1915); to her
daughter Margaret Gray Thomas (1871-1951);
Telfair Museum of Art.
Bequest of Margaret Thomas, OT 1951.32*

131

Unknown maker
French or English
The Dying Gaul
early 19th c.
Bronze; marble
Statue: 10 ⅛ x 3 ⅞ x 5 ⅝ in. (25.7 x 10 x
14.3 cm.) Base: 11 ¹¹/16 x 5 3/16 x 3 5/16 in.
(29.7 x 12.9 x 8 cm.)

Provenance: *George Welshman Owens
(1786-1856); to his daughter Margaret
Wallace Owens Thomas (1829-1915); to her
daughter Margaret Gray Thomas (1871-1951);
Telfair Museum of Art.
Bequest of Margaret Thomas, OT 1951.34.1-2*

132

Unknown maker
American
Window cornices (pair)
c. 1830
Pine; gesso; gilt
65 ½ x 6 ½ x 4 in. (166.4 x 16.5 x 10.2 cm.)

Provenance: *George Welshman Owens
(1786-1856); to his daughter Margaret
Wallace Owens Thomas (1829-1915); to her
daughter Margaret Gray Thomas (1871-1951);
Telfair Museum of Art.
Bequest of Margaret Thomas, OT 1951.103.1-2*

133

Unknown maker
American
Carved and molded window cornices (pair)
c. 1820-1830
Pine; gesso; gilt
4 ½ x 67 x 7 in. (11.4 x 170.2 x 17.8 cm.)

Provenance: *George Welshman Owens
(1786-1856); to his daughter Margaret
Wallace Owens Thomas (1829-1915); to her
daughter Margaret Gray Thomas (1871-1951);
Telfair Museum of Art.
Bequest of Margaret Thomas, OT 1951.102.1-2*

134

Unknown maker
American
*Shaped decorative fascia boards for
venetian blinds*
c. 1810-1830
Pine
8 ⅜ x 44 ¾ x ¼ in. (21.3 x 113.7 x .64 cm.)

Provenance: *found in the Richardson-Owens-
Thomas House attic, 1984.
Richardson-Owens-Thomas House Study
Collection, Telfair Museum of Art*

135

Unknown maker
English
Silver chest with fitted inserts
c. 1825
Mahogany; brass; green velvet
27 x 50 x 39 ½ in. (68.6 x 127 x 100.3 cm.)

Provenance: *William Scarbrough (1776-1838)
and/or Godfrey Barnsley (1805-1873); descend-
ed in the family of Godfrey Barnsley; Mrs.
Bulow Campbell, 1930s; to her daughter Mrs.
Richard Courts; Historic Savannah
Foundation, 1971; Telfair Museum of Art.
Transfer from Historic Savannah
Foundation, 1991.5.6*

136

Harvey Lewis and Joseph Smith (active in
Philadelphia 1805-1811)
American (Philadelphia)
Partial tea and coffee service (three pieces)
c. 1810
Sterling silver
Coffeepot with filter: 14 x 12 ¼ x 7 ½ in.
(35.5 x 31.1 x 19 cm.); teapot: 7 ½ x 10 ½ x
6 ¾ in. (19 x 26.7 x 17 cm.); sugar bowl and
cover: 7 ⅞ x 9 x 6 ¾ in. (20 x 22.9 x
17.1 cm.)

Mark: *verso, on coffee pot, rough engraved
"40..12/oz/oMF"; verso, on sugar bowl, rough
engraved "9,4-2"; verso, on teapot, embossed
without frame "Lewis & Smith" and in rectangle "PHILA"*
Inscription: *recto, on all three pieces engraved
in script in cartouche on decorative band on
front "TER" [Thomas/Elizabeth Rice]*

Provenance: Elizabeth Dews Rice (d. 1824)
and Thomas Rice (d. 1817) of White Bluff
(near Savannah); Telfair Museum of Art.
Gifts of Hesse Pringle Mitchell Troy, Sarah
H. Pinney and H. Rees Mitchell, 1986.2-4
Illustrated in Coleman, 1992, p. 103

137

Unknown maker
American
Nutmeg grater in shape of urn
c. 1810
Sterling silver; tin
3 ½ x 1½ in. (8.8 x 3.8 cm.)

Mark: None
Inscription: recto, engraved in script
"MEHW"

Provenance: descended in the Jones family to
Frances Noble Jones Luquer (Mrs. Evelyn P.)
(b. 1905); Telfair Museum of Art.
Gift of Mrs. Evelyn P. Luquer, 1977.65

138

Samuel Child Kirk (1792-1872)
American (Baltimore)
Waiter
c. 1828
Sterling silver
9 dia. x ⅞ in. (22.8 x 2.2 cm.)

Mark: verso, in rectangle "Sam^L Kirk", in rec-
tangle "S.K", in rectangle "11.OZ", oval stamp
quartered with fleur de lis and stripes, and
incised in Roman capital without a frame
"F".
Inscription: recto, c. engraved in Gothic script
"Porter"; verso, rough engraved "241"

Provenance: part of the original furnishings of
the Telfair House, completed 1819; Telfair
Museum of Art.
Bequest of Mary Telfair, 1875, 00.445
Illustrated in Coleman, 1992, p. 103

139

William Thomson (active in New York
1810-1845)
American (New York)
Teaspoons (eight)
c. 1815
Sterling silver
5 ¹⁵/₁₆ x 1 ¼ in. (15.1 x 3.2 cm.)

Mark: verso, in script in rectangle "W.
Thomson"
Inscription: recto, engraved in script on
handle "O"

Provenance: George Welshman Owens
(1786-1856); to his daughter Margaret
Wallace Owens Thomas (1829-1915); to her
daughter Margaret Gray Thomas (1871-1951);
Telfair Museum of Art.
Bequest of Margaret Thomas, 1951, S-169-176
Illustrated in Coleman, 1992, p. 82

140

David B. Nichols (1791-1860)
American (Savannah)
Teaspoons (three)
c. 1815-1820
Sterling silver
5 ¹¹/₁₆ x 1 ⅛ in. (14.5 x 2.9 cm.)

Mark: verso, in Roman capitals in rectangle
"D.B. NICHOLS"
Inscription: recto, engraved in script on
handle "LCW"

Provenance: Laura Cornella Winkler
(1834-1925); to her son Armin Butler Palmer
(1860-1927); to his daughter Laura Knapp
Palmer Bell (1885-1972) and Malcolm Bell, Sr.
(1886-1962); to their four children Katharine
Lambert Bell Ellis (b. 1910), Malcolm Bell, Jr.
(b. 1913), Laura Palmer Bell Barrow (b. 1914),
and Frank Greenhalgh Bell (b. 1926); Telfair
Museum of Art.
Gift of the children of Mr. and Mrs. Malcolm
Bell, Sr., 1969.3.1-3
Illustrated in Coleman, 1992, p. 82

141

Moses Eastman (1794-1850)
American (Savannah or New York)
Teaspoon, King's pattern
c. 1825
Sterling silver
5 ½ x 1 ¾ in. (14 x 4.5 cm.)

Mark: verso, in Roman capitals in rectangle,
star or eagle in circular field, and three
impressed pellets in form of triangle "EAST-
MAN"
Inscription: recto, engraved in script on
handle "AWH"

Provenance: Ann Wylly Adams Habersham
(1795-1876); to Josephine Habersham
Habersham (1821-1898); to Anna W.
Habersham Jones (1849-1888); to George
Noble Jones (1874-1955); to Caroline W. Jones
Wright (b. 1911); to Anna Habersham Wright
(b. 1950).
Loan from Anna Habersham Wright

142

(Peter?) Griffen
American (New York)
Soup spoon, King's pattern
c. 1825
Sterling silver
6 ⅞ x 1 ½ in. (17.5 x 3.8 cm.)

Mark: verso, incised in Roman capitals
without frame "GRIFFEN", incised in
Roman capitals without frame "EYLAND
& CO.", and (on its side) incised on shaft "Y"
Inscription: recto, engraved in script on
handle "AWH"

Provenance: Ann Wylly Adams Habersham
(1795-1876); to Josephine Habersham
Habersham (1821-1898); to Anna W.
Habersham Jones (1849-1888); to George
Noble Jones (1874-1955); his daughter to
Caroline W. Jones Wright (b. 1911); to Anna
Habersham Wright (b. 1950).
Loan from Anna Habersham Wright

177

143

Moses Eastman (1794-1850)
American (Savannah or New York)
Butterknife, King's Pattern
c. 1825
Sterling silver
7 x 9/16 in. (17.8 x 1.4 cm.)

*Mark: verso, in Roman capitals in rectangle
"M.EASTMAN"*
*Inscription: recto, engraved in script on
handle "G.J."*

*Provenance: Senator George Jones (1766-
1838); to his son Noble W. Jones (1787-1818);
to his son George Noble Jones (1811-1876);
to his son George Fenwick Jones (1841-1876);
to his son George Noble Jones (1874-1955); to
his daughter Caroline Jones Wright (b. 1911).
Loan from Caroline Jones Wright*

144

Moses Eastman (1794-1850)
American (Savannah)
Sauce ladle
c. 1830
Sterling silver
7 ¾ x 2 ½ in. (17.7 x 6.4 cm.)

*Mark: verso, in Roman capitals in rectangle
"M·EASTMAN"*
*Inscription: recto, engraved in script on
handle "O"*

*Provenance: George Welshman Owens
(1786-1856); to his daughter Margaret
Wallace Owens Thomas (1829-1915); to her
daughter Margaret Gray Thomas (1871-1951);
Telfair Museum of Art.
Bequest of Margaret Gray Thomas, 1951,
OT S-140
Illustrated in Coleman, 1992, p. 78*

145

Penfield & Co [Josiah Penfield (1785-1828)
and Frederick Marquand (1799-1882),
active 1820-1826; Josiah Penfield and
Moses Eastman (1794-1850), active
1826-1828]
American (Savannah)
Tablespoons (six)
c. 1820-1828
Coin silver
8 ¾ x 1 ¾ in. (22.2 x 4.5 cm.)

*Mark: verso, in rectangle, stamped "PEN-
FIELD & CO"*
Inscription: engraved, in script "Davenport"

*Provenance: descended in the Davenport
family to Mrs. Charles Bunker, 1965; Historic
Savannah Foundation.
Loan from Historic Savannah Foundation,
Isaiah Davenport House Museum*

146

Unknown maker
English
Cream pitcher
c. 1800
Sterling silver
4 ¾ x 4 ¾ x 2 ⅜ in. (12.1 x 12.1 x 6.1 cm.)

*Mark: verso, in Roman capitals without
frame "H" over "W", lion passant, crowned
leopard's head, sovereign's head, in Roman
capital in rectangle "C"*
*Inscription: engraved in script under spout,
in cartouche "M W J" [Mary Wallace
(Savage) Jones]*

*Provenance: Dr. George Jones (1766-1838); to
Noble W. Jones (1787-1818); to George Noble
Jones (1811-1876) and Mary Wallace (Savage)
Jones (1812-1869); to George Fenwick Jones
(1841-1876); to Mary Savage Jones (Mrs.
Clarence Gordon Anderson) (1873-1958); to
her niece Caroline Jones Wright (b. 1911).
Loan from Caroline Jones Wright*

147

Unknown maker, (IM or JM?)
American
Silver tobacco box
c. 1796-1803
1 1/4 x 6 1/8 x 2 3/4 in. (3.2 x 15.6 x 6.9 cm.)

*Mark: recto, left of c., on lip of body of box,
stamped in shield-shaped field "IM"*
*Inscription: entire box covered in decorative
engraving; on raised circular medallion on
top, engraved in script "John
Barnard/Wilmington Island" around
central motif of eagle with foliated branch
under sixteen stars*

*Provenance: probably belonged to Major
John Barnard (1750-1819) or his son John
Washington Barnard (1783-1826) [possibly
related to Timothy G. Barnard (6)]; descended
in an African American family in Georgia;
Mr. and Mrs. O. O. Thompson, Jr.
Loan from Mr. and Mrs. O. O. Thompson,
Jr., American Antiques*

148

Attributed to Philip Rundell (1743-1827)
English (London)
Soup tureen and cover
1819
Sterling silver
11 ¼ x 10 ½ x 20 in. (28.5 x 26.6 x 50.8 cm.)

*Mark: verso, on cover in Roman capitals in
rectangle, lion passant "PR", and in small
Roman in shield "d"; recto, on tureen body
near handle in Roman capitals in rectangle,
lion passant, crowned leopard's head in shield
"PR", and in small Roman in shield "d"*
*Inscription: recto, on cover engraved in script
c. "LPGJFM" [Louisa Porter Gilmer (1852-
1921) and Jacob Florance Minis (1852-1936)]*

*Provenance: descended in the Minis family;
Telfair Museum of Art.
Gift of the Minis Estate, 1938.10
Illustrated in Coleman, 1992, p. 98*

149

Attributed to T. Cox Savory (active 1827)
Dessert spoon
1827
English (London)
Sterling silver
8 ¾ x 1 ¹⁵/16 in. (22.2 x 4.9 cm.)

Mark: verso, of handle in Roman capitals in rectangle with incised pellet above center of rectangle "T.C.S.", lion passant, leopard's head, "o" in small Roman, sovereign's head in oval Inscription: engraved griffen on handle

Provenance: William Scarbrough (1776-1838) and Julia Bernard Scarbrough (1786-1851); to their daughter Julia Henrietta Scarbrough Barnsley (1810-1845); to her son George Scarborough Barnsley (1837-1918); to his daughter Elizabeth Agnes Barnsley Holland (1884-1936); to her five children: Marjorie Bowe Holland (George Barnsley Holland's widow), Harold Barnsley Holland, Julia Margaret Holland MacDonell, Robert Barnsley Holland, and Mary Holland Grizzle; Georgia Historical Society.
Loan from Georgia Historical Society

150

Unknown maker
Covered coffee urn
c. 1820-1830
English (Sheffield?)
Plated silver
Urn: 14 x 17 in. (35.5 x 43 cm.);
base: 7 x 7 in. (17.7 x 17.7 cm.)

Provenance: Ellen McGinnis McAlpin (Mrs. Henry McAlpin) (c. 1799-1831); to her daughter Ellen McAlpin (1822-1866); to her daughter Emma W. Schley (1865-1927?); to her daughter Alice Hunter (1887-1966); to her daughter Marjory Heyward (b. 1918).
Loan from Mrs. M. Heyward Mingledorff

151

John Settle and Henry Wilkinson
(active c. 1828-1831)
Cruet stand with castors
1830-1831
English (Sheffield)
Silver plate, glass
Stand: 10 ⅛ x 10 in. (25.7 x 25.4 cm.)

Mark: recto, on stand to left of cartouche, in quatrefoil "I" and "S" over "H" and "W", lion passant; recto, on stand to right of cartouche, sovereign's head in oval, crown and in small Roman in rectangle "h"; mustard lid: in quatrefoil "I" and "S" over "H" and "W", lion passant, sovereign's head in oval, crown and in small Roman in rectangle "g"; shaker lid: in half of quatrefoil "I" and "S", lion passant, sovereign's head, crown and in small Roman in rectangle "h"

Provenance: George Welshman Owens (1786-1856); to his daughter Margaret Wallace Owens Thomas (1829-1915); to her daughter Margaret Gray Thomas (1871-1951); Telfair Museum of Art.
Bequest of Margaret Gray Thomas, 1951, OT S-60
Illustrated in Coleman, 1992, p. 103

152

Unknown maker
French (Paris)
Vase (one of a pair)
c. 1825
Hard-paste porcelain with overglaze enamels and gilt
12 ⅝ x 3 ¾ x 3 ¾ in. (32 x 9.5 x 9.5 cm.)

Source of print: possibly a scene from Shakespeare

Provenance: George Welshman Owens (1786-1856); to his daughter Margaret Wallace Owens Thomas (1829-1915); to her daughter Margaret Gray Thomas (1871-1951); Telfair Museum of Art.
Bequest of Margaret Thomas, 1951.43.2

153

Unknown maker
French (Paris)
Vase
c. 1825
Hard-paste porcelain with overglaze enamels and gilt
9 x 3 ½ x 5 in. (22.9 x 8.9 x 12.7 cm.)

Source of print: possibly adapted from Nicolas Poussin, The Ashes of Phocion Collected by His Widow, France, 1648.

Provenance: Mary Elizabeth Dulles Cheves (d. 1837); to her daughter Louisa S. Cheves McCord (1810-1879); to her daughter Louisa Rebecca McCord Smythe (1845-1928); to her daughter Hannah McCord Smythe Wright (1874-1955); to her son David M. Wright (1909-1968); to his wife Caroline Jones Wright (b. 1911).
Loan from Caroline Jones Wright

154

Unknown maker
English (?)
Dessert plate
c. 1810
Hard-paste porcelain with overglaze enamel and gilt decoration
7 ⅛ dia. x ¾ in. (18.1 x 1.9 cm.)

Inscription: c., in script "OES"

Provenance: Oliver Sturges (1779-1824); to his daughter Elizabeth Sturges Hunter (Mrs. William Presstman) (1803-1872); to her daughter Sarah Campbell Hunter Claghorn (Mrs. Joseph Samuel) (1828-1886); to her son Rufus Samuel Claghorn (1849-1916); to his daughter Marguerite Claghorn Gilchrist (Mrs. Robert) (1889-1952); to her daughter Margaret Claghorn Gilchrist Livingston (Mrs. Lorton Stoy) (b. 1919).
Loan from Mrs. Lorton Stoy Livingston

155

Unknown maker
French
Serving platter
c. 1830-1840
Porcelain with enamel and gilt overglaze
decoration
13 ½ x 19 ½ x 2 ⅛ in. (34.3 x 49.5 x 5.4 cm.)

Provenance: descended in the Jackson family
of Savannah.
Loan from Michael Everett Collins

156

Unknown maker
Chinese, for export
Punch bowl
c. 1790-1800
Porcelain with gilt and overglaze
enamel decoration
15 x 7 in. (38.1 x 17.8 cm.) base
dia. 7 ⅝ in. (19.4 cm.)

Print source: one side panel illustrates the
story of Neptune and Caenis from Ovid's
Metamorphosis, *xii, p. 193 ff; a second panel*
is based on the story of Perseus and
Andromeda, as painted by Titian (c. 1562-
1565); the third panel shows Phaethon, son of
Helios and Clymene, driving the solar chariot
(Ovid, Metamorphosis, *i., p. 750 ff)*

Provenance: William Glen (1701-1785); to his
son John Glen (1744-1799) [mentioned in Will
June 3, 1799, "large 2 gallon china bowl to my
daughter Margaret Hunter wife of Mr. Wm
Hunter," and in Inventory June 3, 1799, "1
large China bowl $4.00."]; to his daughter
Margaret Glen Hunter (1775-1836); to her son
William Presstman (1799-1869); to his daugh-
ter Sarah Campbell Hunter Claghorn (Mrs.
Joseph Samuel) (1828-1886); to her son Rufus
Samuel Claghorn (1849-1916); to his daughter
Marguerite Claghorn Gilchrist (Mrs. Robert)
(1889-1952); to her daughter Margaret
Claghorn Gilchrist Livingston (Mrs. Lorton
Stoy) (b. 1919).
Loan from Mrs. Lorton Stoy Livingston

157

Unknown maker
Chinese, for export
Covered soup tureen and stand
c. 1800
Porcelain with gilt and overglaze blue
enamel decoration
Stand: 15 ¾ x 13 ⅜ x 2 in. (40 x 34 x
5.1 cm.); tureen with cover: 10 ½ x 15 x 8 in.
(26.7 x 38.1 x 20.3 cm.); o.h. 11 in.
(27.9 cm.)

Inscription: no longer legible, recto, c., in
oval cartouche, gold script "O E S"

Provenance: Oliver Sturges (1779-1824); to
his daughter Elizabeth Sturges Hunter (Mrs.
William Presstman) (1803-1872); to her
daughter Sarah Campbell Hunter Claghorn
(Mrs. Joseph Samuel) (1828-1886); to her son
Rufus Samuel Claghorn (1849-1916); to his
daughter Marguerite Claghorn Gilchrist
(Mrs. Robert) (1889-1952); to her daughter
Margaret Claghorn Gilchrist Livingston
(Mrs. Lorton Stoy) (b. 1919).
Loan from Mrs. Lorton Stoy Livingston

158

Attributed to Bakewell, Page and
Bakewell (1808-1882)
American or Anglo-Irish (possibly
Pittsburgh)
Sugar bowl with cover
c. 1820-1830
Cut glass
8 3/16 x 5 ⅛ in. (20.8 x 13.1 cm.)

Provenance: descended in the Telfair family;
Telfair Museum of Art.
Bequest of Mary Telfair, 1875, 00.96
Illustrated in Coleman, 1992, p. 114

159 a,b

George Gemenden & Co.
American (Savannah)
Glass soda bottles (two)
c. 1840
Green bottle glass with molded eagle
and flag motif
7 ½ x 2 ½ in. (19.1 x 6.4 cm.)

Inscriptions: verso, raised lettering "GEO.
GEMENDEN [& Co?],
SAVANNAH/GEO"

Provenance: excavated from privy site in
Savannah, on Indian Street, 1960s.
Loan from H. Paul Blatner

160 a,b

Philip Young & Co.
American (Savannah)
Glass soda bottles (two)
c. 1840
Green bottle glass with molded eagle
and flag motif
7 ½ x 2 ½ in. (19.1 x 6.4 cm.)

Inscriptions: verso, raised lettering "PHILIP
YOUNG/& Co./SAVANNAH/GA"
Loan from H. Paul Blatner

Provenance: a. saratoga top, double collar:
excavated from Civic Center site in
Savannah; b. blob top: excavated from a site
in Savannah, on the corner of Jones and
Barnard Street.

161

Unknown maker
English
Fender with two brackets, tongs and shovel
c. 1820
Brass, iron
Fender: 15 x 52 x 13 in. (38.1 x 132.1 x
33 cm.); tongs: o.l. 29 in. (73.7 cm.);
shovel: o.l. 30 ½ in. (77.5 cm.)

Provenance: George Welshman Owens
(1786-1856); to his daughter Margaret
Wallace Owens Thomas (1829-1915); to her
daughter Margaret Gray Thomas (1871-1951);
Telfair Museum of Art.
Bequest of Margaret Thomas, OT 1951.5.1-4

162

Unknown maker
American or English
Wire fire screen with iron swags
1800-1820
Brass and iron
51 x 9 in. (129.5 x 22.9 cm.)

Provenance: originally in the Bulloch-Habersham house on Orleans Square; Telfair Museum of Art.
Gift of Mrs. Lindsey Henderson, 1958.10

163

Unknown maker
English
Fire tools and implement holder
c. 1820
Stand: 27 x 11 in. (68 x 27 cm.); shovel:
28 in. (71 cm.); tongs: 26 in. (66 cm.)

Provenance: descended in the Jones family.
Loan from Caroline Jones Wright

164

Unknown maker
American
Coal grate and ash pan (one of a pair)
1830
Brass
Grate: 25 ½ x 33 x 18 in. (64.7 x 83.8 x 45.7 cm.); ash pan: 6 ½ x 25 ¾ x 15 ½ in. (16.5 x 65.4 x 39.3 cm.)

Provenance: the grate was originally in the house of Isaac (1780-1856) and Dinah (Cohen) Minis (1787-1874) on the NW corner of Hull and Barnard; to Abraham (1820-1889) and Lavinia Minis (1826-1923); to Abram (1859-1939) and Mabel Amelia (Henry) Minis (1870-1971); to their sons H. Philip (b. 1908) and Abram Minis, Jr. (1903-1971).
Gift of H. Philip Minis, 1951, OT 1958.1-2

165

Unknown maker
American
Pineapple mold
c. 1800-1850
Tin
7 x 4 ⅜ x 2 ⅛ in. (17.8 x 10.8 x 5.4 cm.)

Provenance: descended in the Telfair family; Telfair Museum of Art.
Bequest of Mary Telfair, 1875, 1900.238.2

166

Unknown maker
American
Belt buckle used by a member of the Savannah Volunteer Guards
c. 1830
Die stamped brass, silver plating
2 ¹³/16 x 2 ¹³/16 in. (7.2 x 7.2 cm.)

Inscription: embossed "SAVH. VOL. GUARDS/ 1802"

Provenance: excavated in downtown Savannah, 1970s.
Loan from H. Paul Blatner

167

Unknown maker
American
Belt buckle used by a member of the Republican Blues
c. 1810
Die stamped brass
2 ¼ x 3 in. (5.7 x 8.2 cm.)

Inscription: embossed on ribbon on shield "REPUBLICAN BLUES" "1808"

Provenance: excavated in Savannah at site of Barracks (DeSoto Hotel), 1960s.
Loan from H. Paul Blatner

168

John Pearson (active 1791-1817)
American (Savannah)
Button
c. 1800-1820
Die stamped brass, gold gilted
1 in. dia. (2.54 cm.)

Inscriptions: verso, embossed "J. PEARSON SAVANNAH"

Provenance: excavated in downtown Savannah, 1970s.
Loan from H. Paul Blatner

169

Moore and Baker
American (New York)
Long arm musket, percussion ignition system
1837
Walnut; iron; silver
Barrel: 42 in. (106.7 cm.); o.l.: 58 in. (147.3 cm.)

Inscription: engraved under silver eagle "Presented by his fellow soldiers to Richard D. Arnold May 1, 1837"; engraved on cheek rest "To defend our country republican blues 1808"; top of barrel engraved in black lettering "Moore & Baker NY"; on lock plate engraved "TD Moore"

Provenance: Richard D. Arnold, M.D. (1808-1876), Mayor of Savannah.
Loan from H. Paul Blatner

170

Edward Lovell (active 1818-1840)
American (Savannah)
Long arm shotgun, percussion ignition system
c. 1840
Walnut; iron; platinum blow out plug
Barrel: 31 in. (78.7 cm.); o.l.: 47 ¾ in. (121.3 cm.)

Inscription: on barrel rib, engraved "LONDON FINE TWIST"; on lock plate, engraved "E. LOVELL S$_{AV}$: Geo"

Provenance: descended in a Savannah family; Atlanta dealer, 1970s; auctioned by Richard Bourne to Norman Flayderman, 1970s; Dutch collector; H. Paul Blatner, 1980s.
Loan from H. Paul Blatner

171

Joseph Cooper
American (New York)
Long arm musket, flintlock ignition system
1833
Walnut; silver; iron
Barrel: 39 9/16 in. (100.5 cm.);
o.l.: 54 ¼ in. (137.8 cm.)

*Inscription: engraved on silver angel "8th
Jany 1833/Presented by the/Republican
Blues/To J.D. H[ug]hes"; on lock, engraved
"JOS^H. COOPER N-YORK"*

*Provenance: purchased from Atlanta dealer
who had purchased it in California, 1992.
Loan from H. Paul Blatner*

172

Unknown maker
American
Badge of the Anacreontic Society
1804-1810
Silver, gilt wash
3 6/16 x 1 ⅞ in. (8.5 x 4.8 cm.)

*Inscription: recto, c., in script
"Oliver./Sturges."; l., in Roman capitals
"SAVANNAH."; r., in Roman capitals
"ANACREONTIC SOCIETY."*

*Provenance: Oliver Sturges (1779-1824); to his
daughter Elizabeth Sturges Hunter (Mrs.
Williams); to her daughter Sarah Campbell
Hunter Claghorn (Mrs. Joseph Samuel)
(1828-1886); to her son Rufus Samuel
Claghorn (1849-1916); to his daughter
Marguerite Claghorn Gilchrist (Mrs. Robert)
(1889-1952); to her daughter Margaret
Claghorn Gilchrist Livingston (Mrs. Lorton
Stoy) (b. 1919).
Loan from Mrs. Lorton Stoy Livingston*

173

Unknown maker
American
Badge of the Anacreontic Society
(1804-1810)
Silver, gilt wash
3 ⅜ x 1 ⅞ in. (8.5 x 4.8 cm.)

*Inscription: recto, c., in script
"W^m/Woodbridge"; l., in Roman capitals*

"SAVANNAH"; r., in Roman capitals
"ANACREONTIC SOCIETY"

*Provenance: descended in the Woodbridge
family; to Mrs. Caroline Lamar Woodbridge;
to Georgia Historical Society.
Loan from Georgia Historical Society*

174

Unknown maker
American
Wedding brooch
c. 1832
Gold, pearls, garnets
2 ½ x 1 ⅝ in. (6.4 x 4.1 cm.)

*Provenance: gift from Robert E. Lee to
Elizabeth Anne MacKay Stiles (Eliza)
(Mrs. Wm. Henry Stiles I) upon her marriage
to William Henry Stiles in 1832; to her
daughter in-law Eliza Clifford Gordon Stiles
(Mrs. Wm Henry Stiles II) (d. 1926); to her
granddaughter Frances Dorothy Stiles White
(1889-1979); to her daughter Mary Elizabeth
White Layton (b. 1925).
Loan from Elizabeth Layton*

175

Unknown maker
Mourning ring
1805
Gold, pearls, black enamel
Sight: ⅞ x ¾ x ½ in. (2.2 x 1.9 x 1.3 cm.)

*Inscription: inside band "Ob^t 9 Jan^Y/1805/act.
73^{Ys}"; recto "NOBLE/WIMBERLY JONES"*

*Provenance: commissioned upon the death of
Dr. Noble Wymberly Jones (1722-1805); found
at an antique show.
Loan from Davida Tenenbaum Deutsch*

176

Unknown
Probably English
*Nymphs Decorating a Term of Ceres
with Flowers*
c. 1800
Wool, silk chenille, and watercolor
on silk; linen backing
10 ¾ x 13 ¾ in. (27.3 x 34.9 cm.)

*Provenance: possibly descended in the
Screven family; Telfair Museum of Art.
Gift of Frank B. Screven in memory of his
mother, Mrs. Frank B. Screven and Gift of
Friends of Miss P. Holst, 1961.28*

177

Frances Tillman
American (Savannah)
Bedspread
1812
Linen, cotton embroidery
Framed: 86 ½ x 81 ½ in. (219.7 x 207 cm.)

*Inscriptions: c., worked "E PLURIBUS
UNUM/Frances Tillman/Mar. 4, 1812*

*Provenance: Price Gilbert; Mrs. Richard
Winn Courts; Westville Historic Handicrafts,
Inc., 1972.
Loan from Westville Historic Handicrafts,
Inc.*

178

Mary Elizabeth Clayton Miller Taylor
(1774-1846)
American (Savannah)
Appliqued quilt, Tree of Life pattern
c. 1824
Glazed chintz printed by John Hewson
(Philadelphia, c. 1745-1821), cotton
103 x 104 ¾ in. (261.2 x 266.1 cm.)

*Inscription: signed in ink under central
appliqué "William Taylor/from his/Grand
Mother/1824"*

*Provenance: Mary Elizabeth Clayton Miller
Taylor; to her grandson William Taylor (1822-
1893); to his niece Mary Dalzelle Taylor
Spence (b. 1881); to her daughter-in-law
Isabel Austin Walker Spence (Mrs. Nelson);
Sotheby Parke Bernet; Davida Tenenbaum
Deutsch; Telfair Museum of Art.
Museum purchase with funds from Albert
Stoddard, 1983.1*

Attributed to Sarah Anderson Stites
Gordon (Mrs. William Washington
Gordon) (1816-1882)
American (Savannah)
Vase of flowers
1831-1832
Framed: 25 3/16 x 15 ⅛ in. (64 x 38.4 cm.)
Silk, wool, silk ribbon, lace, other fibers

Provenance: found in the attic of the Wayne-
Gordon House (1953); assumed to have
descended in the Gordon family.
Loan from Juliette Gordon Low Birthplace

180

Unknown maker
American or English
Leaf of stationery with embossed
classical motif
c. 1812
Paper
7 ¾ x 4 15/16 in. (19.6 x 12.5 cm.)

Inscriptions: "The officers of the Chatham
Regiment/request the honor of Thoˢ. Chase
Esqʳ's company/to dinner on Friday next at
half past three/O'clock P.M. at the Exchange
Coffee house/Savᵇ. Decʳ. 2ⁿᵈ 1812 Lieut.
Gaston/"Rahn/"Thoˢ. Gribbin Stewards"

Provenance: Jermiah T. and Richard Chase
papers, MS. 278, Manuscripts Division,
Maryland Historical Society Library.
Loan from Maryland Historical Society

181

Fairman, Draper, Underwood & Co.
(active 1823-1827), engravers and printers
American (Philadelphia)
Engraved certificate of 10 shares in the
Bank of the United States
c. 1823-1827
Paper
7 ½ x 9 ¾ in. (19 x 24.7 cm.)

Inscription: "UNITED/BANK OF THE
UNITED STATES OF AMERICA/Nᵒ
35.828 Be it known that Margaret
Telfair/of Savannah, Geo. is/entitled to
Ten/Shares in the Capital Stock of the

Bank of/the United States transferable
at the/said Bank by the said Margaret
Telfair/or her Attorney./Witness the Seal
of the President Directors and Company
of/the Bank of the United States at
Philadelphia the/Eighth day of February
1831/W. McIlvaine Cashier N. Biddle
President/Fairman Draper Underwood
& Cᵒ."
In foreground: Lady Liberty in classical garb
holding a spear in her left hand and her right
arm is draped over the neck of a bald eagle on
a Federal shield; in middleground: ship in
water/mouth to a river; in distance: light-
house and lighthouse building on an embank-
ment at mouth to river

Provenance: descended in the Telfair family;
in Telfair papers on deposit at the Georgia
Historical Society.
Loan from Georgia Historical Society

182

Unknown maker
English (possibly Birmingham)
Retailed by J. & I. Cox (James & John
Cox, active 1819-1830)
American (New York)
Two arm Argand lamp
c. 1825-1830
Bronze; reproduction glass shades
26½ x 17 in. (67.3 x 43.2 cm.)

Marks: on each burner, embossed on brass
labels "J & I COX/NEW YORK"

Provenance: George Welshman Owens
(1786-1856); to his daughter Margaret
Wallace Owens Thomas (1829-1915); to her
daughter Margaret Gray Thomas (1871-1951);
Telfair Museum of Art.
Bequest of Margaret Thomas, 1951.26

183

Unknown maker
English or American
Sunumbra lamp
c. 1825-1840
Gilt over bronze; reproduction glass shade
31 x 7 in. (78.7 x 17.8 cm.); globe 11 ¼ x
10 in. (28.5 x 25 cm.)

Provenance: associated with the Harrison
family, Savannah.
Loan from Juliette Gordon Low Birthplace

184

Unknown
English
Tripod candlesticks (pair)
c. 1800-1810
Brass
11 9/16 in. (29.4 cm.)

Provenance: purchased at the Robert
Habersham house sale, 1916; gift in memory
of Madeline Dub Spiegelberg by her children
to Historic Savannah Foundation; Telfair
Museum of Art
Transfer from Historic Savannah
Foundation, 1991.5.2.a-b

185

Unknown maker
English
Candlestick
c. 1800-1820
Brass
12 ½ x 4 ⅜ in. (31.8 x 11.1 cm.)

Provenance: excavated from a privy in
Savannah at Juliette Gordon Low site c. 1967;
H. Paul Blatner, 1994.
Loan from H. Paul Blatner

Account of the Reception of General Lafayette in Savannah on Saturday, March 19, 1825. (Savannah: W. T. Williams, 1825).

Ackermann, Rudolph. *The Repository of Arts, Literature, Commerce, Manufactures, Fashions, and Politics.* (London, 1809-1828).

Adams, Elizabeth Bryding. *The Dwight and Lucille Beeson Wedgwood Collection at the Birmingham Museum of Art.* (Birmingham, AL: Birmingham Museum of Art, 1992).

Alexander, Forsyth M. "Cabinet Warehousing for the Southern Atlantic Ports 1783-1820." *Journal of Early Southern Decorative Arts,* v. 15, # 2 (November, 1989), pp. 1-42.

Arrowsmith, James. *An Analysis of Drapery, or the Upholsterer's Assistant.* (London, 1819; reprinted New York: Acanthus Press, 1993).

Avery, Catherine B., ed. *The New Century Classical Handbook.* (New York: Appleton-Century-Crofts, Inc., 1962).

Baker, W. D. John and Warren. *Old English Lustre Pottery.* (Newport, GB: R. H. Johns, Ltd., 1951).

Barnard, Harry. *Chats on Wedgwood Ware.* (New York: Frederick A. Stokes Company, Publisher, 1924).

Barquist, David. *American Tables and Looking Glasses in the Mabel Brady Garvan and Other Collections at Yale University.* (New Haven, CT: Yale University Press, 1992).

Bassett, Beth. "Edgerton Chester Garvin: Photographer." *Brown's Guide to Georgia.* v. 8 , # 6 (June, 1980).

Beard, Geoffrey. *Craftsmen and Interior Decoration in England 1660-1820.* (London: Bloomsbury Books, 1981).

_____ and Christopher Gilbert, eds. *Dictionary of English Furniture Makers 1660-1840.* (Leeds, GB: Furniture History Society, 1986).

Beasley, Ellen. "Samuel Williamson: Philadelphia Silversmith, 1794-1813." (Unpublished M.A. Thesis, University of Delaware, Winterthur Program in Early American Culture, 1964).

Beecher, Catherine and Harriet Beecher Stowe. *American Woman's Home.* (New York: J. B. Ford and Co., 1869).

Bell, Malcolm Jr. "Ease and Elegance, Madeira and Murder: the Social Life of Savannah's City Hotel." *Georgia Historical Quarterly,* v. 76, #3 (Fall, 1992), pp. 551-76.

_____. *Major Butler's Legacy: Five Generations of a Slave-holding Family.* (Athens, GA: University of Georgia Press, 1987).

Bénézit, E. *Dictionnaire critique et documentaire des Peintres, Sculpteurs, Déssinateurs et Graveurs.* (France: Librairie Grund, 1948-1955).

Birmingham Trade Catalogue...The Argand or Air Lamps, among the following patterns are represented with glasses ... lamps of every description for use and ornament. (Birmingham, GB: c. 1812).

Bishop, Robert. *Centuries and Styles of the American Chair 1640-1970.* (New York: E. P. Dutton & Co., Inc., 1972).

Bivins, John. "A Catalog of Northern Furniture with Southern Provenance." *Journal of Early Southern Decorative Arts,* v. 15, # 2 (November, 1989), pp. 43-91.

Bloit, Michel. *Trois Siècles de Porcelaine de Paris.* (Paris: Editions Hervas, 1988).

Bloom, Eric ed. *Grove's Dictionary of Music and Musicians.* (New York: St. Martin's Press Inc., 1954).

Boggs, Marion Alexander, ed. *The Alexander Letters 1787-1900.* (Athens, GA: University of Georgia Press, 1980).

Bolton, Henry Carrington and Reginald Pelham Bolton. *The Family of Bolton in England and America, 1100-1894.* (New York: Privately printed, 1895).

Bolton, Robert T. *Genealogical and Biographical Account of the Family Bolton in England and America.* (New York: A. Gray, 1862).

Bolton, Theodore. *Early American Portrait Painters in Miniature.* (New York: F. F. Sherman, 1921).

_____ and George Groce. "John Wesley Jarvis." *Art Quarterly.* v. 1 , # 4 (Autumn, 1938).

Bolton-Smith, Robin. *Portrait Miniatures in the National Museum of Art.* (Chicago: University of Chicago Press, 1984).

Bragard, Professor Roger and Dr. Ferdinand J. De Hen. *Musical Instruments in Art and History.* (London: Barrie and Rockliff, 1967).

Braynard, Frank O. *S. S. Savannah: The Elegant Steam Ship.* (Athens, GA: University of Georgia Press, 1963; reprinted, New York: Dover Publications, Inc., 1988).

Bright, Marion Converse. *Early Georgia Portraits 1715-1879.* (Athens, GA: University of Georgia Press, 1975).

Brilliant, Richard. *Pompeii: The Treasury of Rediscovery.* (New York: Clarkson N. Potter, 1979).

Britt, Albert Sidney, Jr. *The Champion-Harper-Fowlkes House: Headquarters Society of the Cincinnati in the State of Georgia.* (Savannah: Society of the Cincinnati, 1988).

Brockway, Jean Lambert. "Malbone, American Miniature Painter." *The American Magazine of Art*, v. 20, # 4 (April, 1929), pp. 185-191.

Bryan, Michael. *Dictionary of Painters and Engravers, Biographical and Critical.* Robert Edmund Graves and George C. Williamson, eds. 5 vols. (London: George Bell, 1903).

Buckingham, James Silk. *The Slave States of America.* (London: Fisher, Son & Co., 1842).

Burton, Milby. *Charleston Furniture 1700-1825.* (Charleston, SC: Charleston Museum, 1955).

Carll, M. Allison. "An Assessment of English Furniture Imports into Charleston, SC, 1760-1800." *Journal of Early Southern Decorative Arts*, v. 11, # 2 (November, 1985), pp. 1-18.

Carson, Marian. "Sheraton's influence in Philadelphia." *The Magazine Antiques*, v. 63, # 4 (April, 1953), pp. 84-87.

Catalano, Kathleen M. "Cabinetmaking in Philadelphia 1820-1840, Transition from Craft to Industry." *Winterthur Portfolio*, v. 13 (1979), pp. 81-138.

_____. "The Empire Style: Philadelphia," in Mary Jane Madigan, ed. *Nineteenth Century Furniture: Innovation, Revival and Reform.* (New York: Art and Antiques, 1982), pp. 10-17.

Cate, Margaret Davis. *Our Todays and Yesterdays.* (Brunswick, GA: Glover Brothers, 1930; Spartanburg, SC: The Reprint Co., 1972), pp. 148-150.

Cheney, Louis T. "The Telfair and Its Paintings." *The Magazine Antiques*, v. 91, # 3 (March, 1967), pp. 33-37.

Chamberlain, Samuel and Narcissa. *Southern Interiors of Charleston, South Carolina.* (New York: Hastings House, 1956).

Christman, Margaret C.S. *The First Federal Congress, 1789-1791.* (Washington, DC: Smithsonian Institution Press, 1989).

Clark, Willene B. *The Stained Glass Art of William Jay Bolton.* (Syracuse, NY: Syracuse University Press, 1992).

Coleman, Feay Shellman. "Mantels by W. and J. Frazee, Alexander Telfair House, Savannah, Georgia." (Unpublished manuscript, Owens-Thomas House files, n.d.).

_____. *Nostrums for Fashionable Entertainments: Dining in Georgia, 1800-1850.* (Savannah: Telfair Academy of Arts and Sciences, Inc., 1992).

Coleman, Kenneth and Charles Stephen Gurr, eds. *Dictionary of Georgia Biography.* 2 v. (Athens, GA: University of Georgia Press, 1983).

Coleman, Kenneth. "Savannah - Georgia's port city." *The Magazine Antiques*, v. 91, # 3 (March, 1967), pp. 322-323.

Collard, Frances. *Regency Furniture.* (Suffolk, GB: Antique Collectors' Club, 1985).

Comstock, Helen. *American Furniture: A Complete Guide to Seventeenth, Eighteenth, and Early Nineteenth Century Styles.* (New York: The Viking Press, 1962).

The Connoisseur's Complete Period Guide to the Houses, Decoration, Furnishing and Chattels of the Classic Periods. (New York: Bonanza Books, 1968).

Cooper, Wendy A. *Classical Taste in America.* (Baltimore: Baltimore Museum of Art, 1993).

Coulter, E. Merton. "Presidential Visits to Georgia During Ante-Bellum Times." *Georgia Historical Quarterly*, v. 55, # 3 (Fall, 1971), p. 329 ff.

Cornelius, Charles Over. *Furniture Masterpieces of Duncan Phyfe.* (Garden City, NY: Doubleday, Page & Company, 1922; reprinted New York: Dover Publications, Inc., 1970).

Cutten, George Barton. *The Silversmiths of Georgia: Together with Watchmakers and Jewelers 1733-1850.* (Savannah: The Pigeonhole Press, 1958).

Davidson, Marshall B. and Elizabeth Stillinger. *The American Wing: The Metropolitan Museum of Art.* (New York: Alfred A. Knopf, 1985).

Davis, Lee H. "The Greek Revival Influence on American Clock Case Design and Empire Clock Case Development." Supplement to the *Bulletin of the National Association of Watch and Clock Collectors, Inc.*, # 18 (Spring, 1991), pp. 9-23.

Davis, Raymond Earle Jr. "Scarbrough House Hosted Fancy Ball." (Unpublished manuscript, Savannah: 1976).

Deak, Gloria Gilda. *Picturing America, 1497-1899: Prints, Maps, and Drawings Bearing on the New World Discoveries and on the Development of the Territory that is Now the United States.* (Princeton: Princeton University Press, 1988).

De Groër, Leon. *Decorative Arts in Europe 1790-1850*. (New York: Rizzoli, 1985).

Dewing, Maria Richards (Mrs. C.W.). *Beauty in the Household*. (New York: Harper and Brothers, 1882).

Dictionary of National Biography. (London: Oxford University Press, 1937-8).

Dietz, Ulysses S. *Century of Revivals: Nineteenth-Century American Furniture from the Collection of the Newark Museum*. (Newark: The Newark Museum, 1983).

Downing, Andrew Jackson. *The Architecture of Country Houses*. (New York: D. Appleton & Company, 1850; reprinted New York: Dover Publications, Inc., 1969).

Ducoff-Barone, Deborah. "Philadelphia Furniture Makers, 1800-1815." *The Magazine Antiques*, v. 139, # 5 (May, 1991), pp. 982-995.

_____. "Philadelphia Furniture Makers, 1816-1835." *The Magazine Antiques*, v. 145, # 5 (May, 1994), pp. 742-755.

Elder, William Voss III and Jayne E. Stokes. *American Furniture 1680-1880 from the Collection of the Baltimore Museum of Art*. (Baltimore: Baltimore Museum of Art, 1987).

Ellet, Mrs. *Women Artists in All Ages and Countries*. (New York: Harper and Brothers Publishers, 1859).

Fales, Dean A., Jr. *American Painted Furniture 1660-1880*. (New York: E.P. Dutton and Company, Inc., 1972).

Farnham, Katharine Gross and Callie Huger Efird. "Early Silversmiths and the Trade in Georgia." *The Magazine Antiques*, v. 99, # 3 (March, 1971), pp. 380-385.

Federal Writers' Project. *Savannah*. (Savannah: Review Printing Co., 1937).

Feld, Stuart P. *Neo-Classicism in America: Inspiration and Innovation 1810-1840*. (New York: Hirschl and Adler Galleries, Inc., 1991).

Fennimore, Donald L. "A Labeled Card Table by Michel Bouvier." *The Magazine Antiques*, v. 103, # 4 (April, 1973), pp. 761-763.

_____. "American Neoclassical Furniture and its European Antecedents." *The American Art Journal*, v. 13, # 4 (Autumn, 1981), pp. 49-65.

_____. "Egyptian influence in early nineteenth century American Furniture." *The Magazine Antiques*, v. 137, # 5 (May, 1990), pp. 1190-1201.

_____. *Silver and Pewter*. (New York: Alfred A. Knopf, 1984).

_____ and Robert T. Trump. "Joseph B. Barry, Philadelphia cabinetmaker." *The Magazine Antiques*, v. 135, # 5 (May, 1989), pp. 1212-1225.

Fielding, Mantle. *Dictionary of American Painters, Sculptors and Engravers*. (New York: J.F. Carr, 1965).

Flanigan, J. Michael. *American Furniture from the Kaufman Collection*. (Washington: National Gallery of Art, 1986).

Flores, Jan. "Archibald Stobo Bulloch." (Unpublished manuscript, History 500, Armstrong State College, Savannah, GA, 1990).

Fore, George T. and Associates. *Architectural Investigations of the Owens-Thomas House, Savannah, Georgia*. (Raleigh, NC, for the Telfair Museum of Art, 1995).

_____. *The Owens-Thomas House, Savannah, Georgia, Conservation Studies, Finishes Analysis*. (Raleigh, NC, for the Telfair Museum of Art, 1991).

Foster, J.J. *A Dictionary of Painters of Miniatures (1525-1850)*. (1926; reprinted New York: Burt Franklin, 1968).

Fraser, Esther S. "Painted Furniture in America: I. The Sheraton Fancy Chair 1790-1817." *The Magazine Antiques*, v. 5, # 6 (June, 1924), pp. 302-306.

_____. "Painted Furniture in America: II. The Period of Stencilling." *The Magazine Antiques*, v. 6, # 3 (September, 1923), pp. 141-146.

Garrett, Elizabeth Donaghy. *At Home: The American Family, 1750-1870*. (New York: Harry N. Abrams, Inc., Publishers, 1990).

Giffen, Lee. "Living with Antiques: Wormsloe, the home of Mrs. Craig Barrow." *The Magazine Antiques*, v. 91, # 3 (March, 1967), pp. 50-53.

Gilchrist, Alexander. *Life of William Etty, R.A.* (London: David Bogue, 1855).

Godden, Geoffrey A. *An Illustrated Encyclopedia of British Pottery and Porcelain*. (New York: Bonanza Books, 1966).

Goldsborough, Jennifer Faulds. *Eighteenth and Nineteenth Century Maryland Silver in the Collection of the Baltimore Museum of Art*. (Baltimore: The Baltimore Museum of Art, 1975).

_____. *Silver in Maryland*. (Baltimore: Museum and Library of Maryland History, Maryland Historical Society, 1983).

Govan, Thomas Payne. *Nicholas Biddle, Nationalist and Public Banker, 1786-1844.* (Chicago: University of Chicago Press, 1959).

Gowans, Alan. "Freemasonry and the neoclassic style in America." *The Magazine Antiques*, v. 77, # 2 (February, 1960), pp. 172-175.

Granger, Mary, ed. *Savannah River Plantations: Savannah Writers Project.* (Savannah: The Georgia Historical Society, 1947).

Grant, Col. Maurice Harold. *A Dictionary of British Sculptors.* (London: Rockliff, 1953).

Green, Robert Alan. "William Gale and Son, New York." *The Magazine Silver*, v. 2, # 2 (March-April, 1978), pp. 6-11.

Griffin, William W., et al. *Neat Pieces: The Plain-Style of Furniture and Nineteenth Century Georgia.* (Atlanta: Atlanta Historical Society, 1983).

Griffiths, William H. *The Story of the American Bank Note Company.* (New York: the company, 1959).

Groce, George C. and David H. Wallace. *The New-York Historical Society's Dictionary of Artists in America, 1564-1860.* (New Haven, CT: Yale University Press; London: Oxford University Press, 1957).

Gross, Katherine Wood. "The Sources of Furniture Sold in Savannah 1789-1815." (Unpublished M.A. Thesis, University of Delaware, Winterthur Program in Early American Culture, 1967).

Hamlin, Talbot. *Greek Revival Architecture in America.* (London: Oxford University Press, 1944; reprinted, New York: Dover Publications, Inc., 1964).

Hardee, Charles S.H. *Reminiscences and Recollections of Old Savannah.* (Savannah: privately printed, 1928).

Hartridge, Walter C. "Architectural Trends in Savannah." *The Magazine Antiques*, v. 91, # 3 (March, 1967), pp. 4-10.

_____. *The Letters of Robert MacKay to His Wife, Written from Ports in America and England, 1795-1816.* (Athens, GA: The University of Georgia Press, under the auspices of The Georgia Society of the Colonial Dames of America, 1949).

Harvey, Lynn. "William Jay: A Conjectural Reconstruction of The Archibald Stobo Bulloch House, Savannah, Georgia." (Unpublished manuscript, Chicago, 1994).

_____. "King Cotton and Its Effect on the Savannah, Georgia of William Jay 1816-1821." (Unpublished manuscript, Chicago, 1995).

Hawley, Henry. *Neo-classicism: Style and Motif.* (Cleveland, OH: Cleveland Museum of Art, 1964).

Held, Julius S. and Donald Posner. *Seventeenth and Eighteenth Century Baroque Painting, Sculpture, Architecture.* (Englewood Cliffs, NJ: Prentiss-Hall, Inc. and New York: Harry N. Abrams, Inc., 1972).

Hevner, Carol E. "Rembrandt Peale, Art and Ambition." *The Magazine Antiques*, v. 127, # 2 (February, 1985), pp. 464-470.

Hewitt, V.H. and J.M. Keyworth. *As Good as Gold: 300 Years of British Bank Note Design.* (London: Published for the Trustees of the British Museum by British Museum Publications, 1987).

Hinton, J.H. *History and Topography of the United States.* (London: I.T. Hinton & Simpkin & Marshall, 1830-1832).

Hitchcock, Hugh Wiley. *Music in the United States: A Historical Introduction.* (Englewood, NJ: Prentice, Hall, 1974).

Hope, Ann M. *The Theory and Practice of Neoclassicism in English Painting: The Origins, Development and Decline of an Ideal.* (New York and London: Garland Publishing, Inc., 1988).

Hope, Thomas. *Household Furniture and Interior Decoration.* (London: Longman, Hurst, Rees and Orme, 1807).

Hunter, Anna C. "Savannah's Musical Heritage." *Savannah Morning News Magazine* (October 26, 1958), pp. 6-8.

Jenkins, Ian Jenkins, "Adam Buck and the vogue for Greek vases." *The Burlington Magazine*, v. 130, # 1023 (June, 1988), pp. 448-457.

Johnson, Dale T. *American Portrait Miniatures in the Manney Collection.* (New York: Metropolitan Museum, 1990).

Johnson, Marilyn A. "John Hewitt, Cabinetmaker." *Winterthur Portfolio*, v. 4 (1968), pp. 185-205.

Johnston, Sona K. *American Paintings 1750-1900.* (Baltimore: Baltimore Museum of Art, 1983).

Joy, Edward T. *English Furniture 1800-1851.* (London: Sotheby Parke Bernet Publications, 1977).

Kayser, J.C. *Commercial Directory of the United States.* (Philadelphia: J.C. Kayser and Co., 1823).

Keefe, John W. "English Lusterware from the Duckworth Collection." *The Magazine Antiques*, v. 96, # 3 (September, 1969), pp. 382-389.

Kelly, Alison. *Mrs. Coade's Stone*. (Upton-upon-Severn, GB: The Self Publishing Association Ltd., 1990).

Kelso, William M. *Captain Jones' Wormsloe: A Historical, Archaeological and Architectural Story of an 18th century Plantation Site Near Savannah, Georgia*. (Athens, GA: University of Georgia Press, 1979).

Kennedy, J. Robie. "Examples of Georgian and Greek Revival Work in the Far South." *Architectural Record*, v. 21, # 3 (March, 1907), pp. 215-228.

King, Thomas. *Modern Style of Cabinet Work Exemplified*. (London, 1835).

Klamkin, Marian. *The Return of Lafayette 1824-1825*. (New York: Charles Scribner's Sons, 1975).

Kole, Kay. *The Minis Family of Georgia 1733-1992*. (Savannah: Georgia Historical Society, 1992).

"The Kollock Papers, 1799-1850," ed. by Edith Duncan Johnston. *Georgia Historical Quarterly*, Part I, v. 30, # 3 (September, 1946), pp. 218-258; Part II, v. 30, # 4 (December, 1946), pp. 312-354; Part III, v. 31, # 1 (March, 1947), pp. 34-79; Part IV, v. 31, # 2 (June, 1947), pp. 121-162; Part V, v. 31, # 3 (September, 1947), pp. 195-232; Part VI, v. 31, #4 (December, 1947), pp. 289-321.

Lafayette, Hero of Two Worlds: The Art and Pageantry of His Farewell Tour of America, 1824-1825. (Hanover and London: University Press of New England, 1989).

Lafayette: The Nation's Guest: A Picture Book of Mementos which Express the Respect and Affection of the American People for Lafayette. (Winterthur, DE: Henry Francis DuPont Winterthur Museum, 1957).

La Mésangère, Pierre. *Collection des Meubles et Objets de Goût*. (Paris, 1802-1835).

Lane, Mills D. *Architecture of the Old South, Georgia*. (New York: Abbeville Press, 1990).

_____, ed. *The Rambler in Georgia: Travellers' Accounts of Frontier Georgia*. (Savannah: The Beehive Press, 1973).

_____. *Savannah Revisited: A Pictorial History*. (Athens, GA: University of Georgia Press, 1969).

Larsen, Ellouise Baker. *American Historical Views on Staffordshire China*. (New York: Doubleday, Doran and Company, Inc., 1939).

Lee, F.D. and J.L. Agnew. *Historical Record of the City of Savannah*. (Savannah: J.H. Estill, 1869).

Lerski, Hanna H. *William Jay, Itinerant English Arthitect, 1792-1837*. (Lanham, MD.: University Press of America, Inc., 1983).

Lewis, Philippa and Gillian Darley. *Dictionary of Ornament*. (New York: Pantheon Books, 1986).

Libin, Laurence. *American Musical Instruments in the Metropolitan Museum of Art*. (New York: W. W. Norton & Company, 1985).

McAlpin, Henry. *Souvenir of the Hermitage*. (Savannah: Privately printed, 1910).

McCaskey, Glen. "Caty Greene: Kiawah During the American Revolution." *Kiawah Island Legends*, v. 1, # 1 (Spring/Summer, 1990), pp. 86-88.

McClelland, Nancy. *Duncan Phyfe and the English Regency, 1795-1830*. (New York: William R. Scott, 1939; reprinted New York: Dover Publications, Inc., 1980).

McDonough, James V. "William Jay, Regency Architect in Georgia and South Carolina." (Ph.d. Dissertation, Princeton University, 1950).

McLeod, Mrs. Hugh (Rebecca Lamar), "The Loss of the Steamer Pulaski." *Georgia Historical Quarterly*, v. 3, # 2 (June, 1919), pp. 63-95.

Masonic Symbols in American Decorative Arts. (Lexington, MA: Scottish Rite Masonic Museum of Our National Heritage, 1976).

Meares, Catherine de Rosset. *Annals of the deRosset Family*. (Columbia, SC: R.L. Bryan, Co., 1906).

Metropolitan Museum of Art. *19th-Century America: Furniture and Other Decorative Arts*. (New York: The Museum, 1970).

Miller, Beth. "The Ridgelys of Hampton: New Perspectives on Musical Life in Nineteenth-Century Baltimore." (Paper delivered at the 1988 annual conference, The American Museological Society).

Miller, Edgar G. *American Antique Furniture*, 2 v. (Baltimore: The Lord Baltimore Press, 1937; reprinted New York: Dover Publications, Inc., 1966).

Mitchell, William Robert, Jr. *Classic Savannah*. (Savannah: Golden Coast Publishing Co., 1991).

Mongan, Agnes. *Harvard Honors Lafayette*. (Cambridge, MA: Fogg Art Museum, Harvard University, 1976).

Monkhouse, Christopher P. and Thomas S. Michie. *American Furniture in Pendleton House*. (Providence, RI: Museum of Art, Rhode Island School of Design, 1986).

Montgomery, Charles. *American Furniture: The Federal Period 1768-1825*. (New York: The Viking Press, 1966).

Montgomery, Horace ed. *Georgians in Profile: Historical Essays in Honor of Ellis Merton Coulter*. (Athens, GA: University of Georgia Press, 1958).

Morley, John. *Regency Design: Gardens, Buildings, Interiors and Furniture*. (London: A. Zwemmer Ltd., 1993).

Naeve, Milo and Lynn Springer Roberts. *A Decade of Decorative Arts: The Antiquarian Society of the Art Institute of Chicago*. (Chicago: The Art Institute of Chicago, 1986).

Nelson, Christina. "Transfer Printed creamware and Pearlware for the American Market." *Winterthur Portfolio*, v. 15, # 2 (Summer, 1980), pp. 93-115.

Nelson, Edna Deu Pree. "When is a Piano?" *The Magazine Antiques*, v. 29, # 6 (June, 1936), pp. 245-249.

The Newark Museum. *Classical America 1815-1845*. (Newark, NJ: The Museum, 1963).

New Oxford Annotated Bible, New Revised Standard Version with Apocrypha. (Oxford: University of Oxford Press, 1991).

The New-York Historical Society. *Catalogue of American Portraits in the New-York Historical Society*. 2 v. (New Haven and London: Yale University Press, for the Society, 1974).

New York Public Library. *One Hundred Notable American Engravers 1683-1840*. (New York: New York Public Library, 1928).

Nichols, Frederick Doveton. *The Architecture of Georgia*. (Savannah: Beehive Press, 1976).

Nicholson, Peter. *Principles of Architecture*. (London, 1798).

Northen, Wm. J. ed. *Men of Mark in Georgia*. 7 v. (Atlanta: A. B. Caldwell, Publisher, 1907-1911; reprinted Spartanburg, SC: Reprint Co., 1974).

Otto, Celia Jackson. *American Furniture of the Nineteenth Century*. (New York: The Viking Press, 1965).

Peabody, Elizabeth. "Elizabeth Peabody's Letters to Maria Chase of Salem, Relating to Lafayette's Visit in 1824." *Essex Institute Historical Collections*, v. 85 (October, 1949), pp. 360-368.

Pearce, John N., Lorraine W. Pearce, and Robert C. Smith, "The Meeks family of cabinetmakers." *The Magazine Antiques*, v. 85, # 4 (April, 1964), pp. 414-419.

Pennington, Estill Curtis. *A Southern Collection*. (Augusta, GA: Morris Communications Corporation, 1992).

Philadelphia Museum of Art. *Philadelphia: Three Centuries of American Art*. (Philadelphia: The Museum, 1976).

Pictorial Dictionary of British 19th Century Furniture Design. (Suffolk, GB: Antique Collectors' Club, 1977).

Pompeii as Source and Inspiration: Reflections in Eighteenth- and Nineteenth-Century Art; An Exhibition Organized by the 1976-1977 Graduate Students in the Museum Practice Program. (Ann Arbor: The University of Michigan Museum of Art, 1977).

Potts, Alex. *Sir Francis Chantrey, 1781-1841*. (London: National Portrait Gallery, 1981).

Priddy, Sumpter. "Fancy, Acceptance of an Attitude, Emergence of a Style." (Unpublished M.A. Thesis, University of Delaware, Winterthur Program in Early American Culture, 1981).

Rainwater, Dorothy T. *Encyclopedia of American Silver Manufacturers*. (Hanover, PA: Everybody's Press, 2nd ed., 1975).

Ralston, Ruth. "The Style Antique in Furniture: II. Its American Manifestation and their Prototypes." *The Magazine Antiques*, v. 48, # 4 (October, 1945), pp. 206-209, 220.

Rediscovering Pompeii: an Exhibition by IBM-ITALIA. (Rome: L'erma di Bretschneider, 1990).

Reid, Jane D. *The Oxford Guide to Classical Mythology in the Arts 1300-1990's*. (New York: Oxford University Press, 1993).

Reilly, Robin and George Savage. *The Dictionary of Wedgwood*. (Suffolk, GB: Antiques Collectors' Club Ltd., 1980).

Reinhold, Meyer. *Classica Americana. The Greek and Roman Heritage in the United States*. (Detroit: Wayne State University Press, 1984).

Rensch, Roslyn. *The Harp, Its History, Technique and Repertoire*. (New York and Washington: Praeger Publications, c. 1969).

Reps, John C. "C2 + L2 = S2?: Another Look at the Origins of Savannah's Town Plan," in Harvey H. Jackson and Phinizy Spalding, eds. *Forty Years of Diversity: Essays on Colonial Georgia*. (Athens, GA: University of Georgia Press, 1984), pp. 101-109.

Reynolds, Graham. *English Portrait Miniatures*. (Cambridge, MA: Cambridge University Press, 1988).

Rice, Foster W. "Checklist of paintings, miniatures and drawings by Nathaniel Jocelyn 1796-1881." *Bulletin of the Connecticut Historical Society*, v. 31, # 4 (October, 1966), pp. 97-145.

Richmond Portraits in an Exhibition of Makers of Richmond 1737-1860. (Richmond, VA: The Valentine Museum, 1949).

Rowland, Lawrence S. "'Alone on the River:' The Rise and Fall of the Savannah River Rice Plantations of St. Peter's Parish, South Carolina." *South Carolina Historical Magazine*, v. 88, # 3 (July, 1987), pp. 121-150.

Roworth, Wendy Wassyng, ed. *Angelica Kauffman: A Continental Artist in Georgian England*. (London: Reaktion Books, in association with Royal Pavillion, Art Gallery & Museums, Brighton, 1992).

Rueger, Christopher. *Musical Instruments and their Decoration: Historical Gems of European Culture*. (Cincinnati: Seven Hills Books, 1986).

Russell, Frank ed. *Architectural Monographs: John Soane*. (New York: St. Martin's Press, 1983).

Rutledge, Anna Wells. "Artists in the Life of Charleston, through Colony and State from Restoration to Reconstruction." *American Philosophical Society Transactions*, new ser., v. 39 (November, 1949), pp. 101-126.

_____. "A French Priest, Painter and Architect in the United States: Joseph-Pierre Picot de Limoëlin de Clorivière." *Carolina Art Association Catalogue* (Charleston, SC: Carolina Art Association, 1936).

Schorsch, Anita. *Mourning Becomes America: Mourning Art in the New Nation*. (Harrisburg, PA: William Penn Memorial Museum, 1976).

_____. "Mourning Art: A Neoclassical Reflection in America." *The American Art Journal*, v. 8, # 1 (May, 1976), pp. 5-15.

Severens, Martha R. *The Miniature Portrait Collection of the Carolina Art Association*. (Charleston, SC: Gibbes Art Gallery, 1984).

_____. *Selections from the Collection of the Carolina Art Association*. (Charleston, SC: Carolina Art Association, 1977).

Shaw, Joshua. *U.S. Directory for the Use of Travellers and Merchants*. (Philadelphia: James Maxwell, 1822).

Shellman, Feay. *The Octagon Room*. (Savannah: Telfair Academy of Arts and Sciences, Inc., 1982).

Sheraton, Thomas. *Cabinet Dictionary*. (London, 1803; reprinted New York: Dover Publications, Inc., 1970).

_____. *Cabinet-Maker and Upholsterer's Drawing-Book*. (London, 1793-1802; reprinted New York: Dover Publications, Inc., 1972).

Sherwood, Adiel. *A Gazetteer of the State of Georgia*. 3rd ed. (Washington City [DC]: P. Force, 1837).

Sloane, Jeanne Vibert. "A Duncan Phyfe Bill and the furniture it documents." *The Magazine Antiques*, v. 131, no. 5 (May, 1987), pp. 1106-1113.

Smith, Alan. *The Illustrated Guide to Liverpool Herculaneum Pottery*. (London: Barrie and Jenkins, 1970).

Smith, George. *Cabinet-Maker's and Upholsterer's Guide, Drawing Book and Repository*. (London: Jones & Co., 1826[8?]).

_____. *A Collection of Designs for Household Furniture and Interior Decoration*. (London: J. Taylor, 1808).

_____. *A Collection of Ornamental Designs after the Manner of the Antique Compos'd for the Use of Architects, Ornamental Painters, Statuaries, Carvers, Castors in Metal, Paper Makers, Carpet, Silk and Printed Calico Manufacturers, and every Trade Dependent on the Fine Arts*. (London: J. Taylor, 1812).

Smith, Jane Webb. *Georgia's Legacy: History Charted Through the Arts*. (Athens, GA: University of Georgia Press, 1985).

Smith, Robert C. "Architecture and sculpture in nineteenth-century mirror frames." *The Magazine Antiques*, v. 109, # 2 (February, 1976), pp. 350-359.

_____. "The Classical Style in France and England 1800-1840." *The Magazine Antiques*, v. 74, # 5 (November, 1958), pp. 429-433.

_____. "The furniture of Anthony G. Quervelle, Part I: The Pier Tables." *The Magazine Antiques*, v. 103, # 5 (May, 1973), pp. 984-994; "Part II: The Pedestal Tables." *The Magazine Antiques*, v. 104, # 1 (July, 1973), pp. 90-99; "Part III: The Worktables." *The Magazine Antiques*, v. 104, # 4 (October, 1973), pp. 260-268.

Sotheby's. *Important Americana: The Bertram K. Little and Nina Fletcher Little Collection, Part I*. Sale # 6526 (January 29, 1994).

Stauffer, David McNeely. *American Engravers upon Copper and Steel*. (Reprint of the 1907 edition; New York: Burt Franklin, n.d.).

Stegeman, John F. and Janet A. Caty: *A Biography of Catherine Littlefield Greene.* (Providence, RI: Rhode Island Bicentennial Foundation, 1978).

_____. "The Cause Célèbre of Caty Greene." *American History Illustrated*, v. 12, # 3 (June, 1977), pp. 8-16.

Talbott, Page. *Furnishing the Music Room (1850-1890).* (Baltimore: Hampton National Historic Site, 1994).

_____. "Seating furniture in Boston, 1810-1835." *The Magazine Antiques*, v. 139, # 5 (May, 1991), pp. 956-969.

Taylor, Snowden. *The Development Era of Eli Terry and Seth Thomas Shelf Clocks.* (Fitzwilliam, NH: Ken Roberts Publishing Co., 1985).

Theus, [Mrs.] Charlton M. "A concise guide to Savannah furniture and cabinetmakers." *Connoisseur*, v. 169, # 680 (October, 1968), pp. 124-131.

_____. *Savannah Furniture 1735-1825.* (Savannah: Privately printed, 1967).

Thieme, Dr. Ulrich and Dr. Felix Becker, eds. *Allgemeines Lexikon der Bildenden Künstler von der Antike bis zur Gegenwart.* (Leipzig, Germany: Veb. E. A. Seeman Verlag, 1907-1947).

Thornton, Peter. *Authentic Decor: The Domestic Interior 1620-1920.* (New York: Viking, 1984).

Bertel Thorvaldsen: Skulpturen, Modelle, Bozzetti, Handzeichnungen. (Köln: Museen der Stadt Köln, 1977).

Toleman, Ruel Pardee. *The Life and Works of Edward Greene Malbone 1777-1809.* (New York: The New-York Historical Society, 1958).

_____. "Newly Discovered Miniatures by Edward Greene Malbone." *The Magazine Antiques*, v. 16, # 5 (November, 1929), pp. 373-380.

Treasures of State: Fine and Decorative Arts in the Diplomatic Reception Rooms of the U.S. Department of State. (New York: Harry N. Abrams, Inc., Publishers, 1991).

Trump, Robert T. "Joseph B. Barry, Philadelphia cabinetmaker." *The Magazine Antiques*, v. 106, # 1 (January, 1975), pp. 94-98.

The Vernacular Architecture of Charleston and the Lowcountry 1670-1990, A Field Guide. (Charleston, SC: Historic Charleston Foundation, 1994).

Voss, Frederick S. *John Frazee 1790-1852 Sculptor.* (Washington, DC and Boston: National Portrait Gallery, Smithsonian Institution and The Boston Atheneum, 1986).

Wagner, Pamela. *Hidden Heritage: Recent Discoveries in Georgia Decorative Art, 1733-1915.* (Atlanta: High Museum of Art, 1990).

Waring, Joseph Frederick. *Cerveau's Savannah.* (Savannah: The Georgia Historical Society, 1973).

Wehle, Harry B. *American Miniatures 1730-1850.* (New York: Garden City Publishing Company, Inc., 1937).

Weidman, Gregory R. and Jennifer F. Goldsborough, et. al. *Classical Maryland 1815-1845: Fine and Decorative Arts from the Golden Age.* (Baltimore: Maryland Historical Society, 1993).

Weidman, Gregory. *Furniture in Maryland 1740-1940.* (Baltimore: Maryland Historical Society, 1984).

Williams-Wood, Cyril. *English Transfer-printed Pottery and Porcelain: A History of Over-Glazed Printing.* (London and Boston: Faber and Faber, 1981).

Wilmerding, John ed. *The Genius of American Painting.* (New York: William Morrow and Company, 1973).

Wilson, Adelaide. *Historic and Picturesque Savannah.* (Boston: Boston Photogravure Co., 1889).

Wittkower, Rudolf. *Art and Architecture in Italy: 1600-1750.* (Baltimore: Penguin Books, 1958).

Young, William, ed. and comp. *A Dictionary of American Artists, Sculptors and Engravers.* (Cambridge, MA: William Young, 1968).